George A. King

St. Charles College

March 6, 1967

CURRENTS AND TRENDS
IN CONTEMPORARY
JEWISH THOUGHT

CURRENTS AND TRENDS
IN CONTEMPORARY
JEWISH THOUGHT

Edited by
BENJAMIN EFRON

Contributing Authors

Herbert M. Baumgard / Jack Bemporad / Arthur A. Chiel
Samuel Chiel / Oscar Cohen / Myron M. Fenster / Arthur
Gilbert / Edward Horowitz / Leon A. Jick / Henry Enoch
Kagan / Kurt Klappholz / Theodore N. Lewis / Alan W.
Miller / Manheim S. Shapiro / Charles E. Shulman
Marshall Sklare / Jack D. Spiro / Richard F. Steinbrink

KTAV PUBLISHING HOUSE, Inc.

NEW YORK

Library of Congress Card Catalog No. 65-21741
Manufactured in the United States of America

Table of Contents

INTRODUCTION

This book, as its title suggests, is aimed at giving our young people of high school and college age a wider knowledge and an understanding of the forces at work in the American Jewish community of which they are a part. Its emphasis is upon the contemporary scene, and it seeks to give perspective on our religion and people. Currents and Trends in Contemporary Jewish Thought, deals, also, with the relationship of Judaism to the general life and culture of our country and time.

To achieve these aims, Mr. Benjamin Efron, as editor, prepared outlines for seventeen articles on various phases of current Jewish life and thought. Seventeen authors and specialists who are, in addition, men of attainment in the Jewish field, were then asked to develop the selected themes. Each author, of course, was to be responsible only for the material appearing in his own article. An eighteenth article appears without benefit of an outline; it is being reprinted in a condensed version from a magazine because it covers so well an important development in Jewish life.

The book is divided into two parts. The first relates to the philosophy and practices of Judaism today, while the second is concerned with secular matters, with cultural activities and interests, and with certain problems the Jews face as a people or ethnic group.

Care has been taken, in the course of the book's progress, to have each article make its special contribution toward an understanding of the total Jewish community of today. We sincerely feel that in its entirety the book makes the contemporary Jewish scene come alive to the reader in a significant manner.

We are grateful, as is Mr. Efron, to the authors who worked so cooperatively in this endeavor. The result is a most readable book that performs, in our opinion, a necessary function for high school, college students, adult education groups, and individuals interested in Judaism.

The Publishers

ACKNOWLEDGEMENTS

AMERICAN JUDAISM, published by the Union of American Hebrew Congregations for permission to reprint part of *Towards A New Jewish Theology.*

BEHRMAN HOUSE, INC., for permission to quote from *The New Haggadah,* edited by Mordecai M. Kaplan, Eugene Kohn, and Ira Eisenstein.

COMMENTARY, published by the American Jewish Committee for permission to reprint part of *Intermarriage and the Jewish Future.*

To the students of the High School Department of Temple Sinai of Roslyn Heights, New York, whose interests and needs over the years helped shape the Editor's plan for this book.

ORIENTATION: TRENDS IN CONTEMPORARY JUDAISM

by Benjamin Efron

BENJAMIN EFRON: Director of Union of American Hebrew Congregations' **COLLEGE OF JEWISH STUDIES** in Los Angeles; degrees from City College and Columbia University; author of **PATHWAYS THROUGH THE PRAYERBOOK, MESSAGE OF THE TORAH, STORY WITHOUT END** and other books.

WHILE the ten articles in this section of the book were written as independent pieces, they were planned as parts of a unified study of the religion of the Jews. Each author was assigned a topic that could make a contribution to a deeper understanding of Judaism as a philosophy as well as a faith.

Jewish educators throughout the country have been reporting a noticeable increase in skepticism toward religion among students of high school and college age. The young people seem to have misgivings not only about some of the practices and traditions of Judaism, but they question, also, the very fundamentals of religious beliefs. The following excerpts from term papers recently written by high school seniors are but a sampling of the doubts being expressed by many of our older students:

> I basically doubt if there is a God and see little consequence if there is one. My belief of a possible God is a deistic one, and is of one who might have created the world but who now is removed from the situation. It makes no difference to me whether the universe always existed or God always existed. In my philosophy, man is God and it is his existence that counts.
>
> * * *
>
> Too often adults feel that prophetic Judaism is too idealistic and totally impractical because it conflicts with their own trivial plans. Unfortunately, the leadership of the older generation, even those who are temple goers, has left much to be desired, because they practice a life filled with hypocrisy.
>
> * * *
>
> It is my belief that one moment of true meditation is

worth more than a year of Sabbath services. It seems to me that most people just read along in the prayerbook and it means little to them.

QUESTIONING AND JEWISH TRADITION

Students and others who question in this manner are well within the Jewish tradition. Rabbis and teachers of the past viewed the "question" as a necessary part of the search for truth. Judaism had no hard and fast dogmas that it required its people to profess, and our rabbis did not proclaim the doctrines of the faith in precise formulations with the idea that any variation—and certainly a contradiction—would be regarded as heretical. Rabbis frequently differed with one another over interpretations and meanings; in fact, the *Talmud* is full of disagreements among even the famous and inspired rabbis whose teachings are quoted in its many volumes. The *Talmud* also reveals how important a part questioning played in the development of post-Biblical Judaism, for out of the answers that the learned rabbis gave to the questioners and doubters among their students flowed the remarkable body of teachings we call Rabbinic Judaism.

This introduction to Part One of the book is not the place to explore the reasons for the apparent increase in skepticism among Jews. It should be noted, parenthetically, that a similar development is taking place among non-Jews. But it is important to note that some of the arguments used by the doubting Thomases among our youth have to do with their disenchantment with the state of affairs the older generation is handing over to them. They mention wars and prejudice and genocide and other man-made catastrophies as dramatic proof that the teachings of religion have failed to affect man's conduct in areas that really count. And they point to the business world, where ethical teachings seem to be ignored, and then ask with raised eyebrow, "Are not the builders of our churches and synagogues the same people who do so well in the business jungle?"

These and other factors that are responsible for the critical attitude of young people toward God and religion suggest that the major concern of the older students is the developing of a philosophy that will lend direction and meaningful purpose to their lives. They are engaged in a kind of testing operation, part of their unending quest for acceptable goals and ideals. What we offer them in our religious schools will be placed under their spiritual microscopes along with other teachings, to be studied and scrutinized with varying degrees of objectivity. It is heartening, in this regard, that a substantial segment of our youth is staying on in our religious schools past Bar Mitzvah and Confirmation. But it becomes more necessary than ever to present Judaism in terms of the contemporary world, in terms of its relevance to life about us.

It was with all this in mind that the section on Jewish religious thought was organized. The first article, TRENDS IN JEWISH RELIGIOUS THOUGHT, introduces the reader to the changes and transformations that have taken place in the Jewish religion from biblical days to modern times. This is followed by a description of the faith as it exists today. Each of the four recognized "denominations" of contemporary Judaism is discussed by a spokesman for his particular branch of the religion.

While it is important to know and understand the forces that brought about the changes that occurred in the concepts and practices of Judaism, one must also appreciate the fact that there are essential and abiding values in the Jewish faith that are common to all the groupings and movements. ETHICAL DOCTRINES IN JUDAISM treats of some of these values, giving their background in ancient events and developments and suggesting their applicability to our own day.

A basic source of most of Judaism's doctrines and teachings is the Bible. In BIBLICAL CRITICISM AND ARCHAEOLOGY the reader will find much that will explain why Jews particularly, and others as well, have paid so much attention to our Holy Scriptures. The author also shows how

the scientific study of the Bible has led to a greater understanding of its importance.

Another common element in the Jewish religion is the
Hebrew language. In DEVELOPMENTS IN THE HE-
BREW LANGUAGE this important but sometimes neglected field of study is reviewed, and the whole subject is
brought into relation with the growth and development of
the Jews and their faith.

DEVELOPMENTS IN JEWISH WORSHIP highlights
still another aspect of Judaism that is shared by all religious
Jews, the conducting of regular prayer services. This article
discusses the prayerbook as part of Jewish religious literature and its evolution to the present time.

Part One of the book is then brought to a close with an
article that concerns itself with the problem of describing
Judaism in terms of its theology. TOWARD A MODERN
JEWISH THEOLOGY focuses attention on the various
considerations one must take into account in defining God
and religion in our time.

It is quite possible, of course, to read the articles in this
section in a different order. One could start with the theology article and then check to see how the spokesmen for
the Orthodox, Reform, Conservative and Reconstructionist
branches of Judaism approach the questions raised by Rabbi
Bemporad. It is not the order but the total effect that counts.
Taken together, the articles seek to help the reader to
understand the dynamics of modern Judaism. As the authors present it, Judaism emerges as the living faith of a
living people. It is a faith that has made significant contributions to the culture and civilization of the world, and
it still has within it the seeds for further growth. It needs
tending and cultivation by people who understand and
value it.

The road to the knowledge of Judaism is, we believe,
well charted in these ten articles and in the accompanying
list of Suggested Readings. It is our hope that with the
deeper knowledge the reader may gain will come a desire
to make its teachings part of his philosophy of life.

TRENDS IN JEWISH RELIGIOUS THOUGHT

by Theodore N. Lewis

THEODORE N. LEWIS: Rabbi of Progressive Synagogue of Brooklyn; a graduate of Hebrew Union College, where he received Doctor of Divinity degree in 1934 and the D.H.L. honorary degree in 1959; author of volume of essays **MY FAITH AND PEOPLE,** and of articles in **JEWISH SPECTATOR, CONGRESS WEEKLY, RE-CONSTRUCTIONIST,** etc.

THOUGH traditional Judaism ascribes the beginning of the Jewish religion to Abraham, Moses was the true founder. How historical the patriarchs are will never be determined, and ultimately the question is of no consequence. Legendary or not, Abraham, Isaac and Jacob live in the heart of every loyal Jew, which makes them important personages in the story of our people.

Out of reverence and love for Abraham, the rabbis speak of him as the first Jew, and ascribe to him not only the original perception of the unity of God, but even the practice of many a *mitzvah* (commandment) not yet ordained. Christian scholars to the contrary, the early Israelites did not appropriate the religious rites of the Canaanites among whom they settled. The practices dedicated to Baal and the other gods they rejected utterly and completely. The talk of syncretism is misleading and without warrant since they did not borrow or adapt any ideas from the religion of the Canaanites.

How then did the early Israelites discover monotheism, that God is One? According to the great Jewish Biblical scholar, Yecheskel Kaufmann, this is indeed a mystery that has not yet yielded to rational or logical analysis. Even more astounding is the fact that our forefathers not only perceived that God is One, but that He is a moral deity, and that His relationship to man is an ethical one.

UNIQUENESS OF JEWISH RELIGIOUS IDEAS

On logical grounds, this unique discovery defies explanation. The religious Jew attributes the event to revelation. There is no other explanation. It is precisely this phenomenon which makes the Jewish religion unique and

9

distinctive, with no relationship to pagan faiths. While Egypt, Babylonia, Assyria and other lands of antiquity did influence the Jew, such influence was purely external—in administrative, legal, social and commercial arrangements. In the realm of the spirit, the Jew borrowed naught from his neighbors. In his conception of God, the Jew remained truly unique.

It is by virtue of this concept of God, this revelation, that the Jew regards himself as "chosen." The term, fiercely maligned by antisemites, denotes only responsibility and duty, and not privilege or favor. The Jew regards himself "chosen" in the sense that through him was the essence of God revealed to mankind.

The man who led the Israelites towards this revelation was none other than Moses, the greatest of all prophets. While the biblical account of Moses includes much legend, the historicity of the man is beyond question. Even without the legendary elements, Moses remains a majestic personality, who transformed a tribal community into a holy people and a kingdom of priests. Such an extraordinary achievement is vouchsafed to only a handful of men.

The essence of the doctrine of Moses and of his successors, the great prophets of Israel, is summed up in two incomparable words—justice and love, or justice and mercy. Moses proclaimed a God of justice and love who hates iniquity and evil and unrighteousness. The Exodus, the most decisive episode in the life and literature of the Jewish people, gives concrete expression to these two aspects of the Divine. God delivers the Jews from Egyptian bondage because He hates oppression and injustice, and is the champion of the persecuted, the downtrodden, and the outcast. Every page of the Bible testifies to His concern for the orphan, the widow and the poor.

The burden of the message of the immortal prophets of Israel is divine justice and divine love, with the natural corollary of the Fatherhood of God and the brotherhood of Man. No one has expressed this universalism more beautifully than the prophet Malachi when he proclaimed,

"Have we not all one Father, hath not one God created us?" (Malachi 2:10).

Moved by the highest ethical considerations, the prophets could not tolerate the injustice and the oppression of their times, which they denounced in burning wrath as transgressions of the will of God. They made it clear that form and practices were not the key elements in the Jewish way of life. The prophets placed ethical considerations above all else. Rituals and ceremonials come after or flow out of the moral teachings of Judaism.

However, before the religious ideas of the prophets could be organized into some kind of orderly system in the Jewish kingdom of Judah, the small state came to an inglorious end in 586 B.C.E. The victorious Nebuchadnezzar destroyed the Temple on Mount Zion and took the people into captivity in Babylon.

What is miraculous is that the people did not forget Palestine or their faith, to both of which they clung fiercely, even vowing on the soil of Babylon never to forget Jerusalem.

After seventy years of exile, the Jews were allowed by a decree of Cyrus, the conqueror of Babylon, to return to their ancient homeland. Not the bulk but a substantial number did return. Judaism as a religion was in a state of transition at the time, influenced on the one hand by the teaching of the prophets, and on the other by the traditions associated with the Temple. The latter was the stronger, and one of the first undertakings of the returned exiles was the rebuilding of the ancient Temple. But the prophetic ideals were brought to their attention too, notably by the great leaders of that period, Ezra and Nehemiah.

Both of these men emphasized the ethical ideas that were so important a part of the written *Torah,* which Ezra had introduced into the lives of the struggling returnees. Thus, there existed for many centuries after Ezra two traditions within the Jewish faith, the rituals and ceremonies connected with the Temple, and the ideas and customs that were developing in relation to the synagogue and the study of *Torah*.

RELIGIOUS DEVELOPMENT AFTER THE TEMPLE FELL

And then came the day, in the year 70 C.E., when the Temple came to a physical end. A whole system of religious expression and devotion passed out of existence with the destruction of the Temple, but by that time the synagogue had developed into an accepted institution, and the study of the *Torah* and the oral interpretations of it had become an integral part of the Jewish way of life.

The destruction of Palestine and the Temple, however, created grave religious and spiritual problems. Many saw no hope for the continuation of Judaism without the Temple, the sacrificial system and the priestly class. But the genius of Jochanan ben Zakkai literally saved Judaism. His emphasis on study, learning and prayer as substitutes for animal sacrifices provided the people with a viable approach to Judaism. Jochanan ben Zakkai and the scholars who associated themselves with the work of the academy at Jabneh looked upon the *Torah* as a living instrument that could be attuned to every new and changing situation. Through their interpretation of the *Torah,* through their religious doctrines and the reforms they instituted, Jochanan and his group laid the foundation for Rabbinic Judaism, the organized body of law and ritual and of periodic revisions of ancient customs and tradition that became the accepted pattern for the Jewish faith.

While ritual remained important, the moral and ethical element in the *Torah* was always given priority. Instead of its being a priestly prerogative, holiness became the obligation for all. Even the humblest Jew could achieve holiness by living on a high moral and ethical plane. Rabbinic Judaism was never content with the negative, with mere prohibitions, but concentrated on the positive and affirmative.

The nobility of Rabbinic Judaism is demonstrated by the

unique religious vocabulary the sages created. Out of their teachings came such terms as *gemilut chessed* (kindness), *tzedakah* (charity), *tzar baalay chayim* (compassion for animals), *tzni-ut* (chastity), and above all *kiddush ha-shem* (the sanctification of the name of God), as well as its obverse, *chilul hashem* (desecration of the name).

Not wishing to let its aims end with abstract and high ideals, the rabbis fashioned the synagogue into an institution through which the Jew could realize and attain them. By providing a place for the people to gather for prayer, for religious instruction, and for spiritual renewal, the rabbis of the Pharisee tradition actually preserved Judaism and the Jew.

Rabbinic Judaism was a process as well as a body of laws. Each great change in history required new interpretations, or perhaps revisions, of previously accepted outlooks or practices. The various laws that had been developed orally through learned discussions of verses of the *Torah* were finally collected by Judah Ha-Nasi (135-216 C.E.), one of the most respected teachers of his time. His collection, known as the *Mishnah,* soon achieved universal acceptance and authority among the people.

The codification of the *Mishnah* gave rise to a glorious period of religious development that culminated with the completion of the *Talmud* about the year 500 C.E. This epoch, covering four or more centuries of concentrated and often inspired thinking about the meaning of Judaism, created a definitive form of Judaism that served the Jews admirably in all their far-flung communities well into modern times. The *Talmud* can be counted as one of mankind's great religious and intellectual achievements.

While the *Mishnah* is the foundation of the *Talmud,* the ultimate source is the Bible, which for the Talmudic sages possessed divine authority. To them, every biblical word and letter was meaningful, indispensable, never superfluous. And yet, in the course of time, the *Talmud* with its derived laws, its doctrines, its legends and myths, as well as its ritual and ethical codes acquired the authority and sanctity which the Bible possessed. As the Bible was "written *Torah*," the *Talmud* became "oral *Torah*," and received the reverence that was given the former.

Halachah (meaning law) refers to the Talmudic legislation which prescribes the path a Jew should follow; it was meant to be his guide in all areas of life, from the important to even the trivial. The Talmudic rabbis aimed at producing specific regulations so that a Jew would know exactly what was required of him in a given situation. The *Torah* was not always so explicit. The Fourth Commandment, for instance, simply says "you shall do no work" on *Shabbat*. But what is work? What forms of human effort were to be prohibited on the Sabbath, which were to be permitted?

Some rabbis strove mightily to keep the day entirely dedicated to God, they went so far as to say that it was unholy and a profanation even to fight to defend one's life on the Sabbath. Other rabbis, the majority, sought to make it a day of spiritual joy and re-creation. They took such passages as "Everyone is to remain where he is; no man is to leave his place on the seventh day" (Ex. 16:29), which would make *Shabbat* a pretty dreary day, and gave them more liberal interpretations. Such rabbis pointed out that the Hebrew word for "place" (*makom*) in the passage quoted is used elsewhere in the *Torah* as a synonym for "city." With such an interpretation, a Jew's scope of movement on the Sabbath was immediately widened to include the entire city. Other rabbis of a still later period broke down the city barrier as well, enlarging the horizon further.

Thus, with great skill and intellectual acumen, the sages defined the meaning of the various laws of the *Torah* and of earlier rabbinic regulations. And as the *Talmud* proceeded in its development it provided a code of law which the Jew could follow no matter where he lived, no matter what language he spoke. Of great service in making the laws more available to people was the codification of the *Halachah* at the hands of scholars like Isaac Alfasi, who died in Spain in 1103, Maimonides, who died in Egypt in 1204; and Joseph Karo, who died in Safed in 1575. (Karo's *Shulchan Aruch* became the most popular of all the codes.)

The *Talmud* had its critics over the years, who unfortunately made it seem as if it was concerned with matters of ritual alone. But actually, ethics and human conduct are placed on a level far above that of ritual. The sages were as keen about achieving moral and ethical perfection as they were about achieving ritual perfection. In truth, Talmudic Judaism is the rightful heir to prophetic Judaism. Even as the prophets, so did the sages hold justice, righteousness, love and mercy to be the very foundations of Judaism, the essence of true religion.

Nevertheless, during the Geonic period, which extended roughly from 600 C.E. to about the time of the Crusades (1096 C.E.), there were divisions within the Jewish community owing to differences in interpretation of biblical and Talmudic passages. One very strong movement, the Karaite group, threatened for a time to split the Jewish world. Thanks to the work of Saadiah ben Joseph (892-942 C.E.), the most distinguished rabbi among the *Geonim,* the spread of the movement was finally halted, and Rabbinic Judaism was again restored to its place as the guide to Jewish belief and practice.

A man of brilliant talents, Saadiah for many years headed the famous academy of Sura. While best known for his philosophic classic *Emunot V'deot* (Dogma and Science), he also enriched Hebrew grammar, biblical exegesis, and indeed almost every branch of Jewish learning. He also introduced the scientific study of Judaism, utilizing his mastery not only of the *Talmud,* but also of the secular learning of that day, which included the best of Arabic and Greek culture and philosophy.

Saadiah had a profound effect upon the thinking of the scholars in the Jewish community the world over, for he was consulted by rabbis and students everywhere upon matters of belief and practice, and his written answers *(Responsa)* were studied diligently.

DEVELOPMENTS IN THE GHETTO CENTURIES

The Dark Ages (from about 800 to 1200 C.E.), a time of ignorance and superstition in the non-Jewish world of Europe, were centuries of enlightenment and spiritual advancement for Jewry. The only darkness the Jews knew in those years was that of oppression and injustice. During the Crusades the Jews of Central Europe were massacred and their religious institutions weakened, and a host of accusations against Jews spread over Europe. These were accusations that could not be "disproven" because of their very absurdity: that Jews used Christian blood to celebrate the Passover; that Jews were responsible for the Black Plague; that they desecrated the host, the wafer used in a Catholic mass. These were "crimes" for which hundreds of Jews paid with their lives.

From 1096 C.E. on, the year of the calling of the First Crusade, the Jews suffered savage persecutions, and economic and social degradation. They were expelled from a number of countries and principalities and decreed out of most professions and occupations. As a result, many Jews began to turn to mysticism in quest of the Messiah, whose miraculous appearance would end the fearful night that had descended upon them. Many Jews practiced fasts and recited formulistic prayers in the hope of hastening his coming.

So much did they concentrate upon the Messiah that they accepted the word of an impostor, Shabbatai Tzevi of Smyrna, that he was the long-awaited savior. For years a bitter conflict raged between those who believed in him and those who did not. Even after Shabbatai Tzevi accepted Islam to escape death, many persisted in believing that he was the Messiah.

Almost a century later, another religious movement was born, sired also by the pressures of those days. Founded by Israel ben Eliezer, better known as *Baal Shem Tov* (Master of the Good Name), Chasidism arose as a protest against the excessive emphasis in Rabbinic Judaism on "learning." By this time, the early 18th century, the Jewish communities in Eastern Europe had declined not only economically but educationally as well.

Chasidism was a religious movement that was directed toward the pious but unlearned masses. *Tzadikim* (saintly men), distinguished for piety and holiness, took the place of rabbis. Instead of learning, Chasidism emphasized communion with God through inspired prayer, often expressed in song and dance, and through meditation. Chasidism also insisted on cheerfulness, as though to say that sadness and melancholy reflected adversely on divine mercy.

Chasidism was more than a protest against the rigors of Rabbinic Judaism. It was also a response to the bitter persecution which the Jews suffered in Poland. Although there were fewer pogroms during the early part of the 18th century, restrictions had grown in number and severity. To the burdened and oppressed Jews, whose daily misery was relieved only by the Sabbath, Chasidism's beliefs and mode of worship brought new hope, serenity and optimism, and above all, fresh faith.

IN THE DAWN OF THE EMANCIPATION

The French Revolution (1789) changed the very character of Europe. Wherever Napoleon and the French armies marched, the revolutionary ideals of liberty, equality and fraternity went with them. Even as it brought enfranchisement and a new dignity to Europeans, so also did it bring the Jews the much sought-after emancipation, the rights of citizenship and a sense of identification with the countries of their residence.

Despite fierce resistance in some areas, new opportunities were opened to Jews. Even in antisemitic Germany, many Jews attained high position in government and politics, and succeeded especially in industry, commerce and the professions.

One of the deplorable consequences of emancipation, however, was Jewish assimilation. As a result of the new freedom, many a Jew suddenly discovered that Judaism was burdensome and unfashionable. Indifference to and neglect of the ancient faith became the fashion for many, and even apostasy and conversion became common, especially in Germany.

Another deplorable result of emancipation was the disruption of the Jewish religious discipline that had been created by the *Shulchan Aruch* of Joseph Karo, which regulated the most minute detail of daily life. Since emancipation, however, Jewish religious life has been disorganized. The old code is no longer universally observed, and a new one has yet to be found or fashioned.

True, many Jews remained loyal to the Judaism that had developed in the ghetto centuries, the way of life that was caught and held fast by *Shulchan Aruch*. But even among those orthodox-minded people there were many questions that needed answering as to how one was to live as a Jew in the changed and changing world in this period of emancipation.

Many organized groups have sought to give the answers during the past 150 years, and the Jews of America are at present evaluating them. The people are seeking their way to a satisfactory Jewish identification and meaningful practice. It is too early, perhaps, to guess the direction the American Jewish community will finally adopt. In the meantime, we do not have a modern *Shulchan Aruch* acceptable to all; we have no *Minhag* America. Religiously, we live in many groupings, each of them hoping to attract the estranged and lost.

SUGGESTED READINGS

STUDIES IN JUDAISM, *Solomon Schechter*, Jewish Publication Society.

THE STORY OF HASSIDISM, *Jacob Minkin*, Harper and Row.

THE PHARISEES, *R. T. Herford*, The Macmillan Company.

THIS PEOPLE ISRAEL, *Leo Baeck*, Jewish Publication Society.

JUDAISM, A PROFILE OF A FAITH, *Ben-Zion Bokser*, Alfred Knopf, Inc.

ORTHODOX JUDAISM

by Kurt Klappholz

KURT KLAPPHOLZ: Rabbi of Congregation Tifereth Israel, Brooklyn; a Doctor of Divinity, was ordained by Rabbinical Seminary of Berlin in 1938; author of **SPIRITUAL AWAKENING** and **THE POWER WITHIN US.**

BEFORE we can proceed to discuss the ideological foundations of Orthodox Judaism, we must examine the meaning of the term orthodox. The term orthodox, in its present usage, is a complete misnomer in designating the belief and the practice of traditional Judaism. The term orthodox was first employed by Abraham Furtado, president of the Sanhedrin called together by Napoleon, in Paris in the year 1807. Subsequently, the term was used by various Jews, sometimes derogatorily, to denote those who adhere strictly to the *Torah* Law.

In the view of some ideologists from the liberal wing of Judaism, Orthodox Judaism is incompatible with progress and liberalism. Until this very day, many non-orthodox Jews are of the impression that theirs is a progressive or liberal Judaism, while orthodoxy is a type of Judaism which is backward and not in keeping with the enlightenment of modern times. We believe that such is not the case and that on the contrary, Orthodox Judaism is perfectly compatible with modern civilization, contemporary thought, the arts and the sciences.

Actually, the term orthodox was borrowed from the ecclesiastic terminology of the Christian church. In Christianity the term orthodox signifies a fundamentalist school of thought which demands rigid adherence to a creed believed to be the infallible truth.

The term orthodox as employed in Christian theology is a contraction of two Greek words: *ortho,* meaning right or proper; and *doxa,* meaning opinion. Some employ the word "*Torah*-true" in place of orthodox, since the term orthodox designates, at best, only those who hold the right opinions and creeds. The word *Torah*-true is a translation of the German term *gesetzestreu,* which was origi-

21

nally employed by the great leaders of *Torah* Judaism in
Germany in the middle and towards the end of the 19th
century.

Men like Samson Raphael Hirsch, the chief exponent
in Germany of modern *Torah* Judaism, and Dr. Ezriel
Hildesheimer, the founder of the orthodox Rabbinical
Seminary in Berlin, rejected the term orthodox as not
being equivalent to the belief and practice of traditional
Judaism, which demands of its adherents total commitment to the *Torah* Law in belief and practice.

BELIEFS OF ORTHODOXY

Orthodoxy maintains that one cannot be an authentic
Jew by merely believing in some fundamental principles
of faith, for Judaism is not confined to the frame of a mere
theology, nor is it a system of dogmas upon which depends
the salvation of the individual. Salvation via belief is a
Christian concept, and is utterly alien to Judaism. Judaism
is not a form of religion, but a way of life.

While Reform Judaism maintains that the *Torah* (Pentateuch) is the literary creation of a divinely inspired
genius, the central belief of Orthodox Judaism is the
divine origin of the *Torah.* God gave His *Torah,* the
written and the oral, to Moses on Mount Sinai when He
revealed Himself to the congregation of Israel assembled
at the foot of the mountain. The written *Torah* is contained in the Five Books of Moses, while the oral *Torah,*
which was given on Mount Sinai simultaneously with the
written *Torah,* is a body of laws, rules and regulations
stemming directly from God.

For generations it was forbidden to put the oral law
into writing; it was transmitted by word of mouth from
generation to generation. When its transmission became
endangered through precarious political conditions, the
rabbis gave permission to put it in writing, so that it might
be preserved for future generations. The oral law in written form is known as the *Mishnah.* The written law, the

oral law, and the regulations and rules arrived at by the rabbis through methods of exegesis and analysis sanctioned by the *Torah* Law itself, together form the *Halachah*.

To the traditional Jew, the *Halachah* points to the proper way of life, to religious conduct and ethical behavior in private and in public. The *Halachah* encompasses all areas of life, for traditional Judaism demands of its adherents nothing less than total and exclusive dedication and commitment.

It is important to keep in mind that the belief in the divine origin of the *Torah* is the keystone of the ideology of Torah-true Judaism. All thinking, reflection and speculation, religious and philosophical, revolves around this central fundamental principle of belief. From it flows the direction of the traditional Jew's religious thought and practice. Since God is eternal, and since the *Torah* stems directly from our Creator, it follows with iron logic that the *Torah* Law has eternal value. The *Torah* Law may be applied at all times and at all places.

Since Reform Judaism believes that the *Torah* is merely the creation of a literary genius, its adherents maintain that the *Torah* Law may be changed and that it may be adapted to changing conditions and times. Orthodox Judaism believes that the *Torah* Law cannot be changed and conditions must be adjusted to the eternal values of the *Torah*.

That does not mean that a traditional Jew cannot wholeheartedly participate in the cultural life of modern society. The contrary is true. *It definitely is possible* for a traditional Jew to harmonize his faith and practice with modern civilization. Nowhere is it stated in the *Torah* that one must not live within the realistic world. Nor does the *Torah* prohibit the full participation of a Jew in areas of modern culture and science, provided that the primacy of the *Torah* is always maintained and everything in life is always viewed by *Torah* standards.

Judaism is concerned with real life in all its aspects.

The tenets of faith cannot be divorced from ritual law, because faith and law form an inseparable unity. Judaism requires its adherents to uphold the supremacy and the sovereignty of the *Torah* in *any* civilization.

TORAH CONCEPT OF SAMSON RAPHAEL HIRSCH

Samson Raphael Hirsch successfully fought assimilation and alienation from Judaism in his time by developing the concept of *Torah im Derech Eretz* (synthesis of *Torah* and secular culture.). In Hirsch's concept, *Torah* is the practice of the Divine Law, and *Derech Eretz* stands for modern education, philosophy and culture. He was deeply concerned with the impact of modern civilization upon the Jewish intellectuals of his day. Many Jews, reared in traditional homes, had become estranged from their faith because they could not see how Judaism and modern culture could be harmonized.

The inner conflict that arose from the apparent incompatibility of Judaism and modern civilization had driven many learned Jews into the arms of assimilation. There was an acute danger that the Jewish intellectual would be lost to his faith and to his people, unless an attempt were made to blend the cultural values of the time with the eternal values of Judaism.

Hirsch taught his followers the importance of secular learning for a better understanding and a clearer appreciation of the *Torah*. He maintained that the future existence of *Torah* could only be safeguarded through the employment of the techniques and methods of modern civilization. He thus brought about a revolution in Jewish education by including secular subjects in the curriculum of the Jewish school. In doing so, he was the pioneer of the modern *Yeshivah* Day School movement, which has experienced phenomenal growth in the past two decades here in the United States.

In his *19 Letters on Judaism,* written in 1836 and recently translated into English, Hirsch skillfully employs

the form of a dialogue, which was first used by the medieval Jewish philosopher, Yehudah Halevi in his *Kuzari*.
In the *19 Letters on Judaism* the dialogue is conducted
by way of a fictitious correspondence between Naftali, a
young rabbi, and his equally young friend Benjamin, who
had become estranged from tradition by his exposure to
the thinking of his time. With brutal frankness Hirsch
makes the young man recount his criticism of traditional
Judaism step by step, and in answer to Benjamin's doubts
and misgivings Hirsch develops the concept of a synthesis
of *Torah*-true belief and practice with modern thinking.

The late Dr. Joseph Wohlgemuth, professor at the Rabbinical Seminary of Berlin and leading religious philosopher in Germany before World War II, assigned far-
reaching importance to Hirsch's thesis by stating that
Hirsch did not attempt to counter the attacks of the non-
traditional Jew through apologetics, nor to conciliate
opponents by means of feeble compromises between faith
and science. Dr. Wohlgemuth states that it was Rabbi
Hirsch's aim to present the Judaism of old in such a light
that the sheer beauty of its form and the sublimeness and
simplicity of its content would win over those capable
of religious feeling. Hirsch believed that a Jew living in
modern times must use modern learning and its methods
to further dedication to the *Torah* and to gain a better
comprehension of the beauty of God's creation.

The concept of *Torah im Derech Eretz* is necessitated
by the fact that man must cope with his existence upon
earth, his destiny and his common life with others, and
that he must achieve this through the earthly means at his
disposal. *Torah im Derech Eretz* is the harmonization of
modern culture with ancient thought, with the recognition of the supremacy and primacy of the word of God as
presented in the *Torah*. Hirsch's philosophy has been a
unique contribution to the reconstruction of Judaism upon
more secure foundations. Through it, the Jew can face
the impact of modern science upon his way of life without
giving up his allegiance to the *Torah*.

The phenomenal growth of the *Yeshivah* Day School movement in the United States during the past few decades bears testimony to the fact that traditional Judaism has not lost its *élan vital.* The curriculum of the modern *Yeshivah* Day School is structured in the image of Hirsch's concept of *Torah im Derech Eretz.* The integrated program comprising Hebraic culture and American civilization has made its impact upon thousands of Jewish families in the United States. It has brought about a rapprochement to traditional Judaism by giving to many an appreciation of its beauty and vital importance in their personal lives.

PHILOSOPHY OF ORTHODOXY

In his book *The Modern Jew Faces Eternal Problems,* Dr. Aron Barth outlines a philosophy of Judaism based upon the *Torah* Law and compatible with modern philosophical thought.

Barth proceeds from the premise that since the *Torah* is God-given, we have no right to change it in order to make it adaptable to any particular time. Nevertheless, he realistically faces the historical fact that Judaism has never been immune to foreign cultural and philosophical influences. Since Jews always lived among other peoples, they were subject to assimilation in a greater measure than were other ethnic groups. Whenever Judaism was confronted by other systems of philosophy or patterns of thinking, our great leaders did not choose to escape from reality, but realistically accepted the challenge.

As a result of these challenges they created immortal works in the fields of religion, ethics and philosophy. To this category of Jewish literature belong Maimonides's *Guide for the Perplexed,* Saadiah's *Beliefs and Opinions* and Yehudah Halevi's *Kuzari,* as well as Bahya ibn Pakuda's religio-ethical treatise *The Duties of the Heart.*

While the applicability of the *Torah* to all situations of life is not negotiable, Judaism grants its adherents a wide latitude in philosophical thought. In the strict sense of the term, Judaism is not a dogmatic religion. There is room in Judaism for widely divergent and at times even opposing views. The practice of Judaism does not permit deviation from the *Torah,* but in the realm of theological thinking it does not impose any definite pattern upon all its adherents.

The Kabbalists engaged in detailed anthropomorphic descriptions of the deity, but Maimonides strongly rejected any corporeality of God as not being in conformity with our view of the Creator. There is also a wide divergence in thinking between the *Chassidim* and the *Mitnagdim* (opponents of the *Chassidim*), and there are differences in outlook between the *Ashkenazic* and *Sephardic* segments of Jewry. However, in their loyalty to the *Torah* and the practice of the *Torah* Law there is no difference between them at all.

The *Thirteen Principles of Faith* of Maimonides have been widely accepted by Jews everywhere as the fundamentals of Jewish traditional faith. Among them are the all-encompassing basic principle of the oneness of God and the divine origin of the *Torah,* as well as the belief in reward and punishment, the belief in the advent of the Messiah and the resurrection of the dead.

Some scholars of great repute strongly opposed the formulation of dogmas such as these, while others reduced their numbers. These differences in theological matters derive from the fact that Judaism is not a theology or a faith, but a way of life. It is not the *thinking* about Judaism that is decisive, but its *practice* in all the ramifications of life. Only from the *Torah* can the authentic view of Judaism be derived.

Judaism teaches that the *Torah* is not the exclusive property of the scholars and the intellectuals, since it was given to all the people and for all generations. Everyone has a share in it, the wise and the simple, the rationalist and the mystic, the wealthy and the poor. No one has a

monopoly on the *Torah;* it is accessible to all and shut
off from none.

Judaism has no ecclesiastical hierarchy. The rabbi holds
no sacerdotal status in the congregation. He does not dis-
pense sacraments. He is primarily the teacher and guide of
his people, and is consulted in all matters pertaining to
the *Torah* Law and its application to life. However, traditional Judaism recognizes only those who have received
the traditional certificate of ordination (*semichah*) as
authentic rabbis. Only *semichah* from recognized rabbinical authorities entitles them to answer questions of ritual
law and practice and to perform rabbinical functions in
conformity with traditional usage and practice.

THE DUTY OF TORAH STUDY

The fact that a congregation has a rabbi does not relieve
its members from studying the *Torah,* and from attaining
erudition in the knowledge of the *Torah.* The study of
Torah being a religious obligation incumbent upon every
Jew, there did develop an aristrocracy of learning which
drew its members from among the people at large.

In years gone by the *talmid chacham* (*Torah* scholar)
enjoyed the highest esteem of the Jewish community. In
addition to its rabbi, each congregation had a sizeable
group of *talmiday chachamim* (*Torah* scholars) who
would set aside definite periods each day for *Torah* study.
The *talmid chacham* did not study for the sake of personal
honor or in order to obtain an academic degree; it was
done "for the exclusive sake of *Torah* itself" (*Torah
lishmah*), because it was one's religious obligation so to do.

Prior to the First World War great centers of *Torah*
learning flourished in Eastern Europe. With the great wave
of immigration about seventy years ago, many European
rabbinic scholars arrived in the United States. At that
time some were of the opinion that *Torah* could not be
transplanted successfully to America, because the American cultural climate did not seem to be conducive to the
establishment of *Torah* study centers. While some *Yeshi-*

vot functioned on American soil before the outbreak of the Second World War, the number of students at these centers of *Torah* was limited and their influence did not transcend the boundaries of the orthodox community.

As it happened, events in Europe prior to the Second World War forced many Talmudic scholars to leave their countries of birth and to seek refuge in the United States. Some brought with them the remnants of their illustrious *Yeshivot* from Eastern Europe. They were joined here by rabbinic scholars coming from Western Europe, who had received their training in the great rabbinic academies of Germany and Austria. Their combined influence in the community resulted in the phenomenal growth of *Torah* centers in America during the past twenty-five years, a rise far exceeding all expectations.

In addition to the schools for higher *Torah* learning (*Yeshivot*) the Day School movement that was founded by orthodox rabbis and laymen developed mightily under the spiritual sponsorship of the outstanding *Torah* leaders of our time. It is estimated that at present the *Yeshivah* Day Schools have an enrollment of 50,000 students throughout the United States. While this is but a fragment of the 1,000,000 Jewish children of school age, the future leadership of the orthodox community is being trained in these schools.

It is a commonly known fact that American Jewish education has for a long time been "a mile long and an inch deep." The result has been the emergence of a lay leadership of synagogues which is totally ignorant of Jewish values. The graduates of *Yeshivah* Day Schools will decisively change the image of the American Jew. These young American Jews and Jewesses who are receiving their Hebraic and secular training in the American *Yeshivot* will, hopefully, help them stem the tide of assimilation and intermarriage which threaten the future existence of American Jewry.

It is noteworthy that as a result of the great impact made by the *Yeshivah* movement, American-born young men and women have come in large numbers to *Torah* institutions such as Yeshivah University, Stern College for Women, and others all over the United States. We find today young orthodox Jews employed in the highest offices of our government and in private industry. And there are strict adherents to *Torah* Law in the fields of physics, chemistry, biology, medicine, the arts and the sciences. These young men and women are on the membership roster of the Association of Orthodox Jewish Scientists, an organization formed a few years ago for the purpose of promoting the interest and the welfare of the Torah-true scientist.

It is no longer unusual to see a Jewish high school or college student wearing his *yarmulke* in public. At many American colleges orthodox students belong to "Yavneh," the organization for orthodox students on the college campus. It cannot be denied even by the prophets of doom that America has become a mighty fortress of *Torah*. What was considered an impossibility sixty years ago is happening right before our eyes, the renaissance of *Torah* on American soil.

SUGGESTED READINGS

TIMELESS TORAH, edited by *Jacob Breuer*, Philipp Feldheim, Inc.

THE SABBATH, *Dr. I. Grunfeld*, Philipp Feldheim, Inc.

FUNDAMENTALS OF JUDAISM, edited by *Jacob Breuer*, Philipp Feldheim, Inc.

THE MODERN JEW FACES ETERNAL PROBLEMS, *Aron Barth*, World Zionist Organization.

REFORM JUDAISM

by Richard F. Steinbrink

RICHARD F. STEINBRINK: Rabbi, Monmouth Reform Temple, New Jersey; fourth generation of family active in Reform Judaism; a graduate of Brooklyn College, he was ordained at N. Y. School of the Hebrew Union College-Jewish Institute of Religion.

THE fact that we speak of Reform Judaism in the present tense and not in the past (reformed) tells us something very important about the philosophy of the movement: namely, that it is an on-going, living, dynamic approach to Judaism, not a past-tense, completed fact. From the beginning, the leaders of Reform looked upon Judaism as a living, adapting, fluid faith which could flourish in any environment.

The founders of Reform in the German-speaking lands of Europe, however, were not thinking in terms of a new "movement" in Judaism. Their work eventually did lead to a new religious denomination, but it was not the central aim of the early leaders. The early "reformers" were essentially *maskilim* (cultured and enlightened people) who were sensitive to special situations in their countries and states. Their suggestions for the practice of Judaism were not a conscious reaction to the antisemitism of 18th century Europe. They did not offer Reform as a way of combating antisemitism; rather they were responding to specific developments in the states of Central Europe, to circumstances that they regarded as requiring new approaches from the Jews.

THE PATH OF REFORM JUDAISM IN EUROPE

Perhaps the most important single event that launched Reform Judaism was the *tolerannzpatent* (Edict of Toleration) of Emperor Joseph II of Austria, issued in the year 1782. This edict abolished the poll tax for Jews, as well as the *ot kalon* (the Jews' badge) which was a "mark of humiliation." It also banned the forced baptism of Jewish children by non-Jewish midwives.

33

Where it had been made to appear shameful to be a Jew
prior to this, a measure of dignity began to be permitted to
our forefathers in Central Europe. Jews had been forbidden to use German in documents and contracts; instead
they had been ordered to draw up their legal contracts in
Yiddish only. This was now negated, and Jews were given
access to the national tongue. Where Jews had been restricted in their occupations and had been prohibited from
working the land, now they were permitted to take up
agriculture. Where Jews had previously been forced to
school their own young, now Jewish children were to be
permitted into the public schools. And where Jews had
been restricted in their travel, and were refused permission
to live within the city limits of Vienna, they were now permitted freer movement within the Empire.

The Edict of Toleration did not actually bring about tremendous differences in the social structure or climate of
Austria, but it is interesting to note some of the reasoning
behind the Emperor's action. As explanation, Joseph II
stated that "to me the Jews are human beings, consumers,
and tax payers and consequently useful if properly kept in
check." It was a change from the past, however, to be
deemed useful human beings.

The newly granted freedom produced in part of the
Austrian Jewish community some profound reactions, one
of them having to do with the attitude toward Hebrew.
There had been a slow but steady decay of Hebrew learning and culture among the Jews of Austria, and with the
granting of some of the new rights in certain of the country's districts there was a move toward the abandonment of
the *lashon hakodesh* (the holy tongue). Some rabbis of
the time, influenced by this new spirit of turning outward
toward the national culture, wrote and preached that Hebrew was no longer necessary for the Jew in his worship.
Rather, these rabbis argued, it would be better to revise
the liturgy, shorten the prayers, and have them delivered in
the vernacular so that they might be truly comprehensible

to those who prayed and to those who would hear the prayers offered in the synagogue.

An important contribution to the development of the vernacular language for religious uses was made by Moses Mendelssohn, who translated the *Torah* into German. His translation was printed in Hebrew letters, however. The German words were transliterated in Hebrew so that the general Jewish reader, not yet equipped with a good knowledge of German, would be able to read the translation. Mendelssohn thus combined the traditional text with the German language, opening a path for the Jews to German, and through that language to secular Western culture.

Someone has said about Mendelssohn that he "called on his fellow Jews to be rational in faith, orthodox in practice, and German in culture." While this sounds like a neatly packaged formula, it does raise the question as to how the German Jew could be all of these things at the same time. Moses Mendelssohn was not able to answer this question for his contemporaries, but he did provide the beginnings for the working out of a solution to the problem.

Another reaction to the Jew's increased freedom and to his closer contact with people in the non-Jewish world was that for the first time in many centuries the Jew was able to observe the Gentile in the practice of his religion. Because the Gentile was so much in the majority his practices were accepted as being indigenous to the country, and many Jews envied the Gentile for his forms of worship. Some of these forms influenced the more educated among the Jews, certainly those who had the greater contact with the Gentile world, and led some Jews to make changes in synagogue practice that brought the worship service closer to the Gentile model.

THE CHANGES THAT WERE INTRODUCED

Noticeable among the reforms was the shortening of the synagogue service. Throughout the centuries rabbis and congregational leaders had expanded the liturgy to the

point where the prayer service was considered to be, at least
in the minds of many Jews, overly long, repetitious, and
perhaps even boring. By comparison with the worship of
non-Jewish religious groups, a service in the synagogue
was poor, and already in those years beginning to be poorly
attended. In some sections of the Jewish community in the
German-speaking states, synagogue leaders therefore began to demand more punctuality in the start of the service,
and more decorous and dignified behavior on the part of
the congregation at prayer.

In time some leaders introduced music, choirs and more
singing in order to make the worship more enjoyable.
Many of the rabbis also began to preach sermons at all of
the regular services so as to bring Judaism and the prayerbook into harmony with the new philosophies that the
people were now in contact with in the world outside.

In addition to this, many changes were made in the
siddur (prayerbook) itself. The newly-liberated Jew, now
that he was an actual part of German society, began to
have second thoughts about the prayers in the *siddur* which
voiced Israel's longing for a return to Zion and the reestablishment of the Temple ritual there once again. It was
not that they necessarily scorned the idea of a return to the
bet hamikdash (the Holy Temple), but that they regarded
it as ungrateful and perhaps even insulting that, having
been newly accepted into the German society, they should
continue publicly to desire to be repatriated to distant and
foreign Palestine.

A very large part of the Jews of Germany and Austria
clung to the traditional practices of Judaism that they had
inherited from the ghetto past, and discussion within the
Jewish community waxed furious and violent on many
occasions over the radical departures from old-line
Judaism.

A final consequence of the new freedom for the Jew was
the inevitability of assimilation and a rise in intermarriage, resulting in the rejection of Judaism by a substantial
number. As a mobile citizen of the country the Jew was

able physically to escape from his ghetto-type environment. Where once some Jews had felt the ghetto-developed rituals and customs to be irksome and "backward," now many found new joy and delight in their heritage as a result of the "reforms" of Jewish practices that had been introduced during the years 1817-1871. Because of them, there can be no doubt that Reform Judaism was responsible for the saving of many of the Jews of Germany from leaving the religion of their fathers.

REFORM COMES TO AMERICA

It should be noted that the modernization of Judaism as it took place in Europe has not been presented as the "Movement" of Reform Judaism. No doubt, it formed the basis for what later on became the Reform Movement, but at the time described previously it would not be correct to refer to the new thinking as anything like a movement. In Central Europe we had mainly individuals who influenced some people to make a shift in their beliefs and practices. But it was not until this philosophy was brought to the shores of America, and not until it was carefully cultivated and given certain organizational forms, did it become, or could it be considered, a real movement.

The new Judaism was more successful in America than in Europe for a number of reasons. In the first place America offered people the ever-shifting frontier; it offered Judaism and other philosophies new frontiers in which to grow. America offered political liberty and economic opportunity, and the Jew, like all the other immigrants, could start life here with a clean slate. It has been said that anything new could have succeeded in America where it had failed in Europe, simply because the country itself was so new.

But, as important as the free intellectual climate of America was for the growth of the Reform Movement, we must also look to the beliefs and activities of that small group of immigrant rabbis who preached the harmony be-

tween American and Jewish ideals. They were able to
enunciate in modern terms ideas they had carried over to
these shores from their native Germany. We must, for example understand the great importance of Rabbi Isaac
Mayer Wise, the organizer and founder of American Reform Judaism. From the moment of his arrival in this
country Rabbi Wise spoke only English. This must be
understood, because it was a contrast to the other rabbis
who had come to America about the year 1846 (not until
1883 did we have ordained American rabbis). Rabbi Wise
wrote and preached in English because he entered into the
spirit and the tempo of American life. He also recognized
that the old European forms would not be adequate for a
viable and meaningful Judaism suited to the American
frontier.

It should be borne in mind that the earliest West European immigrants moved out, for the most part, into the
Middle West, there to become prosperous businessmen who
sought to become thoroughly Americanized in every aspect
of their lives. In the America of that day, which had had no
history of enforced ghettos or second-class citizenship (except in the case of Negro slaves), interaction between Jew
and non-Jew was an everyday occurrence. There was of
course an image of the Jew that non-Jews had acquired
from their religious training, but in America the patterns
of the past were not usually mechanically reproduced. Jew
and non-Jew met on the soil of America in those frontier
days with less sting to the prejudices and distrust that had
developed into a way of life in Europe.

The early Reform rabbis had no parochial, no limited
view of Judaism. They preached the universalism of the
Torah, the ethics of the prophets, and the antiquity of the
Talmud (but not its binding authority). The early Reform
rabbis were selective in what they chose from the Jewish
tradition to teach here in America. This was in keeping
with the way American culture in general was developing,
for people in general were retaining from their multi-

cultured backgrounds that which they considered important, and which fitted in with their American experience.

CUSTOMS AND PRACTICES: THE REFORM VIEW

Since much of Reform Judaism has to do with changes
in customs and practices it would be preferable, before
attempting to define Reform as a religious movement, to
show how it approached the various rituals and ceremonies
of Judaism. We must observe a note of caution, however:
one can speak only of the majority of Reform congregations, not for the movement as a whole. Rabbis and congregations, even within the Reform family, may or may not
observe a specific practice, or they may perform a ceremony
in their own way. That such differences exist within Reform relates to one of the important underlying principles
of the Movement of which we will speak later.

A. *The Sabbath*

For the majority of Reform Jews, the major observance
of the Sabbath is the late Friday evening service. Jews
used to hold a short service on Friday before nightfall, but
Reform Judaism introduced a formal one after supper on
Friday night. It did so at a time when the Jewish community of America as a whole was neglecting the Saturday
morning service, which had been the high point of Sabbath observance in the old country. What seemed to appeal
to people was the opportunity to end the week by attending the synagogue on *erev Shabbat* (Sabbath Eve), and
worshiping together. The late Friday service was one of
the innovations that Reform pioneered, and because of its
success it was adopted by other Jewish groups as well.

Most Reform Jews drive cars and cook on the Sabbath
and other holidays, activities that the traditional definitions
of "work" would seem to prohibit. In addition, organ or
other instrumental music is common in the synagogue on
Shabbat, for it is the Reform viewpoint that these things
are not deleterious to the spirit of the Sabbath, and they
are certainly in harmony with modern American life, and

in the case of synagogue music help to make the Sabbath
more beautiful and inspiring to the worshiper.

B. *Holidays and Festivals*

Reform Jews follow the *biblical* Festival calendar in the
main. Consequently, *Rosh Hashanah* and *Shavuot* are celebrated on the first day only, *Succot* on the first and eighth
day, and *Pesach* on the first and seventh day.

C. *Bar Mitzvah and Confirmation*

Bar Mitzvah is observed in the majority of Reform congregations, *Bat Mitzvah* to a lesser degree. In Reform, however, the age of thirteen takes on no special significance.
If a boy becomes *Bar Mitzvah,* and this is optional, it usually signifies not the attainment of manhood, but the first
step in a long path toward responsible Jewish adulthood.
The educational programs of most Reform congregations
take the teenager well into his High School years. It is in
these important years that the teenager has many questions
and doubts of a maturer level than those of the intermedi-
ate grades. Consequently, in Jewish Reform congregations
instruction continues on until Confirmation, usually at the
end of grade ten, and for many until the completion of
Senior High School. In any event, becoming *Bar Mitzvah*
does not signify the end of the Reform Jewish teenager's
religious education.

Confirmation is an innovation within our tradition,
originally conceived in Germany. One of the principles of
Reform was the belief in the religious equality of women
with men. If Jewish boys were to be given the opportunity
for study toward *Bar Mitzvah,* then equal opportunity had
to be offered to girls. The first Confirmation Class in Jewish
history that consisted of both boys and girls was confirmed
in their faith by Rabbi Israel Jacobson in Germany, in
1822. Rabbi Isaac M. Wise introduced it in America in his
congregation in Cincinnati, and it has become one of the
most important aspects in the Reform movement's educational program since.

In the congregation where this writer serves, the Confirmation Class is taught exclusively by the Rabbi. The course of study is comparative religion. The teenager who has spent ten years in our school completes his educational process by understanding his religion against the religious backgrounds of his neighbors. We do not teach other religions per se, but we teach about them in order to help the young Jewish mind to understand the uniqueness of his own religion, to help him appreciate the differences, and to give perspective to the similarities. During the Confirmation ceremony, which occurs on the Festival of *Shavuot,* the students confirm their faith and belief in the religion into which they were born. They freely accept Judaism as their religion in adult life and become Junior Members of the Congregation.

D. *Hats and the Talit in the Synagogue*

There is nothing in Jewish law which dictates that a man must cover his head while at prayer; even in traditional circles the *yarmulke* has only the cloak of custom, not law. The early Reformers, as we have seen, removed those traditions which tended needlessly to separate the Jew from his non-Jewish neighbor. In western culture, it was argued, one uncovers the head as a sign of respect, as for instance in saluting a woman or the flag. To many Jews it seemed consistent with this custom to remove one's head covering while paying respect to God at prayer.

Today most Reform congregations do not require the worshipers to cover their heads; most of our congregants prefer to pray without any head covering, but in many one is free to worship with or without. Many rabbis continue to wear *yarmulkes* or pulpit caps. A well-known leader in Reform recently wrote about this subject in the following manner: "While not a matter of law but of social propriety, it has come to be the source of serious conflict and heated emotions. As such, Reform has come to stress that it not serve as the point of bitter controversy, that men be permitted to worship as they wish, with head covered or uncovered, and that energies should be dedicated instead to the sincerity and regularity of prayer, and the enactment of the ideals enunciated in the prayers in individual lives."

Concerning the *talit,* however, more ought to be said. Its origin in the Exodus, with the fringes taken as a sign of freedom, make of it a significant symbol. It is not widely worn among Reform Jews today, but perhaps its wearing should be reconsidered; at least this writer would tentatively suggest it. What would be a necessary concomitant, however, in the light of our view on the equality of women in religion, would be to have them wear it at prayer as well as the men, if the custom is reintroduced.

One final word about Reform customs concerning prayer. Our views on religious equality make it logical for women and men to sit together at worship. Sectioning women off, in whatever manner and for whatever reason, violates a principle of great significance for our time.

THE PRINCIPLES OF REFORM JUDAISM

The underlying principle on which Reform Judaism was founded, and by which it continues to be guided, is that the Bible is the most magnificent document created by *man.* On the surface this does not appear to be a great enough truth upon which to base an entire religious movement, yet the implications of this statement are far-reaching and important.

In the first place this means that the Bible was not divinely revealed by God to Moses and then to the children of Israel. It does mean that it constitutes the efforts of an ancient people to set down their ideas, and questions and beliefs about God and the universe and about life and death, something the Hebrews did in a manner that no others have ever equaled. Nevertheless, with all its beauty and wisdom, we must realize that the Bible is the product of humans. And since it is a human document it is subject to both the greatness and the weakness of the men who created it.

The Bible is also the product of a particular era of time. Reform holds that not everything in Holy Scriptures is of equal value. Specifically, the ethical and moral teachings must be separated from the ritual and ceremonial traditions. The ethical teachings are timeless, unchanging, eternally valid. The ritualistic practices which are prescribed are the products of a definite time and location, related to specific economic and political conditions. The rituals and ceremonies are subject to change and in fact did change even within biblical times. Moses, although traditionally not the first Jew, introduced practices that were quite different from, and even unknown in, the days of the Patriarchs. And the practices of priests, aristocrats and commoners in the days of the kings, much decried by our Prophets, were already different from those Moses taught in the desert. And when the Temple fell whole sections of the Scriptures became obsolete, while the rise of the Synagogue, another of Judaism's great contributions, is not even depicted in the Bible. All the rituals and practices are therefore not necessarily equally valid in every age and in every country.

To phrase all of this differently, it means that each generation, and each individual for that matter, while striving to live within our ancient traditions also has the right and duty to examine and harmonize the tradition with the contemporary scene. This of course needs to be done with *knowledge* and with sympathetic understanding of Judaism's essence. This is the basic principle underlying the entire Reform Movement.

Reform Jews act as their own authority in all religious matters. The traditional sources of law and custom are always consulted and evaluated, but they are not necessarily binding. Every congregation within the Reform Movement is autonomous, as is each individual Jewish congregant. There are obvious difficulties inherent in this liberal approach to Judaism, but they are more than compensated for by the deeply, personally satisfying individual faith and devotion which it gives rise to, and which is

characteristic of most of the dedicated, religiously committed Reform Jews who profess its beliefs.

THE INSTITUTIONS AND ORGANIZATIONS OF REFORM

In the structure of the Reform Jewish community in
America, there are three major organizations and institutions: The Hebrew Union College-Jewish Institute of Religion (HUC-JIR); The Union of American Hebrew Congregations (UAHC); and the Central Conference of American Rabbis (CCAR).

The HUC-JIR is the oldest Rabbinic seminary in the
western hemisphere. Reform rabbis are college graduates
who then receive professional training for the rabbinate at
the HUC-JIR. The school has three branches, in Los Angeles, Cincinnati, and New York. A fourth, a School for
Biblical and Archaeological Study, was recently established
in Jerusalem. Both David Ben Gurion and Levi Eshkol
have remarked publicly that the Jerusalem School of the
HUC-JIR demonstrates the close link that exists between
the Reform Movement and the State of Israel.

The Union of American Hebrew Congregations is the
congregational arm of the Reform Movement. There are
nearly seven hundred congregations in the United States
and Canada which are affiliates of the UAHC. Located in
the beautiful "House of Living Judaism" in Manhattan,
the UAHC services its member congregations by providing special surveys and information, by publishing text
books, and by acting as consultants on all matters pertaining to synagogue life and administration. Further, it is
the parent organization for the National Federation of
Temple Sisterhoods, the National Federation of Temple
Brotherhoods, the National Federation of Temple Youth,
the National Association of Temple Educators and the
National Association of Temple Administrators.

The Central Conference of American Rabbis is the
organization of Reform rabbis. There are some 850 members of the CCAR at the date of this writing (1965), and it

has become one of the great organizations on the American scene. The resolutions it enacts at its annual conventions set a high standard for the Reform Jewish Movement in America. Indeed, its pronouncements are generally highly regarded over the entire country, both by Jews and non-Jews alike.

SUGGESTED READINGS

THE STORY OF JUDAISM, *Bernard Bamberger,* Union of American Hebrew Congregations.

REFORM JUDAISM: A Guide for Reform Jews, *Abraham J. Feldman,* Behrman House.

REFORM JEWISH PRACTICE AND ITS RABBINIC BACKGROUND, *Solomon Freehof,* Union of American Hebrew Congregations.

IN THE HOUSE OF THE LORD, *Solomon Freehof,* Union of American Hebrew Congregations.

CONSERVATIVE JUDAISM

By Samuel Chiel

SAMUEL CHIEL: Rabbi, Malverne Jewish Center, L. I.; a graduate of C. C. N. Y., he was ordained by Jewish Theological Seminary, 1952; program editor for the Eternal Light Television Series sermons included in **BEST JEWISH SERMONS OF 1954** (also 1960).

THE religious picture of American Jewry at the end of the nineteenth century presented a scene of two opposing camps at either end of the religious spectrum.

On the one hand, there was the Reform group, which in 1885 had adopted the Pittsburgh Platform, stating that the ceremonial laws were no longer to be accepted as binding and that the Jewish people had no national aspiration as implied in the traditional desire to return to Palestine.

On the other hand, the Orthodox group attempted to recreate the life of Eastern Europe in America without taking into account the changed environment, the inroads of the majority culture, and the strenuous efforts needed to fashion a new life in a strange environment.

Confronted by these two extremes, the early leaders of Conservative Judaism were convinced that neither represented a true version of traditional Judaism. Men like Sabato Morais, Alexander Kohut, H. Pereira Mendes and Benjamin Szold felt that Reform Judaism, by its radical changes, had eliminated some of the most essential fundamentals of Judaism. The *Mitzvot Maasiot* (ritual commandments) were part of the basic structure of our religion and reflected the particular genius of Judaism in its attempt to hallow all of life. To eliminate them was to cut a limb from the living organism of our faith.

These men also recognized that changed circumstances demanded new approaches and a willingness to confront the American civilization and face the challenges it presented. They knew that American rabbis of the future

47

would be able to communicate with their congregants only if they were trained in the English language and were conversant with the best that American education and culture were able to offer.

In truth, the early leaders of Conservative or Historical Judaism, as they called their point of view, did not intend to create a new movement in Judaism. In the Inaugural Address by Solomon Schechter at the organizing convention of the United Synagogue, he emphasized:

> Let me premise that this United Synagogue has not been called into life with any purpose of creating a new division. While it will, as its name implies, unite us for certain purposes, which we deem sacred and indispensable to the welfare of Judaism, it is not our intention to enter into a feud with the existing parties. Life is too short for feuds, and the task before us is so great, so manifold, that we must spare all our faculties and save all our strength for the work of a positive nature.

Instead, they hoped to create a kind of center position which would attract both extremes to it. However, this hope was not realized.

In 1886, these rabbinic leaders of traditional congregations organized the Jewish Theological Seminary of America in New York as a school for the training of rabbis and teachers. The charter of the Seminary explains that it was founded for "the preservation in America of the knowledge and practice of historical Judaism." But it was not until 1902, when Solomon Schechter was invited to come from Cambridge to become the President of the Seminary, that this institution began to wield its great influence on the American religious scene.

Schechter was the single most important influence in the growth and influence of Conservative Judaism. He was brought up in Rumania and received an intensive education in an atmosphere of Jewish learning and piety. Subsequently, he studied in Vienna and Berlin, learning there the scientific approach to the study of Judaism. In

England he became Reader in Rabbinics at Cambridge University.

Schechter, as President of the Seminary, transformed it into an outstanding academic and religious institution. He set rigorous standards for students who would enter its Rabbinical School. He engaged the greatest Jewish scholars as professors of Bible, *Talmud,* History, Philosophy and Hebrew Literature.

In addition to placing the Seminary on a solid academic base, Schechter created what he termed "the greatest bequest that I shall leave to American Israel," the United Synagogue of America. It is this organization, with its modest beginnings of twenty-two constituent congregations, which ultimately gave to the movement its broad base of support without which it could not have functioned.

In his remarkable Inaugural Address at the founding of the United Synagogue on February 22, 1913, Schechter outlined the most important guiding principles of Conservative Judaism. He stressed the importance of English sermons at the services. He insisted on order and decorum in the synagogues. He called for the use of scientific methods of study in the Seminary, as well as in the *Talmud Torahs.* All of these he recognized as being essential elements in the attempt to recapture the loyalty and respect of young American Jews for the teachings of the *Torah* and Jewish tradition.

In addition, he emphasized the importance of the religious education of women, which had in the past been all too often neglected. He declared:

It should again be the duty of this Union to make its influence felt with regard to the religious education of women, which is sometimes so woefully neglected in many old congregations. It is through them that we reach the children in a country like America, where the husbands are busy all the week. It is through them that we can save a great part of the Sabbath, and it is through them that the dietary laws will be observed in our homes. I would even suggest that the Union assign a certain portion of its work to women, and give them regular shares in its activities. They can become more than an auxiliary to us; indeed helpful in many respects where, as conditions are in this country, their influence is more far-reaching than that of their husbands.

He spoke further of the need for bringing Judaism back into Jewish homes with the observance of the rituals, such as the dietary laws. He called for the preparation of new textbooks for the congregational schools, and stressed the teaching of the Hebrew language.

Cyrus Adler became President of the Seminary in 1915 after Schechter's death. He helped to consolidate the position of the Seminary, in its financial structure and in its goal of graduating rabbis and educators for the Conservative Movement.

Dr. Louis Finkelstein succeeded Cyrus Adler as President of the Seminary. Under his brilliant leadership, the Seminary has continued to be an outstanding school of Jewish learning and scholarship, but in addition it has become an even more vital force in its impact upon the Conservative Movement, the American Jewish community and the general American scene.

Though its founders intended otherwise, Conservative Judaism in the last sixty years has grown and flourished into a great religious movement, embodied in a threefold organizational structure consisting of three primary parts: a Seminary, a professional association and member synagogues.

THE SEMINARY

The Jewish Theological Seminary has become one of the outstanding institutions of learning in the world. The Seminary ordains the rabbis who serve Conservative congregations. In addition, the Teachers Institute prepares young men and women for the Hebrew teaching profession, as well as for administrative positions in Jewish education. The Cantors Institute provides the training for the *chazzanim* of Conservative synagogues. In addition, there are classes at the Seminary for adults who are interested in deepening their knowledge of Judaism on a non-professional basis.

The Seminary maintains the largest Jewish library in the world, containing more than 200,000 books of Judaica and 10,000 rare manuscripts. The Jewish Museum is another of its endeavors, displaying the beauty of Jewish ritual and art objects. In Los Angeles, the Seminary has created a western branch known as the University of Judaism, which maintains classrooms, workshops, a theatre, a museum and a library for the 1,600 students enrolled there.

Through its program "The Eternal Light," the Seminary has been bringing to millions of Jews and non-Jews the message of Judaism through radio and television. With its Institute of Social and Religious Studies, it has provided a forum for the exchange of religious and philosophical insights with clergymen of other faiths. In recent years, the Seminary has created a network of seven Ramah Camps, where 2,000 young people spend their summer in a unique Hebraic and religious setting, combining study and recreation.

THE RABBINICAL ASSEMBLY

The Rabbinical Assembly of America is the rabbinic organization of the Conservative Movement. It consists mainly of Seminary graduates, as well as others who have joined the association. It is concerned with the problems confronting the rabbinate and has been active in the study and evaluation of the Jewish law in relation to the needs of the members of its congregations.

THE UNITED SYNAGOGUE

The third major element of the Conservative Movement

is the United Synagogue of America, which acts as a unifying organization of the member congregations, for the purpose of serving and guiding them in the achievement of higher standards in congregational life.

Its major emphasis, in consonance with Schechter's original guiding principles, has been in the field of education. Its Commission on Jewish Education has developed standards and curricula for the congregational schools, has published many textbooks and other educational materials, and has stimulated the congregations to provide more intensive education for their children.

The Commission's counterpart on the adult level is the National Academy for Adult Jewish Studies, which is providing similar services to the Adult Education programs of the congregations.

In the area of informal education for young people, the Department of Youth Activities directs the national youth organization known as the United Synagogue Youth. It schedules national conventions, area-wide conclaves and summer encampments. Recently it has formed a new group called *Atid,* for the college-age youngsters of the United Synagogue.

The Joint Commission on Social Action attempts to translate the ethical teachings of Judaism into concrete actions of social concern in areas such as civil rights, separation of church and state and many others.

The Committee on Congregational Standards provides guidance to the congregations in their adherence to basic principles of the Movement in areas such as Sabbath, *Kashrut,* fund raising, relationships with other congregations and the general community.

In 1957 the World Council of Synagogues was organized to serve as a unifying force for Conservative Congregations in other parts of the world. It has attracted congregational affiliation in Latin America, India and Israel.

Though each of the synagogues is in the final analysis autonomous, these three organizations help to create a general consensus among the constituent members. The

Conservative Congregational service is generally characterized by the use of Hebrew and English prayers, the men wear a *talit* and *yarmulke,* and men and women are seated together at the services.

IDEOLOGY

Though in our study of Jewish religious ideologies we accentuate the differences between us, it is well to recall that we are united on many more beliefs than those in which we differ. Religious Jews agree on the basic principles of our faith: the belief in One God and the important corollaries that stem from that belief, the unity and dignity of mankind. In addition, we all see the role of man as being a co-worker with God in the process of perfecting ourselves, mankind and the universe.

However, we differ from Orthodoxy and Reform in laying particular stress upon certain parts of the tradition, which we consider to be central to Judaism. Three of these aspects of special emphasis are: the concept of Catholic Israel, the viewpoint of Positive-Historical Judaism, and the idea of Unity in Diversity.

CATHOLIC ISRAEL

It was Solomon Schechter who used this term as a translation for an ancient concept in our tradition known as *Klal Yisrael*—the importance of the totality of the Jewish people. To clarify the emphasis of Conservative Judaism on this concept, we need first to be reminded of another basic idea taught by a medieval Jewish sage when he asserted that Israel, God and the *Torah* are One. By this he meant to say that Israel's task as a people was to fulfill its covenant with God, to become a holy people through the teachings and guidance of the *Torah*. These three elements are inseparable parts of our religion.

It appeared to the founders of Conservative Judaism that both Orthodoxy and Reform had emphasized one part of this triad to the virtual exclusion of one or both of the other elements.

Reform Judaism, in the early part of this cenutry, placed its greatest emphasis on the belief in God and the need for ethical living. However, it negated the authority of the *Torah* in its ritual commandments, as well as the whole body of Jewish interpretation of the *Torah* through the centuries in the *Talmud* and the Codes. Furthermore, Reform denied the concept of an indivisible bond between segments of the Jewish people by asserting that Jews were a religious group only, without the affirmation of nationhood reflected in the Jewish hope for the restoration of Zion.

Orthodoxy, on the other hand, emphasized faith in God and the authority of the *Torah,* but in its rigid adherence to Jewish law and its refusal to countenance change in the law, neglected to take into account the third part of the triad—Israel, the Jewish people in its present context on the American scene.

Conservative Judaism agreed on the primacy of belief in God and the authority of the *Torah,* but also insisted that the national aspects of Jewish history must not be neglected. The Bible, the *Talmud,* the liturgy, all speak of Israel's sorrow at the exile of our people from the Holy Land and consistently voice its longing for the return to Zion. Conservative Jews felt that to eliminate this aspiration for a physical homeland of the Jewish people and the spiritual influence which could emanate from it to Jews throughout the world, would be untrue to Jewish tradition. It is therefore easy to understand why Conservative Judaism has been from the outset in the forefront of the Zionist Movement to reestablish the State of Israel.

In line with this same stress on *Klal Yisrael,* the Conservative Movement has placed great emphasis on the study of the Hebrew language in its schools, as well as its use in the liturgy. This stems from a recognition of the fact that one of the great bonds which unites the

Jewish people, wherever they reside, is the language of the Bible and the prayerbook.

POSITIVE-HISTORICAL JUDAISM

It was Zechariah Frankel (1801-1875), a great German scholar and rabbi, who was the creator of the "positive-historical" school in Judaism. His thinking and writing had a profound influence upon the Conservative Movement,

It consists of the view that though we are always prejudiced in favor of the tradition, because of the great values it possesses and because of its hallowed usage by our people, Judaism has never remained static as a religion. It has changed in adjusting to the needs of new generations and new developments in our history.

This change, however, has not been revolutionary or haphazard. It has been a slow, evolutionary process created within the framework of Jewish law and guided by the requirements of Jewish life.

This attitude of Conservative Judaism is well reflected in the title of an excellent book on the development of Conservative Judaism, edited by Rabbi Mordecai Waxman: *Tradition and Change.* It differs from Reform Judaism's attitude in that Reform has rejected the binding authority of Jewish law. It differs from Orthodoxy, which is reluctant to permit any changes in Jewish law.

Conservative Judaism believes that the law must be examined in the light of modern needs. If changes are required, they should be made through the *Halachah,* the legal system created by our tradition.

An example of this approach may be seen in a responsum written by members of the Law Committee of the Rabbinical Assembly some years ago, which was approved by a majority of that committee. Since it was not adopted unanimously, by the rules of the Rabbinical Assembly, this responsum does not have official status. Yet at the same time, being the result of the cumulative efforts of three leading members of the Conservative Rabbinate, it gives us an excellent example of the Conservative approach to Jewish law.

The responsum deals with Sabbath Observance. The major part of this document provides an analysis of the reasons for the breakdown in the observance of the Sabbath, and is coupled with a positive program and strong appeal for the revitalization of the Sabbath in the life of the American Jew. Then, in regard to the question of the permissibility of riding to the Synagogue on the Sabbath in order to attend Services, the responsum declares:

As we have already indicated, participation in public service on the Sabbath is in the light of modern conditions to be regarded as a great mitzvah, since it is indispensable to the preservation of the religious life of American Jewry. Therefore it is our considered opinion that the positive values involved in the participation in public worship on the Sabbath outweigh the negative values of refraining from riding in an automobile. When attendance at services is made unreasonably difficult, without the use of an automobile, such use shall not be regarded as being a violation of the Sabbath.

The rabbis point out that this easement should be understood in the light of the total program of Sabbath revitalization, as part of the attempt to make the Sabbath central in the life of the American Jew.

The responsum exemplifies the serious attempt on the part of Conservative Judaism to evaluate Jewish law in the light of modern circumstances, where Jews sometimes live at great distances from the synagogue, and to recommend changes in the law when they are felt to be necessary.

UNITY IN DIVERSITY

A third aspect of the ideology of Conservative Judaism

is the idea of retaining unity within the Movement while yet permitting a certain amount of diversity for individual congregational expression as well.

In the Preamble to the Constitution of the United Synagogue of America, after the basic standards for congregational practices are established, which include "loyalty to the *Torah* in its historic exposition; to further the observance of the Sabbath and the Dietary Laws; to preserve in the service the reference to Israel's past and the hopes for Israel's restoration," it continues:

> *It shall be the aim of the United Synagogue of America, while not indorsing the innovations introduced by any of its constituent bodies, to embrace all elements essentially loyal to traditional Judaism and in sympathy with the purposes outlined above.*

This statement gives recognition to the fact that at times certain synagogue practices develop, not through the interpretation of the law alone, but from the attempts on the part of the congregations together with their spiritual leaders to give some varied expression to the ritual in the context of the times. Thus, for example, the *Bat Mitzvah* ceremony is an innovation created by Dr. Mordecai M. Kaplan, one of the great philosophers of the Conservative Movement, in an attempt to give equal status to girls and to afford them an opportunity for affirming their faith at the same age as is offered to boys through the *Bar Mitzvah*. What began as an innovation, apparently answered a felt need among American Jews, so that this Ceremony is not only practiced among Conservative Jews, but is becoming an accepted practice by others as well.

Another example of this kind of creative diversity is reported by Dr. Robert Gordis, Professor of Bible at the Seminary and outstanding expositor of the Conservative Movement. In his book *Judaism For the Modern Age,* Dr. Gordis describes an innovation on the holiday of *Sim-*

chat Torah which was introduced in one synagogue and has now been adopted in others as well. Traditionally, each male of *Bar Mitzvah* age and over is called to the *Torah* on this day of Rejoicing over the *Torah*. In addition, after the adults have been honored, all the children are called to the *Torah* to recite the blessings in unison with an adult.

As a result of a question by a group of women as to whether they, too, had a share in the *Torah,* one rabbi introduced the practice of calling all the women to the *Torah* to recite the blessing together with a male member of the congregation. A number of congregations have now adopted this innovation, enabling the women to rejoice equally with the men and children in the affirmation of their love for the *Torah*.

Diversity is creative and can add new vitality, but it must not be permitted to become chaotic. Unity must be maintained as well. This is accomplished by what Rabbi Mordecai Waxman terms as a "generally sensed set of standards" throughout the Movement. These standards, as reflected for example in the use of the prayer book published by the Rabbinical Assembly and the United Synagogue, used by most Conservative Congregations, would indicate both the desire to maintain the traditional structure, pattern, and warmth of the service together with some modifications that make the service even more relevant for our day.

RELIGIOUS JEWRY TODAY

The complexion of Jewish religious life which confronted the founders of Conservative Judaism in this country has changed considerably. The extremist positions taken by Reform and Orthodoxy have been modified through time and experience on the American scene.

In the Reform Movement, there has been a greater return to the traditional forms and expression of our faith. The Hebrew language is being taught in Reform congregational schools and has been increasingly introduced in the synagogue service. Its attitude toward the rituals has become more positive even though it may not accept their binding character. In addition, the Reform Movement, with very few exceptions, has changed its approach to Zionism and Israel and has adopted a pro-Zionist, pro-Israel position.

Orthodoxy too, with the exception of small extremist groups, has modified its approach to the American environment and experience. Its rabbis now generally combine a *Yeshivah* and university training and are fully conversant with the modern scene. Many Orthodox rabbis have accepted pulpits in congregations with mixed seating. Though the service remains predominantly Hebrew, English readings have been introduced as well.

In a sense, it appears that though the original hope of the founders of Conservative Judaism to rally all Jews to its course of traditional Judaism failed, yet in the six decades of its active growth, both extremes have moved closer to the Conservative position in their approach to Jewish life. This would tend to indicate the wisdom and foresight of the early leaders of Conservative Judaism in their attempt to create a religious pattern in consonance with the tradition, and at the same time, in harmony with modernity.

THE CHALLENGES

Despite the growth of the Conservative Movement to its present size of a million and a half adherents, and despite the proliferation of its synagogues throughout the country, its leaders recognize that its work has only begun. In the second half of the twentieth century, the challenges that confront it are very great.

Together with its Reform and Orthodox counterparts, Conservative Judaism faces the problem of trying to make Judaism become a live option in the lives of its adherents. Most congregants are still indifferent to the religious and cultural offerings of the synagogue. Most are still operating with a minimal knowledge and understanding of their faith. Some of their children are tragically cutting themselves off from the Jewish community by becoming partners in mixed marriages which often result in a dissolution of ties with the Jewish people.

The challenge that faces Conservative Judaism is to convey to each of its adherents the beauty, truth and inspiration of his faith and his heritage. It lies in making the faith in one God and in one humanity real in the thoughts and actions of each person. It consists of showing its adherents the great value of the *mitzvot,* both as ethical instruments as well as positive sources of Jewish identification. It involves making the ethical imperatives of Judaism significant guideposts in the conduct of each person's life.

In short, Conservative Judaism must now prove itself by creating Jews who are fully committed to God, *Torah,* and the people of Israel.

SUGGESTED READINGS

TRADITION AND CHANGE, *Mordecai Waxman,* Burning Bush Press.

THE EMERGENCE OF CONSERVATIVE JUDAISM, *Moshe Davis,* Jewish Publication Society.

CONSERVATIVE JUDAISM, *Marshall Sklare,* The Free Press.

ARCHITECTS OF CONSERVATIVE JUDAISM, *Herbert Parzen,* Jonathan David Company.

RECONSTRUCTIONISM

by Alan W. Miller

ALAN W. MILLER: Rabbi, Society for the Advancement of Judaism; educated at University College, London and Balliol College, Oxford; received Minister's Diploma from Jews' College, London; lecturer in Hebrew and Midrash at Leo Baeck College, London.

RECONSTRUCTIONISM is a religious-humanist philosophy which seeks to define the function of Judaism in the modern world. As a religious philosophy it is dedicated to reinterpreting Jewish tradition in order to make it vital for the daily life of the Jew as a member of the Jewish people. As a humanist philosophy it suggests that the proper goal of human activity in general and of Jewish activity in particular is the perfectibility of society.

The philosophy of Reconstructionism was developed by Mordecai M. Kaplan. Dr. Kaplan was born in Europe in 1881 and emigrated to America as a boy. The Pale of Settlement in which he had been born was only in a chronological sense part of the late nineteenth century. From the point of view of being a Jew it was, to all intents and purposes, pre-modern. The New World of America presented a complete contrast, politically, economically and culturally.

The tensions generated by the obvious disparity between the pre-modern world of his early years and the modern world he experienced in America aroused in him a burning desire to reconcile the two. Since in him the wish to remain a Jew in the modern world burned equally fiercely with the desire to be ruthlessly honest in his search for the truth, the philosophy of Reconstructionism, which grew out of his search, came to be both a diagnosis and a prescription for Judaism. The very term "Reconstructionism" is an implied evaluation of the past, in that it suggests that we cannot accept the past uncritically, that it is in need of reconstruction. It also suggests that the operation may best be performed through conscious and deliberately planned action.

WORK OF MORDECAI KAPLAN

Kaplan's thinking was increasingly reflected in his teaching and writing over the years. In 1922 he founded the Society for the Advancement of Judaism to serve, among other things, as a laboratory for experimentation in Jewish group expression. Out of the Review of that Society grew the *Reconstructionist Magazine* (founded January 1935), a bi-monthly which sets forth the ideology of Reconstructionism and reflects its principles through creative comments on and interpretations of Jewish life.

The Jewish Reconstructionist Foundation was established in 1940. Since it is a basic tenet of Reconstructionism that Jewish religion grows out of the collective civilizational experience of the Jewish people, the early Reconstructionists regarded themselves mainly as a school of thought, and not as a fourth denomination in American Jewish life. In fact, they considered the stress on denominationalism detrimental to the higher interests of Judaism. Reconstructionists therefore worked first within the existing organizations of the Jewish community. In recent years, however, the denominations within Judaism have tended to harden into monolithic and self-perpetuating groupings, and gradually Reconstructionism has begun to develop into a specific religious movement. This is reflected in the growth of institutional organizations like the Federation of Reconstructionist Congregations and Fellowships, the Reconstructionist University Fellowship, the Reconstructionist Press, the Reconstructionist Rabbinical Fellowship and a projected Reconstructionist Institute of Judaism.

As Dean of the Teachers Institute of the Jewish Theological Seminary of America, as Professor of Homiletics, and as a prolific writer and speaker Dr. Kaplan influenced large numbers of Jews, laymen as well as rabbis. His pupils, notably Eugene Kohn (former Managing Editor of the *Reconstructionist Magazine,* and Editor of the Reconstructionist Press), Ira Eisenstein (President of the

Reconstructionist Foundation and Editor of the *Reconstructionist Magazine*), Jack J. Cohen, and the late Milton Steinberg, collaborated with him in many of his publishing ventures.

In 1934 Kaplan's greatest work was published: *Judaism as a Civilization*. Other important books followed, such as *The Meaning of God in Modern Jewish Religion*, and *The Future of the American Jew*. In association with his colleagues he also revised the basic texts of Jewish worship in *The New Haggadah* (1941), the *Sabbath Prayer Book* (1945), the *High Holiday Prayer Book* (1947), the *Festival Prayer Book* (1958), and the *Daily Prayer Book* (1963).

PHILOSOPHY AND IDEOLOGY

The philosophy of Reconstructionism is perhaps most clearly manifest in *The New Haggadah*. In line with its religious-humanist view of history, which conceives of God as a force operating *through* man rather than a personal Supreme Being operating *on* man, Moses, who is not mentioned in the traditional *Haggadah*, is in *The New Haggadah* restored to his rightful place as an inspired leader of the Jewish people. For to ascribe glory *only* to God, Reconstructionists feel, reduces man to a passive, abject creature whose efforts are worthless in making the world a better place to live in. Such a downgrading does nothing to strengthen man in the battle against war, poverty, sickness and ignorance.

Again, *The New Haggadah* replaces a number of superfluous (from a modern point of view) sections in the traditional *Haggadah* by excerpts from Rabbinic literature, describing Moses as conceived in legend by the Jewish people. Most important of all, prayers dealing with the Messianic redemption of the future are translated into modern idiom and refer to freedom for all men from contemporary tyrants. Slavery is understood not merely literally as in "we were slaves in Egypt," but also metaphorically:

We have dedicated this festival tonight to the dream and the hope of freedom, the dream and the hope that have filled the hearts of men from the time our Israelite ancestors went forth out of Egypt. Peoples have suffered, nations have struggled to make this dream come true. Now we dedicate ourselves to the struggle for freedom. Though the sacrifice be great and the hardships many, we shall not rest until the chains that enslave all men be broken.

But the freedom we strive for means more than broken chains. It means liberation from all those enslavements that warp the spirit and blight the mind, that destroy the soul even though they leave the flesh alive. For men can be enslaved in more ways than one.

Men can be enslaved to themselves. When they let emotion sway them to their hurt, when they permit harmful habits to tyrannize over them—they are slaves. When laziness or cowardice keeps them from doing what they know to be the right, when ignorance blinds them so that, like Samson, they can only turn round and round in meaningless drudgery— they are slaves. When envy, bitterness and jealousy sour their joys and darken the brightness of their contentment—they are slaves to themselves and shackled by the chains of their own forging.

Men can be enslaved by poverty and inequality. When the fear of need drives them to dishonesty and violence, to defending the guilty and accusing the innocent—they are slaves. When the work men do enriches others, but leaves them in want of strong houses for shelter, nourishing food for themselves and for their children, and warm clothes to keep out the cold—they are slaves.

Men can be enslaved by intolerance. When Jews are forced to give up their Jewish way of life, to abandon their Torah, to neglect their sacred festivals, to leave off rebuilding their ancient homeland—they are slaves. When they must deny that they are Jews in order to get work—they are slaves. When they must live in constant fear of unwarranted hate and prejudice—they are slaves.

How deeply these enslavements have scarred the world: The wars, the destruction, the suffering, the waste: Pesah calls us to be free, free from the tyranny of our own selves, free from the enslavement of poverty and inequality, free from the corroding hate that eats away the ties which unite mankind.

Pesah calls upon us to put an end to all slavery: Pesah cries out in the name of God, "Let my people go." Pesah summons us to freedom.

(The New Haggadah, pp 11-13)

GOD AS PROCESS

A basic concept in Reconstructionism is that there is a principle of polarity at work in the cosmos whereby everything that exists is itself, and is also inextricably related to everything else. This cosmic principle of independence and interdependence is manifested in the sphere of natural affairs in what are known as the laws of nature, which include man in terms of his physical self. In man, conceived from a human point of view, this principle is manifested as human responsibility. In the same way, for example, that the galaxies and the solar system in which we live came into existence through the operation of the law of gravity, which is the cosmic principle of polarity operating in the sphere of physical nature, so also, it is believed, human society as we know it came into existence through the operation of this principle in the

sphere of ethical behavior. What is meant by God is the
process whereby this cosmic principle becomes manifest in
human experience through ethical behavior.

Where, in the physical universe, a star or a stellar
system is to be found, the principle of polarity operating
as gravity is at work. When in society, love, loyalty, integrity, responsibility and compassion are to be found,
the principle of polarity operating as God is at work.
God is thus conceived not as a Supreme Personal Being
who operates on the universe and on man from outside,
to whom we can address our petitionary prayers and who
can hear us. God is conceived as a process that is manifest
throughout the cosmos, operating in a specifically human
context and recognized as such.

The reality of God is thus conceived and experienced on
the level of the reality of gravity. When the ancient referred to the need of living in accordance with the will
of God he was, in the Reconstructionist view, referring
to the same need experienced by modern man who, in
the spirit of humanism which characterizes our age, refers
to the need of seeing the purpose of human existence in
terms of the happiness and perfection of man and society.
The uniqueness of the Jewish people lay in the fact that
they alone in the ancient world became aware of the
authentic relationship between a people and their God.
But other peoples also can and must experience that relationship. The fact that the Jewish people were the first
to discover it does not make it an exclusively Jewish
experience.

There can be no denying that superficially a great gulf
exists between the traditional view of God and the one
outlined above. According to Jewish tradition there exists
a Supreme Personal Being who created the world and
humanity. He is Omniscient, Omnipotent, Omnipresent
and Omnibenevolent. He chose, from among all peoples,
the Jewish people and gave them His *Torah*. Because they
failed to follow its precepts, God exiled them and if they
would only repent and observe that *Torah*, He would

redeem them and gather them into Zion through the agency of the Messiah. How can such a world outlook be reconciled with the naturalistic world outlook presupposed above, in which God is thought of as a process within nature, not as an entity external to it?

RECONSTRUCTIONIST VIEW OF JEWISH PEOPLE

According to pre-modern Judaism and its modern equivalents it is the Jewish people which exists for Judaism. According to Reconstructionism, however, it is Judaism which exists for the Jewish people. This revolutionary idea was sparked in the thought of the founder of Reconstructionism through the impact of the thinking of three men on his already questing mind, steeped in traditional Jewish values. From Ahad Ha-Am, Kaplan absorbed the importance of a Jewish people with its spiritual center in Zion. In Emile Durkheim he found confirmation of his own insights into the relationship of peoplehood to religion. And from John Dewey he learned the implications of modern scientific method in the sphere of philosophy, which led him to distinguish sharply between "ideation" as the classical method of philosophy and the functional approach which alone could be acceptable to modern scientific man. From these and other sources an all-embracing view of Judaism was formulated.

Judaism was seen as the evolving religious civilization of the Jewish people. The people were the permanent factor in Jewish experience, the theology merely relative. Ideas of God, for example, had altered radically over the ages. The religious differences between the Biblical and the Rabbinic periods could almost warrant our referring to two entirely different religions in these two periods. Only the fact that the same living people identified itself with both periods enabled the Jewish religion to undergo radical changes and yet still remain the Jewish religion.

Since the emancipation of the Jew in the modern world, he is faced with an entirely unprecedented situation. Not only does he exist as a member of his historic people, with its own Jewish religion as a primary element in its evolving religious civilization, but he also exists as a member of the national people among whom he finds himself. Since, according to Kaplan, a living people expresses its transcendental or transnatural concerns in religion, the modern Jew who is also an American finds himself living in two civilizations, a member of two peoples and in possession of two religions, Jewish and American.

Whenever the Jew lives in two civilizations, the very demographic nature of the situation demands that the non-Jewish civilization—the American, for example—be the primary one for him. In one country only is the Jew able to live in a primary *Jewish* civilization, in Israel, where the predominantly Jewish state places the *non-Jew* in a two-civilizational situation in which the Jewish one is primary. Kaplan was among the first in America to see the spiritual potentialities for the Jewish people as a whole of a Jewish majority in a state in Palestine, which would be a focal point of the transnational Jewish community. There would be creative reciprocity between all parts of the Jewish people, but especially creative would be those impulses emanating from the historic homeland of the Jewish people.

Most religions are natural outgrowths of the collective experience of a people. After a period of existence, a people tends to commemorate certain events, heroes, objects and texts as embodying the highest ideals known to that people and symbolic of its loftiest aspirations. In ancient times, however, our ancestors were entirely unaware of what we can now, through modern scientific insights, see to have been the natural origin of Jewish religion. In common with the rest of mankind, they tended to project onto the canvas of the external world ideas which originated in the collective experience of their own people.

When considered from this point of view, the gulf between the idea of God in Jewish tradition and that propounded by Reconstructionism is seen to be more apparent than real. The constant factor in Jewish history has always been the Jewish people. They maintained their identity through radical change in much the same way as the individual maintains his identity through the years by constantly reevaluating fixed points on the horizon of life. The evolving Jewish people constantly reevaluated and reconstructed themselves, albeit unconsciously. The Sabbath, for instance, underwent a radical transformation from what it had originally been in Bible times, as well as in later Apocryphal and Rabbinic times. The people maintained their identity by reinterpreting this basic element in their religion, and thus brought about continuity between one phase of its existence and the next. Other *sancta* (coined from "sanctum"—the holy things) that have undergone radical transformation in the course of Jewish history are God, Moses, *Torah,* Passover and worship, to mention but a few. All peoples develop sancta. They form the basis of religion.

A philosophy, once its basic propositions are altered, is no longer the same philosophy. A non-indigenous religion, such as Christianity, once its basic dogmas are removed or interpreted away, is a different religion. But a living people, such as the Jewish people, can undergo radical religious metamorphosis, and yet still remain in possession of what can quite legitimately be referred to as its religion. An interesting case of how this process operates on the level of the individual is brought out in Jean Anouilh's play, *Le Voyageur Sans Bagage.* There a man who suffers from serious amnesia becomes someone else to all intents and purposes by deliberately rejecting his own personal "sancta" (his parents, his past history, etc.), and by adopting those of someone else.

With the coming of the modern world it is no longer possible for many Jews who accept the scientific outlook to continue in the animistic paths of antiquity. They cannot explain the phenomenon of past and present Jewish history by the hypothesis of a Supreme Personal Being who has watched over them, a God who can operate on history from outside of Nature. Reconstructionism has a radically new approach. The facts of Jewish experience cannot be altered, but they can be explained more effectively.

By way of analogy, the ancients explained lightning as bolts thrown from heaven by some angry deity. Modern meteorology tells a different story. The phenomenon of lightning has not changed since time immemorial, but modern man is reasonably certain that the new scientific hypothesis accounts for it more adequately today than the old mythical hypothesis. He is also reasonably certain that it accounted for the phenomenon in the past, even when men believed in bolt-throwing deities.

JUDAISM AS A RELIGIOUS CIVILIZATION

While a new hypothesis about Judaism as an evolving religious civilization as opposed to a Revealed Religion cannot alter the past, but can merely account for it in terms more acceptable to modern scientifically oriented man than the pre-modern explanation, it is the essence of Reconstructionism that Judaism is currently in need of deliberate and calculated reconstruction. The new hypothesis has experimental implications for the present and future.

As seen by Reconstructionists, Jewish civilization evolved unconsciously; first there was a national phase of existence, which lasted until the Babylonian Captivity of 586 B.C.E., when religion was but one of several collective expressions, along with politics, secular literature and music. Then came the period of our subjection to the Persians, Greeks and Romans, when religion became a primary collective preoccupation of our people. This era, which lasted until the destruction of the second Temple in 70 C.E., is referred to as our ecclesiastical stage because in it the head of the Jewish people was a High Priest operating, in theory at least, under God. Apart from the short-lived Hasmonean episode there was no political leader such as a king. After the year 70 C.E. the effective leaders of the people were the rabbis, who functioned in terms of Rabbinic law. During this phase which lasted up to about 1800, our people were deprived not only of political autonomy and homeland but also, for the most part, of any political or human status whatsoever; religion became their sole preoccupation.

We are now, claims Reconstructionism, entering a fourth phase of our existence, a democratic phase in which the Jew will live in two civilizations, that of his country of domicile and that of Judaism. However, a civilization can function only if the people which lives in it also functions. Since the emancipation, the Jewish people can be said to exist and function as Jews, but not specifically as a Jewish people. The corporate status of the Jewish people, recognized by both Jews and non-Jews in the pre-modern period, no longer exists. Under democracy Jewish affiliation is of necessity voluntary, and those institutions to which the affiliation is normally made, the synagogue for example, are not representative of the people as a whole. Accordingly, Reconstructionism looks forward to the conscious and deliberate reconstitution of the Jewish people in the modern world, with an internationally recognized corporate status, as a prime means to the reconstruction of Jewish religion. Only insofar as Jewish religion grows out of the normal collective experience of the people as a whole can it effectively satisfy modern needs.

In the meantime Reconstructionism advocates the richest possible identification with Jewish civilization even though, in the absence of a reconstituted people and organic communities, such a civilization in the modern world can only be regarded as still in the making. The observance of all traditional ritual practices is strongly endorsed where they can be meaningfully maintained, not as decrees of a Supreme Being but as Jewish folkways expressive of the people's will to live—"religious poetry in action," as Kaplan has described them.

Especially does Reconstructionism stress that Judaism, as a civilization, is more than Jewish religion. All expressions of Jewish life in the sphere of art, music, and literature are encouraged as basic to the collective experience of that civilization. Thus Reconstructionism has constantly supported areas of Jewish life not specifically "religious" in character, in its belief that every creative Jewish endeavor, whether secular or sacred, enhances the collective status of the Jewish people and ultimately enriches its religious aspect. Even non-observant Jews who are nevertheless conscious Jews are welcomed to its ranks.

There is no doubt that the Reconstructionist approach appeals to many Jews today, especially the intellectual element, who are repelled by the prevailing expressions of Jewish life. Yet, Reconstructionism and its approach are for *Klal Yisrael,* and not just for its intelligentsia. Nevertheless, as Kaplan has repeatedly pointed out, unless a people can provide a meaningful *raison d'être* for its intellectuals, the quality of its collective life will inevitably deteriorate. The facts all point in one direction— that the lack of reconstruction in contemporary Jewish life has indeed meant a wholesale exodus of creative minds from the ranks of the Jewish people. Unless this can be stemmed, the future of the Jewish people remains uncertain. Yet the obstacle to the large-scale acceptance of the Reconstructionist approach lies not so much in the intellectual demands that its philosophy makes, as that in every area *except* the religious, modern man adopts the scientific outlook. In the sphere of the spirit alone is the constant cry, "Give me that old-time religion."

In the past, religion believed that one of its prime purposes was to explain away all the mysteries in life, or at least to account for them. The Bible thus provides answers to all sorts of ultimate question such as "Who created the world?" "How is it that there are different people in the world?" "How did the Jewish people become what it is?" "Why do men suffer?" The modern naturalist approach, implicit in Reconstructionism, does not deny the reality of these questions. It simply affirms that a bad hypothesis in this area of human speculation is worse than no hypothesis. The old answers are no longer satisfactory and no new answers are forthcoming simply because nobody really knows the answer to these questions; perhaps nobody ever will.

Reconstructionism is not perturbed by the fact that we cannot answer these ultimate questions. Transcending all these mysteries which man, if he is honest with himself, may never solve, Reconstructionism considers the primary questions for man as being: "What ought we to be doing to make the universe a better place than it now is, more fit for human habitation, and what ought we to be doing to make of human society an arena in which man can to an ever growing degree satisfy his will to salvation, which is a reflection, through his people, of the Divine Process at work in the universe?" Rather than concerning ourselves with the question "why do men suffer," Reconstructionism, without for one moment denying that it is a real question, suggests that we would better occupy our brains and hands by trying to build a world and a society in which men will behave more and more in such a way as to make the asking of that question unnecessary. Of course, man-made suffering is only a portion of the evil in the world. There are also "Acts of God," as the insurance companies call them. Yet we would do far better if we left the discussion of the problem of evil to a time when most man-made evil will have been eradicated.

The Reconstructionist position is a frankly religious-humanist one. It believes that man cooperating with God can move toward a more perfect society. It is a call to action in terms of ethical behavior, rather than to quiescent metaphysical speculation. If it does not appeal to all modern Jews, it may well be that all modern Jews are not thoroughly modern—that is, they have not yet applied to the sphere of religion what they know and practice in all other areas of their lives. To have raised the challenge "Think modern and act modern also" in the sphere of Judaism and Jewish religion, is the lasting contribution which Reconstructionism has made to Jewish life in the twentieth century.

SUGGESTED READINGS

QUESTIONS JEWS ASK: RECONSTRUCTIONIST ANSWERS, *Mordecai M. Kaplan.*

THE MEANING OF GOD IN MODERN JEWISH RELIGION, *Mordecai M. Kaplan.*

RELIGIOUS HUMANISM; A JEWISH INTERPRETATION, *Eugene Kohn.*

CREATIVE JUDAISM, *Ira Eisenstein.*

THE CASE FOR RELIGIOUS NATURALISM, *Jack J. Cohen.*
(all from Reconstructionist Press.)

ETHICAL DOCTRINES IN JUDAISM

by Arthur A. Chiel

ARTHUR A. CHIEL: Rabbi, Congregation B'nai Jacob, Wood-bridge, Conn.; ordained at J.I.R. in 1946 and received Doctor of Hebrew Letters degree at Jewish Theological Seminary in 1960; author of **JEWISH EXPERIENCES IN EARLY MANITOBA,** and the **JEWS OF MANITOBA** in 1961; lectured in Cantor's Institute of J.T.S.

BACK in the second century, Rabbi Judah Ha-Nasi, editor-in-chief of the *Mishnah,* raised the all-important question: *"Which is the right way that a man should choose for himself?"* (Pirke Avot, 2:1). Rabbi Judah was hardly the first man to seek the answer. Thinking men had pondered the same question long before him and they continue to do so down to our own day. To Aristotle, the great Greek philosopher, we are indebted for the term that designates this search after the "right way." Aristotle called it *Ethics.* It has come to mean the principles of right action. Ethics is concerned, then, with man's moral ideals and goals, with the constant challenge of making the proper choice.

AN ANCIENT QUEST

When the Hebrews made their appearance on the historic scene, some thirty-five hundred years ago, there had already been considerable attention given to the questions of what makes for the good man, what makes for the good life. Thoughtful Egyptians wrestled with these problems as did also their contemporaries, the Babylonians. In the four-thousand-year-old Gilgamesh Epic of Babylonian source the quest for answers led to the conclusion that life is brief, so why spend energy on the search for immortality. Rather let man eat and be merry by day and by night, let him rather acquire for himself a gay wardrobe and live happily with wife and family.

In the Egyptian Admonitions of Ipu-wer of approximately four millenia ago, the author characterized his fellow-men as indolent, corrupt, skeptical. The solution: let a strong leader come forward and determine for men their way of life. There are available to us for consideration a variety of ancient evaluations and proposals for "the right way."

ENTER THE HEBREWS

For a people that was eventually to influence at least one-third of Western civilization in its ethical thinking, the Hebrews made their appearance in a rather unspectacular manner. Compared with the Egyptians and the Babylonians, the Hebrews might be called latecomers on the historic scene. When these empires were long thriving polities, the Hebrews were but an inconspicuous band of nomads. When the Hebrews finally settled down permanently in their land, it was a tiny country. Looking back, it becomes obvious that neither by their antiquity did the Hebrews make their impact, nor by their military might. The Hebrews' influence was made felt through their religio-ethical breakthrough.

Einstein discovered a general system of mathematical equations which present a common background for all physical action. This comprehensive framework for the expression of the physical laws of the universe is known as the Unified Field Theory. In a sense the Hebrews "discovered" a kind of unity, a "Common Source" for all of existence. That source was *He-Who-Is-One*. Monotheism, the faith in a unique, single, supreme, nature-transcending will—this was Israel's revolutionary message to mankind. The One God is the focus of all that is and all that shall be. The recognition of His will "as the focal point from which understanding and thinking, acting and hoping" is Judaism's point of departure in all of its ethical approach to life.

There is *purposefulness* in existence. God did not end His role in human history after He brought the universe into being. He is continuously, actively involved in the world of change and struggle. In Hinduism the world of sense experience is considered an illusion (Maya) and therefore the religious man tries to gain release from the wheel of life. The ideal, then, is uninvolvement of the individual in the illusion, in life, with the goal of fading into the World Soul, Brahma. Quite the opposite is the understanding in Judaism. God is a reality, active, involved in what we see about us. He is a God of Justice who calls to man to help in the unfolding of a worthwhile existence through the guidelines which He has revealed to man.

MAN, THE PARTNER

In an interview during World War II, President Roosevelt was asked why America was involved in the war. He responded: "In defense of one verse in Genesis, 'God created man in His own image.' " The president was affirming a basic ethical concept of Hebrew origin, a concept which has been incorporated into American democracy.

The earliest chapters of Genesis offer insight into the status of man within God's total scheme. Having created a purposeful universe that was in its completeness "very good," man was brought forth as the climax to the creation process. To him was given the gift of life, to take that gift and make something worthwhile of it. Judaism thinks of man as "a partner of God in fulfilling the purpose of creation." His every act should be geared accordingly.

The *Talmud* summarizes man's unique qualities—he can stand erect, he can speak, he uses his intellect and he can look forward and upwards. All of these enable him to choose the right way. Again, the *Talmud* informs us that man also shares qualities in common with animal life—eating, drinking, procreating and dying. Man must then choose for himself, either the forwards-and-upwards goal, becoming the Psalmist's ideal of "little lower than the angels," or the behavior of an animal, becoming no more than primitive.

The problem of translating ethical ideals into practical application has been a mighty challenge to man. It is one thing to proclaim magnificent principles for society; it is quite another to make such principles concrete in day-by-day existence. Judaism aimed to wed the real to the ideal. It accepted what it believed to be divinely inspired law as a tangible expression and fulfillment of ethics. *Torah* was the repository of ethic-law. The commandments placed before Israel by Moses were a unique blending together of ethic-law. Moreover, Israel, having entered into a binding covenant with God, took upon itself the sacred obligation of its fulfillment.

Israel was charged: "You shall love your neighbor as yourself: I am the Lord." To love one's fellow man was the ethical imperative. But left alone by itself it would have become a hollow sentiment. The *Torah* code of Moses rescued it from such an unhappy fate. There were promulgated for the people binding laws which made of love for neighbor a reality:

> *You shall not reap the corners of the field nor gather the gleamings of your harvest.... You shall leave them for the poor and stranger. . . . You shall not steal, nor deal falsely, nor lie to one another. . . . You shall not oppress your neighbor or rob him. The wages of a hired servant shall not remain with you all night until the morning. You shall not curse the deaf or put a stumbling block before the blind. . . . You shall do no injustice in judgment; you shall not be partial to the poor or defer to the great, but in righteousness shall you judge your neighbor. You shall not go up as a slanderer among your people, and you shall not stand against the blood of your neighbor. . . . You shall not hate your brother in your heart but you shall reason with your neighbor. . . .* (Leviticus 19:10-17).

These and an evolving code of law were the concrete fulfillment of the ethical ideal of loving one's neighbor as oneself. Chief Justice Warren has rightfully said: "In civilized life, law floats in a sea of ethics. Each is indispensable to civilization. . . . Without ethical consciousness in most people, lawlessness would be rampant."

Judaism early recognized this complementary relationship of law and ethics. When God entered into a covenant with Abraham, He called upon the founding father of Israel and upon his descendants to make known to human-kind the way of the Lord, to do *Tzedakah* (Righteousness) and *Mishpat* (Justice) (Genesis 18:19). Righteousness becomes a fact through the discipline of law. Without law righteousness becomes merely a slogan.

EDUCATION IN ETHICS

Judaism was uniquely successful in developing agents and their methods for transmitting ethical principles. The Bible reveals who they were and how they proceeded. They were Moses and the successive prophets over seven centuries. Their methods were those of preaching, exhorta-tion and example. In turn, these prophets were succeeded by legislator-teachers who became known as the rabbis, who built on biblical foundation the body of interpreta-tions leading to legal ordinances known as the *Halachah* (Law). Their centuries' long teachings have come to us through the *Mishnah* and the *Talmud*.

The Age of the Prophets, then, was followed by the Age of the Rabbis. But Judaism early recognized that mere preachment and exhortation were not enough. In the Age of the Rabbis there was launched among the people the program of universal education. The *Torah* was not merely to be believed in, it was to be studied through a lifetime. The first century of the Common Era saw the realization of a full system of education for young and old.

Moreover, "audio-visuals" were gradually developed as instruments for ethical education. These were the symbols and ceremonies which vividly brought home to the people various concepts of the faith: of rest through the Sabbath, of *Rosh Hashanah* and *Yom Kippur* for introspection and repentance, of the *Mezuzah* on the door-post of every home in which is contained the declaration of God's oneness and His universal presence, summoning man to act accordingly in his daily existence. The *Ahavah Rabbah* prayer puts it clearly: "Inspire us to understand

and discern, to perceive, to learn and teach, to observe, do, and fulfill gladly the teachings of Thy *Torah*." The ethical way is one that must be steadily studied and deepened and carried into every area of life.

The rabbis believed that the prophets before them had reached the highest summit in ethical ideas and goals. They felt it their task to realize in practice these ethical teachings of the prophets. "Study is valuable," they said, "only because it is conducive to good deeds." Beautiful ideas professed by man are hardly enough. They must be converted to common use by humanity.

The aim and the purpose of the *Torah* commandments was to establish peaceful and friendly relations between man and man. The ultimate goal is the perfect society. The *Torah* is the means to a great end—the prophetic ideal of a Messianic era when peace and neighborly love will prevail among all people. "In the Messianic Age the *Mitzvot* will be suspended," the *Talmud* boldly suggests. Man will finally become so thoroughly ethical as to eliminate the need of law and commandments.

REGARD FOR LIFE

The idea expressed in the biblical story of Creation that *all* men are created in the image of God is considered as a basic principle of Judaism. Every human being has within him the divine spark and is capable of helping to realize God's plan in the universe. It is this belief in the God-like nature of man that attaches the highest value to human life. It follows then that the life of a human being is to be saved at almost any cost and his health is to be preserved even at the sacrifice of all laws and commandments. (The exceptions to this ethical principle of life-preservation are three: incest, murder and idolatry).

Jewish ethic teaches that all laws of the *Torah* can be ignored when the life or the health of a human being is involved. Sacred as the Sabbath is in Judaism's reckoning, it can be violated to save human life. The *Halachah* (Law) is guided by the over-riding ethical principle of the value of human life. The tremendous interest in medicine among Jews from an early period and right down through the ages has been no matter of accident. It is a direct outgrowth of this ethical ideal: the conservation and enhancement of life.

THE DIGNITY OF MAN

"The honor and personal dignity of any human being," declared the *Talmud*, "are to be so highly regarded as to set aside any prohibitory law of the *Torah*." Bearing in mind the sacred character of the law this ethical principle laid down by the rabbis is a clear indication of their powerful feeling for the dignity of humans. It suggests that if the observance of a particular ritual law is apt to bring shame to a man, that law might be temporarily dispensed with. The consideration for personal dignity must be extended even to him who has lost his dignity by committing a crime. This principle finds its expression in the biblical law: "If a man shall steal an ox or a sheep, and kill it or sell it, he shall restore five oxen for an ox and four sheep for a sheep" (Exodus 21:37). Even the thief must have his honor guarded!

The fine for stealing a sheep is smaller than for stealing an ox, suggest the sensitive teachers, because in stealing the sheep the thief was probably obliged to carry the animal on his shoulders. He suffered therefore a certain indignity. It is this humiliation that was reckoned with and caused the reduction of the fine. Moreover, the dignity of the criminal was given due consideration in the matter of punishment meted out to him. The thief who was sold into servitude must not be insulted by being called "slave." (Consider the hateful distortion of the word, Negro, and the derogatory terms used for Puerto Ricans.)

The biblical prohibition of slandering humans is interpreted by the *Talmud* to include Jew and non-Jew. As for shaming a man in public, such an act is adjudged in Talmudic ethics as the shedding of blood. Singular care must be taken not to hurt the feelings of aliens who are particularly sensitive to their new and, therefore, strange environment. Above all, even when provoked, one must not embarrass the alien by reminding him of his foreign origins. By the same ethical reasoning one must not bring up to a reformed person his one-time delinquencies. At all times and under all circumstances must the dignity of a human be assured.

ACTION SPEAKS

Someone has spoken of ethics as "doing the truth." Judaism is in accord with this approach. It demands action of us. There is wrong in society and it is man's duty to overcome it. Of course, man cannot eradicate death or the accidental tragedies that occur. These are built into man's existence. But there is the expectation that man will endure these with courage and dignity. Where, however, man can act to reduce or to eliminate evil, it is his ethical obligation to do so. Man can reduce the ravages of disease and accidents. Man can lessen suffering and pain. Man can bring social evils under control. He can eliminate poverty and war. Consistently our Bible urges: "And you shall uproot evil from your midst."

Merely to believe in the Fatherhood of God and the Brotherhood of Man is far from enough. These are but points of departure. The real task is to make these professions dynamic realities in man's midst. Isaiah demands action of his people: "Seek justice, relieve the oppressed, judge the fatherless, plead for the widow." Amos stresses the urgency of right action among men as the foundation of society. Privilege without responsibility, he warns, can only lead to disaster. In the light of knowledge that is given to men and nations, they are ethically obliged to live up to their high standards of opportunity and privilege.

When the poor among the people were being exploited in the market place, sold as slaves for debts amounting to no more than the value of a pair of sandals, while those who exploited them lived in luxury and corruption, Amos called for a radical change. It was time for action and not pious mouthings. "Take away from Me the noise of the songs, for I will not hear the melody of your viols. But let judgment run down as the waters, and righteousness as a mighty stream" (Amos 5:23-24).

"Poverty," the *Talmud* states "is more grievous than fifty plagues." The Bible treats poverty as a terrible social ill. The Book of Proverbs repeats again and again the theme of poverty and its terrible consequences. To cite but two of Proverb's evaluations: "All the days of the poor are evil" (Proverbs 15:15); or "The ruin of the poor is their poverty."

The poor have their rights in Jewish ethical thought. They must not be allowed to fall into circumstances where they must beg for assistance. At harvest time, by law, the corners of the fields were to be left for them. Also, to the poor rightfully belonged whatever fell on the ground or was overlooked by the reapers.

To help the needy to help themselves is the ethical ideal in Judaism. "And if thy brother grow poor . . . you shall uphold him" (Leviticus 25:35). Certainly the social legislation of the Bible illustrates again and again Israel's systematic effort against human distress. Israel is instructed: "You shall not harden your heart, nor shut your hand from your needy brother; but you shall surely open your hand to him, and shall surely lend him sufficient for his need in that which he wants" (Deuteronomy 15:7-8).

Maimonides emphasizes that the highest degree of *Tzedakah* is to help the needy to help themselves. In a daring statement to his disciples, Rabbi Moshe Leib, a Chassidic leader, had this ethical recommendation to offer: "If someone comes to you and asks your help, you shall not turn him away with pious words by saying: 'Have faith and take your troubles to God.' You shall act as if there were no God, as if there were only one person in all the world who could help this man—only yourself."

Judaism is an ethically-activist religion. When evil is found it must be dealt with. In the powerfully ethical Chapter Nineteen of Leviticus this dynamic quality of

Judaism is clearly enunciated in a variety of ethical imperatives.

The key phrase to all of this ethical mandate to Israel is "Neither shall you stand idly by the blood of your neighbor" (Leviticus 19:16).

FREEDOM AND RESPONSIBILITY

Ethics implies responsibility on the part of man. The individual is responsible for his own welfare and for the well-being of his fellow humans. Responsibility, in turn, implies freedom to choose, to act in order to bring about the Good Society. Judaism maintains that God has given man freedom of will to choose between right and wrong, between good and evil. Near the end of his farewell address to Israel, Moses says to his people: "I call heaven and earth to witness against you this day, that I have set before you life and death, the blessing and the curse; therefore choose life, that you may live and your children" (Deuteronomy 30:19).

Judaism is at odds with philosophies which argue that man is a helpless subject of forces beyond his control. It differs from religions which have maintained that man is a plaything of the gods. To "choose life" means that there is freedom for man to make choices during a lifetime. In a discussion of this important issue, the third century Rabbi Chanina ben Poppa held that even before a human being was conceived God had already determined "whether he shall be strong or weak, intelligent or dull, rich or poor. But whether he shall be wicked or virtuous is not pronounced."

Other rabbis argued against Rabbi Chanina's theory about the predetermination of a man's strength, intelligence and economic position. But they agreed completely with Rabbi Chanina that God leaves to man the freedom to choose between the ethical way and the unethical way.

There are many things that may be beyond man's control or talent; however, in making judgments which determine the course of action man is the chooser. In his farewell address, Moses tells Israel: "It is not in heaven.

. . . Neither is it beyond the sea. . . . But the thing is close by you, in your mouth, and in your heart, that you may do it" (Deuteronomy 30:11-14).

In its long and sometimes turbulent historic course, Judaism has had to battle hard to uphold the principle of man's free will. The Sadducees, for example, strongly insisted that man's destiny is completely dependent on chance. The Essenes believed that all of man's actions are subject to predestination and Divine Providence. But the conviction that prevailed was that man can make ethical choices and decisions. Maimonides, who devoted considerable attention to this important issue, came forward with the proposition that free will is within the reach of every man: "If he desires to incline towards the good way, and be righteous, he has the power to do so; and if he desires to incline towards the unrighteous way, and be a wicked man, he has also the power to do so."

Of course man has marvelous "dodge devices" whereby he tries to shift responsibility and blame for ethical failure from himself to others. When God asked Adam whether he had eaten the forbidden fruit, Adam protested: "It's the woman that you put at my side—she gave me of the tree, and I ate it!" And when God asked Eve, she hastily shifted the blame too. "The serpent talked me into it!" But these are excuses out of weakness. Man can choose otherwise. He can choose the right way. The rationalization for the unethical way, that everybody else is doing it, is decried by Judaism. "You shall not follow the multitude to do evil," is Moses's warning to Israel (Exodus 23:2). Mob rule is hardly just rule. Mass hysteria often runs counter to ethical choice.

Human freedom is a cherished principle of Judaism. It rejects a doctrine like Original Sin which suggests that there is something ingrained in all humans which forces them to do wrong whether they want to do so or not. True, the Bible declares that "the imagination of the heart of man is evil from his youth," which suggests that man is drawn towards wrongdoing. It implies, however, only a tendency on the part of man but not that he is doomed to wrongdoing from birth. "From his youth" is the biblical phrase, implying that even the tendency towards wrongdoing can be constructively guided in the direction of rightdoing by a process of sound ethical upbringing at the childhood level, before the challenging youth-stage of man.

Finally, Judaism understands well that man's freedom of will is not absolute. We are free agents to make the choice between the right and the wrong. Though we have our limitations, our problems of physical and mental inadequacies, of environmental circumstances be they of poverty or riches, there is "open space." Rabbi Milton Steinberg called this "the arena of moral decision" and while "it may be cramped and narrow . . . it is large enough for man's size, and broad enough to show his mettle. The direction he takes, how far he goes along it, how hard he tries to move (even when he fails to budge an inch), suffice to establish his quality and worth."

IN SUMMARY

Judaism is an ethic-centered religion. The sacred biblical commandments of "You shall be holy" and "You shall love your neighbor as yourself" were not mere pronouncements to be left suspended in limbo above Mount Sinai. The ethical genius of Judaism strove to bring these ideals down to earth as dynamic principles among living men, women and children. The Bible, as the revelation of He-Who-Is-One to His chosen people, has as its prime purpose the education of that people toward a full consciousness and achievement of a total ethical existence. Chosen to be a special task force in history, Israel is to help bring about mankind's redemption by serving as a model to the nations.

The *Talmud* evolved and expanded the ethical ideals set forth in the Bible. Its expositors, the *Tannaim* and the *Amoraim,* teachers of the good life all of them, provided a full system of laws, customs and principles that sought to elevate human life to worthy advantage. They took the biblical precepts of charity and benevolence, the responsibility to consider the feelings and sensitivities of others, the virtues of modesty, mercy, patience and humaneness and made them concrete for everyday fulfillment.

The Jewish theologian-philosophers who followed, after the close of the Talmudic era, undertook the task of systematizing the ethics of Judaism, Saadiah, Bachya ibn Pakuda, Solomon Gabirol, Yehuda Halevi, Maimonides and other religious thinkers examined Jewish ethics and analyzed the foundations on which these had evolved. They sought to demonstrate by logic that the *Mitzvot,* those revealed by God and those established by man, could be harmonized into a whole system. They maintained that the system of Jewish ritual was an excellent means through which to express ethical truths.

The ethical concern of Jewish thinkers has continued uninterrupted down to our modern day. Obviously, circumstances under which Jewry lives today have given rise to a large variety of ethical challenges. Judaism, with its unique understanding of God, man and society has much to offer to the further development of ethics.

The world is strongly dominated by pessimistic theologies and philosophies with a concept of human nature as hopeless, sinful, destined to doom. Judaism, fully recognizing the shortcomings and perplexities of man, nevertheless holds out hope for man's better future.

SUGGESTED READINGS

RABBINIC ESSAYS, *Jacob Z. Lauterbach,* Hebrew Union College Press, "The Ethics of the Halacha," pp. 259-296.

PATTERNS OF ETHICS IN AMERICA TODAY, edited by *F. Ernest Johnson,* The Institute for Religious and Social Studies.

JUSTICE AND JUDAISM, *Albert Vorspan* and *Eugene J. Lipman,* Union of American Hebrew Congregations.

EVERYMAN'S TALMUD, *A. Cohen,* E. P. Dutton & Co., Inc.

BASIC JUDAISM, *Milton Steinberg,* Harcourt, Brace, World and Company.

BIBLE CRITICISM AND ARCHAEOLOGY
by Jack D. Spiro

JACK D. SPIRO: Rabbi, Anshe Emeth Memorial Temple, New Brunswick, N. J.; a graduate of Tulane University, was ordained at H.U.C. in 1958, and received Doctor of Hebrew Letters there in 1962; author of **THE LIVING BIBLE** and articles in **THE JEWISH DIGEST, PASTORAL PSYCHOLOGY, C.C.A.R. JOURNAL,** etc.

THE Bible has exerted a greater influence on mankind generally and the Jew in particular than any other book. It has affected our own English language and literature, supplied ideals and principles to the development of democracy, and served as the foundation of all forms of Judaism and Christianity.

Because of its importance for the development of Western civilization and for our personal lives, it is understandable that we would want to know as much about the Bible as possible. We are interested not only in its ideas and history, but in its creation, its origins, its authorship. We would also like to know how it was preserved through the centuries and whether the Biblical narratives are accurate. Then we would have a better understanding of the Bible.

Actually, the Bible is similar to an anthology, for it is a collection of writings by different authors who were concerned with the theme of the relationship between God and man. There is, however, an important difference between the Bible and other anthologies. We do not know the names of most of the Biblical authors, while the usual collections and treasuries carefully list the authors and the dates when the stories were published.

In *all* ancient literature, not only the Hebrew writings, few names are given for authorship. The probable reason is that authors in ancient times received no payment for their writing nor were there any copyright laws as we have today. Also, since most of the biblical writings, and the literature of other peoples as well, were handed down by word of mouth for generations before they were reduced to writing, it became difficult to determine who the real author was. In most cases the scribe who finally put out a written version of the orally transmitted book was not the original composer.

INCONSISTENCIES IN THE TORAH

Many questions concerning authorship come to the mind of the student as he reads the preserved text of the Bible. In the familiar story of Noah and the flood in the Book of Genesis, for instance, we are told that "the rain was upon the earth forty days and forty nights" (Gen. 7:12). Just a few lines later we read that "the waters remained upon the earth a hundred and fifty days" (Gen. 7:24). In the same story, further, one passage says that two of every kind of animal were taken into the ark (Gen. 6:19), but elsewhere Noah is commanded to take seven males and seven females of certain kinds of animals (Gen. 7:2).

Another example of inconsistency shows up in the story of Jacob and Esau. Esau was jealous of Jacob and wanted to kill him. When Jacob, in fear of his life, fled from his brother Esau, Scriptures say in one passage that Jacob went to the city of Haran (Gen. 27:43), but in another that he came to Paddan-aram (Gen. 28:2).

One of the most popular stories in the Bible is that of Joseph and his brothers. When Joseph was cast into a pit by the brothers, Judah decided to sell him to a group of merchants. These merchants eventually brought Joseph to Egypt and sold him to Potiphar, one of Pharaoh's officers. In one place we read that the merchants were called Midianites (Gen. 37:37), while in another passage they are known as Ishmaelites (Gen. 39:1).

These few examples, of the many that scholars have pointed out, show that one author could hardly have written the different versions of the same story. Since the variations appear within single books of the Bible, it seems quite obvious that more than one author was responsible for producing the *Torah,* the first five books of the Bible. The traditional view was, however, that God transmitted the *Torah* directly to Moses at Mount Sinai.

The inconsistencies and repetitions did not go unnoticed.

As far back as the 12th century they disturbed a great Jewish scholar. Abraham ibn Ezra noted in those days that Chapter 34 of Deuteronomy contains a description of the death of Moses and the author's reaction to the death. He asked how Moses could possibly have written them, and suggested that another author besides Moses must have written the passage.

The Jewish philosopher Baruch Spinoza of the 17th century also tended to doubt the single authorship of the *Torah* and stated, "I determined to examine the Bible afresh in a careful, impartial, and unfettered spirit, making no assumptions concerning it, and attributing to it no doctrines which I do not find clearly therein set down."

In the 18th century a French physician, Jean Astruc, following in the tradition of Spinoza's critical attitude, noted that two different names are employed in the book of Genesis when referring to God. *Elohim* is one of them, while the other is made up of the Hebrew letters "JHVH" (which Christians pronounce "Jehovah" although the probable pronunciation was once *Yahveh,* and which Jews traditionally read as *Adonai*). Astruc separated the passages containing each, and discovered that they were not interchangeable but that each name was often consistently used in a parallel story.

A good example that illustrates this consistency is the creation story in Genesis. There are passages where the term "God" (for the Hebrew *Elohim*) is used and other passages with the expression "Lord God" (for *Adonai Elohim*). When we separate one from the other, two different interpretations of the creation of man are discernible: Genesis 1:27 states "And *God* created man in His own image, in the image of *God* created He him; male and female created He them." Later, in Genesis 2:21-22, there is a somewhat different account of man's creation: "And the *Lord God* caused a deep sleep to fall upon the man, and he slept; and He took one of his ribs, and closed up the place with flesh instead thereof. And the rib, which the *Lord God* had taken from the man made He a woman and brought her unto the man."

Another example pertains to the number of animals of each species brought into Noah's Ark prior to the great flood. In Genesis 7:1-2, where the word "Lord" is used the number is seven. In Genesis 7:9, the number is two and the word "God" is used!

The Wellhausen Theory

Although Astruc's theory has been seriously challenged, he is still credited with giving the critical study of the Bible great impetus. Since his time an attitude of objectivity has been maintained toward Scriptures and scientific methods of literary investigation have been applied to Biblical study. Rabbis and scholars had accepted the Bible for hundreds of years as the divine word of God, but few today would proclaim that it was written by God Himself. Most scholars have concluded that the Bible was written by many authors over a period of about two thousand years.

The school of literary investigation from Spinoza and Astruc to the present is known as "Biblical Criticism." Through analysis of the content, personalities, and literary style of the Scriptural books, the objective critics have made many contributions towards a clearer understanding of the Bible. While the names of many biblical authors are still unknown, the scholars have been able to divide various books and sections of the Bible into several "schools" of authorship.

Every passage in the Bible has been studied carefully in regard to ideas, vocabulary and grammar. By doing this scholars have been able to decide the passages that have been written by a certain author, even though we do not know his name. Some scholars suggest that there may have been a "board of editors" for a group of passages which show similarity in thought and style. They may not have sat together to decide the correct way to tell their story in writing, but they agreed pretty closely in their ideas and interpretations. The theory establishing these schools of thought is known as the "documentary hypothesis," developed in the 19th century largely by Julius Wellhausen and therefore sometimes called the "Wellhausen Theory."

The "documentary" approach to biblical development asserts that there are four basic schools represented in the *Torah,* which are identified by the following letters: J, E, D, and P. The passages in the Bible which belong to J (the oldest) and E (the second oldest), say the advocates of the Wellhausen theory, were written down between 900 and 700 B.C.E. The third document or group of passages, D, was written around 650 B.C.E. And the last group of passages, P, was written late in the 6th century B.C.E.

The following chart will help to clarify the development of the *Torah* and other Biblical books that the Wellhausenites attribute to these schools:

Schools	*Date*	*How the Letters Came to be Used*
J	about 850	The word "Jehovah" is a mistaken transliteration for the Hebrew word Yahveh, meaning "God." The authors of the "J" school used this word as the name of God. So the passages they wrote are known as J.
E	about 750	Another name for God is "Elohim," which the authors of the "E" school used most often. Therefore, their passages are known as E.
D	about 650	Virtually the whole book of Deuteronomy was written by a school known as the "Deuteronomic" writers.
P	about 550	The letter represents the Priestly Code, the writings of the Priesthood. Most of the sacrificial regulations, for example, were written by the school of P.

THE SCHOOL OF LITERARY CRITICISM

Through the use of the techniques of literary criticism, scholars also determine with a reasonable degree of accuracy when the various books, and the three sections of the Bible (Torah, Prophets and Writings), were completed. The following is a brief survey of the work of the "literary critics" school of biblical study, in their establishing of completion dates for different sections of the Bible.

1. Torah. In Chapters 22 and 23 of II Kings, which is in the Prophetic section of the Bible, a memorable event is described that happened in the reign of King Josiah, in the year 621 B.C.E. The High Priest Hilkiah, while workmen were repairing the Temple in Jerusalem, discovered a book that had been either purposely or accidentally lost in one of the Temple rooms. He delivered the book to Josiah, who read it with great interest. From the biblical description of this book, modern scholars have concluded that it must have been the Book of Deuteronomy, the fifth book of the *Torah*. The fact that it was not known to the king of the people suggests that it was but newly written. It could also have been an ancient book that was neglected and in time forgotten, but this seems unlikely because it contains so many basic teachings of Moses and the *Torah*. Most scholars incline to the strongly held belief that the book of Deuteronomy was therefore written sometime in the 7th century B.C.E.

The *Torah* in its entirety (the five books) were not accepted as holy and binding until the 4th century B.C.E. The book of Nehemiah (chapters 8 to 10) suggests this in the story of how Ezra, a scribe and leader of the Jews of Palestine, read the "book of the law" to the people. On that important day the Jewish people made the decision to accept the "law." From the description in Nehemiah scholars have concluded that the "law" in those days meant the *Torah,* the first section of the present Bible.

2. Nevi'im, or Prophets. By the 4th century B.C.E. there were Jews living not only in Palestine but in many other parts of the world. A large group of Jews was settled in the Egyptian city of Alexandria, most of whom did not know Hebrew. They spoke and read Greek since this was the vernacular of the time.

The Alexandrian Jews were unable to read the biblical books because they were written in Hebrew, so they appointed a board of scholars to translate the Scriptures of those days into Greek. They completed the Greek version, known as the Septuagint, in the 3rd century B.C.E.

Several of the books in the Septuagint are not included in our present day Hebrew Bible, and others that are in the Bible are not to be found in the Septuagint. This indicates that by the 3rd century there was still no firm or completed Bible.

From other sources we learn that the "Prophets" (or second section of the Bible) was finally completed sometime in the 2nd century B.C.E. Since it is widely accepted by Bible scholars that the book of David was written about 170 B.C.E., and since it is not included among the Prophetic books of the Bible, we must assume that the "Prophets" was completed before that date.

3. *K'tuvim, or Writings.* Flavius Josephus, a Jewish historian of the 1st century C.E. gives us a clue in one of his books to the date when the third section (or *k'tuvim*) was completed. In describing the Bible of his time he states that "We do not have many books disagreeing and contradicting each other, but only *twenty-two books* containing the record of all time, and which are rightly believed in. Of these, five are those of Moses, which contain the laws and the tradition as to the origin of mankind till his death . . . the prophets who came after Moses wrote of the things that came to pass in their time. . . . There is practical proof of how we treat these same writings, for though so long a time has now elapsed no one has dared either to add to them or to make any change. But it is natural for all Jews ever since the day of birth to consider these as teachings of God, to stand by them, and if necessary gladly die on their behalf."

We learn from this passage of Josephus that in his day twenty-two books were considered to be authoritative and holy. But we know that there are twenty-four books in the Hebrew Bible; therefore two books that we now have were not part of the Bible in the 1st century C.E.

A passage in the *Mishnah* reveals that several rabbis around the year 100 C.E. had a debate over which books in the third section could be accepted as holy. Most of the discussion centered around two books, the "Song of Songs" and "Ecclesiastes." The decision was finally reached, after many hours of weary debate, to include them both in the Bible. The addition of these two books gave us the twenty-four that we now have. Thus, from material in Josephus and the *Mishnah* we are able to conclude that the third section, and with it the whole Bible, was finally completed sometime at the beginning of the 2nd century C.E.

These are, in brief, some of the contributions made by Biblical Criticism to our understanding of the Bible. We can now determine with some degree of accuracy the dates of most of the passages and sections of the Bible as well as information about their authorship. Knowledge of the approximate date of any particular part of the Bible leads to a better appreciation of its ideas, since the historic setting helps us to know why a passage was written and what it was intended to do. And knowing that the writing of the Bible proceeded over a long period of time, we can learn much about the growth and development of ideas in the biblical era.

Before the development of Biblical Criticism, the *Torah* was always considered the most ancient section of the Bible. But now that a more scientific study has taken place, greater importance has been given to the Prophets of Israel. Many believe that the books of the Prophets may be among the oldest in the Bible, and that they even influenced the ideas and beliefs expressed in the *Torah*. Amos, for instance, wrote his book around 750 B.C.E., and was therefore available to the writers of at least two of the "schools" (D and P). One finds in the book of Deuteronomy, which is from the D school, many ideas similar to those expressed by the prophets Amos, Hosea, Micah, and

Isaiah, testifying to the impact they must have had upon Jewish thought and history.

RECENT DEVELOPMENTS IN BIBLICAL CRITICISM

The basic theories of the Wellhausen school of literary criticism have been generally accepted. However, in relatively recent times, decades after the Wellhausen hypotheses were originally postulated, another school of criticism arose. It is known as the "Scandinavian School" because of the many Bible scholars of the Scandinavian countries who have developed its basic theories, the most prominent being I. Engnell.

The Scandinavian School has attempted to cast doubt on the Wellhausen method of literary criticism and emphasizes instead the importance of oral tradition. This school argues that the Wellhausen approach is based on a fallacy in our western thinking. Without reflecting on the matter, western man considers the primary method of transmitting knowledge and ideas to be the written word. But this method was not the common one in ancient times.

The Bible scholars of the Scandinavian School do not necessarily reject the Wellhausen theory of literary strands in the *Torah*. But they do take issue with the approximate dates given by Wellhausen for the origin of the literary strata. They contend that the bulk of the *Torah* was transmitted orally for a long period of time before it was ever written down. Therefore, when we try to determine the origin of the *Torah* (or its parts), we should not be concerned only with the time it was written down but also with the history of its oral transmission prior to actual writing. It is possible, according to this school, that the narratives of the *Torah* could have been transmitted orally for centuries before they were ever committed to writing. The Scandinavian scholars, therefore, give support to the traditional view that the *Torah* is the earliest section of the Bible and that it developed prior to the prophetic portion.

A Jewish scholar of the bible, Yechezkel Kaufmann, supports the theory that the *Torah* predates the prophets.

But he goes further by arguing that the *Torah* narratives were actually transmitted in writing and not just orally from early times. In his great work on biblical origins and history, he offers a criticism of the Wellhausen theories. He does not reject the theory of the primary sources of the *Torah;* that is, J, D, and P. The principal question he asks, stated in his own words, is this: "To what extent can the *Torah* be used as a source for the earliest stage of Israelite religion; is its monotheism preprophetic?"

Kaufmann then gives his answer: "The *Torah* cannot be understood as a later outgrowth of prophetic faith. Literary prophecy cannot, then, be considered the fountainhead or 'ideal source' of Israelite monotheism. The development of Israelite faith was, indeed, more ramified and intricate than either tradition or modern criticism has recognized. A stratum of tradition, independent of literary prophecy, is evident in the literature of the Torah-group. From the viewpoint of the evolution of Israelite religion this stratum belongs not after, but before literary prophecy. It is the literary product of the earliest stage of Israelite religion."

His voluminous work on the Bible attempts to confirm this viewpoint in critical detail. Both Kaufmann and the Scandinavian School offer some indication of a trend towards a more conservative or traditional approach to the Bible. However, no school of Biblical Criticism has yet to offer a serious alternative to, or a profound departure from, the primary theories of Wellhausen in regard to the various documents which were eventually compiled into an integrated work.

ON THE ACCURACY OF THE BIBLE

In addition to advancing our comprehension of biblical ideas, we are also interested in determining the accuracy of the many historical narratives and events mentioned in the Bible. For most of this material there are very few contemporary records, so that the question of accuracy is not easily settled. In recent years, however, archaeology has come forward to help us in establishing whether or not the events and stories recorded in the Bible actually happened.

The world has never possessed as large a body of literature from other ancient people as it does from the Hebrews. Therefore, we have always known more about the Hebrew people through the Bible than about other national groups from ages past. Until archaeology began to supply contemporary records, however, we had very little to support the accuracy of the events which are recorded in the Bible. Also, archaeology has provided us with better understanding of the ways of living that are described in the Bible. A few examples will show how invaluable has been the aid of this science.

After the Hebrews had wandered through the desert for forty years, they tried to enter the land of Canaan from the eastern side. When Joshua led them across the Jordan River into Canaan they had to face their first real danger, the well-fortified city of Jericho. Within its high walls the Canaanites were prepared for the Hebrews' attack. Now, the Bible tells us that Joshua ordered all the Hebrews to surround the city, and to shout and blow the ram's horn as loudly as they could. "And it came to pass, when the people heard the sound of the trumpet, and the people shouted loudly, that the wall fell down flat. Then the people went up into the city, every man directly, and they seized the city. . . . And they burnt the city with fire and all that was inside (Josh. 6:20-24). (The Book of Joshua does not state whether the reverberation from the *shofar* blasts razed the walls, or that God directly destroyed them after the priests encompassed the walls seven times.) This battle has become famous, and it is the subject of a popular Negro spiritual. But over the years scholars have wondered how true it all was.

From 1907 to 1909, archaeologists were carefully investigating the area of land which the Bible describes as the city of Jericho. With great pains and labor they dug through layers of soil until, much to their amazement, they uncovered two huge walls that had been levelled to the ground. These walls, made of sun-dried brick, were each twelve feet high and stood twelve feet apart.

The archaeologists who made the great discovery stated that the outer wall "fell" about 1200 B.C.E., and therefore must be the city wall which Joshua destroyed. When these walls were examined carefully, they revealed traces of a tremendous fire. Also, the ancient homes that lay behind the walls were burned to the ground. This recalls the line from the Bible quoted above: "And they burnt the city with fire and all that was inside." The battle of Jericho was thus verified through archaeology.

FAMOUS ARCHAEOLOGICAL DISCOVERIES

We have already referred to the famous story of Noah and the great flood which supposedly destroyed the whole world (Genesis 6-9). Other ancient books also had similar stories about floods, and several years ago a famous archaeologist named Woolley decided to find out if there was any truth in the biblical story. After a time of searching he discovered something which seemed too fantastic to believe.

Beneath many layers of soil, he came across a huge deposit of muddy clay which was different in composition from all the other soil in the area. This suggested that an enormous flood, like the one described in the Bible, had transported the soil from other areas and finally deposited it in this distant place. After further investigation, Woolley found out that this ancient flood covered an area about 400 miles long and 100 miles wide. This may not seem very large today, but to people in ancient times it must have appeared to be the whole world. With the help of Woolley's find we can now accept the idea that a flood like that of the time of Noah could really have happened.

Archaeology also shed some light on the prediction by Joseph that the Egyptians would experience seven years of famine (Genesis 41). We have not yet found records to corroborate that Joseph was really a leader in Egypt, but we do have proof that Egypt experienced starvation and poor crops many times. A very ancient letter from Egypt was recently discovered which describes one of these famines in the following way: "My heart is heavy over the terrible failure of the Nile floods for the past seven years. There is little fruit; vegetables are in short supply; there is a shortage of food generally. . . . The storehouses have been opened, but everything that was in them has been consumed." Therefore, we now have evidence that the kind of famine recorded in the Bible actually happened in Egypt.

Perhaps one of the most noted archaeological finds was the locating of King Solomon's mines. The great archaeologist Nelson Glueck was actually looking for the place called Ezion-geber in the Bible, where Solomon was supposed to have kept his navy. The Bible tells us that "King Solomon made a navy of ships in Ezion-geber, which is beside Elath, on the shore of the Red Sea, in the land of Edom" (I Kings 9:26). Dr. Glueck therefore organized an expedition to Aqabah, which is the biblical Elath, to see if he might be able to discover traces of Solomon's navy in order to verify the biblical passage. During the investigation that followed, the archaeological team uncovered tiles, remnants of walls, and copper fishhooks. From the potsherds that were found around the wall foundations it was determined that the date of construction was about 1000 B.C.E., the time of Solomon's reign.

Eventually Dr. Glueck discovered a large gateway, the entrance to which contained a lockfast. This gateway was the type used in large and active seaports. He had succeeded in revealing the exact spot which the Bible describes as the place of Solomon's "navy of ships in Ezion-geber."

The findings of copper slag, however, led Dr. Glueck to ask another question. Where were the workshops which produced this copper? In time he discovered the copper refineries and smelting furnaces where Solomon's laborers produced the metals that permitted this king to become one of the most powerful monarchs of his time.

Glueck has written: "Ezion-geber was the result of careful planning and was built as a model installation with remarkable architectural and technical skill. In fact practically the whole of town of Ezion-geber, taking into consideration place and time, was a phenomenal industrial site, without anything to compare with it in the entire history of the ancient Orient. Ezion-geber was the Pittsburgh of old Palestine and at the same time its most important seaport."

For a long time before these discoveries at Ezion-geber, scholars and archaeologists had puzzled over this Biblical verse: "For the Lord thy God bringeth thee into a good land . . . a land whose stones are iron and out of whose hills thou mayest dig brass" (Deut. 8:7-9). There were many doubts about the presence of copper and iron in Palestine and scholars therefore found it difficult to believe this passage. But the work of archaeology has verified the passage and dispelled the doubts.

DECIPHERING ANCIENT INSCRIPTIONS

In II Kings 20:20 it is mentioned that King Hezekiah constructed a pool and conduit in Jerusalem so that the city would be provided with water in case of a siege. Many centuries later, in the year 1880, a small boy was playing in water that flows into a pond called the Pool of Siloam. He slipped and fell into a tunnel, where he noticed an inscription on the wall. This proved to be a record of the work done to cut Hezekiah's tunnel: "Now this is the way the cutting through happened. While yet the masons were wielding the pick, each toward his fellow, and while there was yet three cubits to be cut through, there was heard the voice of someone calling to another, for there was a fissure in the rock on the right hand. Then, on the day that the cutting-through was completed, the stone-cutters struck, each to meet his fellow, pick against pick. So the water flowed from the source to the pool, 1200 cubits. And 100 cubits was the height of the rock above the head of the diggers."

Several inscriptions on stone have been found such as this one, each confirming some biblical event or other.

One of the most famous inscriptions is the Moabite Stone, discovered by the Frenchman Clermont-Canneau in the late 19th century. As soon as he saw the stone, in the possession of desert Arabs, he knew it was valuable, but the hostile Arabs blew it to pieces with gunpowder. This did not stop Clermont-Ganneau; like a single-minded scientist he set out to retrieve all the fragments. When he successfully completed his search he sent the reassembled pieces to the Louvre.

The inscription on the stone was written in the name of Mesha, king of Moab, and says in part: "I am Mesha, son of Chemosh (Moabite god), King of Moab . . . Omri was the king of Israel and oppressed Moab many days, for Chemosh was angry with his land. And his son succeeded him and he also said, I will oppress Moab. In my days he said this; but I got the upperhand of him and his house . . ."

Although some of the details are set forth in a different manner in the Bible, the Moabite inscription confirmed the following biblical record of the same episode; thus giving further proof of the historical accuracy of the Bible: "Now Mesha king of Moab was a sheep-master; and he rendered unto the king of Israel the wool of a hundred thousand lambs, and of a hundred thousand rams. But it came to pass, when Ahab was dead, that the king of Moab rebelled against the king of Israel" (II Kings 3:4-5).

Many inscriptions such as these, which gave corroboration to biblical references, have been uncovered through archaeological investigation. Some, like the letters discovered at Tell-el Amarna in 1887 and the Nuzi clay tablets from Northern Mesopotamia, are extremely valuable for other reasons: their language is so closely related to biblical Hebrew that they help us to understand certain Hebrew words that had been obscure or unintelligible before the discovery. By turning up these ancient writings, therefore, archaeology has served to make the Bible more understandable by clarifying difficult words.

For example, an ink inscription was recently found at Arad, a city mentioned in the Bible. The jar on which it was found dates back to the 6th century B.C.E. The in-

scription gives a date, the third day of the month of *Tzach*.
Now, there is a phrase in Isaiah 18:4, "chom tzach," which
has never been translated correctly since the Hebrew
word "tzach" was unknown. But now that we know from
the Arad inscriptions that the word *tzach* refers to a month
in the ancient Hebrew calendar, the phrase can be accu-
rately translated as "the heat of *Tzach*" (which was in all
probability a summer month).

Another example can be seen in the differing translation
of the word "tis-charu" in Genesis 42:34, which has Joseph
say to his brothers, "And bring your youngest brother unto
me; then shall I know that ye are no spies, but that ye are
upright men; so will I deliver you your brother, and *ye
shall traffic* in the land." This is in the Jewish Publication
Society Bible of 1917. But in the new translation of the
Torah in 1962, the word "traffic" has been changed to
"move about." The reason for this change also derived
from archaeological findings.

The background of the verse quoted above is that
Joseph's brothers had come to Egypt in an attempt to get
some food for their families at home in Canaan. They had
not come to settle there, or to go into business as the old
translation implies when it used the word "traffic." Scholars, however, came to a different understanding of the
verb *sachar* (of which "tis-charu" is the form for the
future, second person, plural), when a very old language
called "Akkadian" was deciphered. In this language there
is a word similar to the Hebrew verb *sachar*. In the Akkadian, which was a language spoken at the same time as
Hebrew, the verb means "to move about." This verb occurs three times in the book of Genesis, and in each case
nothing could suit the text better than the translation "to
move about." In the verse under question, what Joseph
was saying to his brothers was simply this, that after they
proved their innocence they would be free *to move about*
in Egypt as they pleased. Thus, another obscure word was
clarified as a result of new knowledge derived from ancient
inscriptions and records.

There are scores of examples that could be given to show
how archaeological discoveries—whether of stone monuments, pottery, or inscriptions—have helped to support
the historicity of biblical events and to shed light on biblical passages. Archaeology has proved to be a most valuable method of investigation. Between it and the knowledge produced by Biblical Criticism a great deal has been
accomplished to make the biblical world come alive. The
work of the scholars in both fields have made the Bible
itself an even more fascinating book, since it contains a
record of the activities of a people, the Hebrews, who lived
right in the midst of throbbing religious and historical
developments. The present-day reader can dip into this
wealth with the aid of the great collection of books called
the Bible, which was produced by the Hebrews, and the
materials developed by Biblical Criticism and archaeologists.

SUGGESTED READINGS

THE ARCHAEOLOGY AND RELIGION OF ISRAEL, *William
F. Albright,* The John Hopkins Press.

PREFACE TO SCRIPTURES, *Solomon B. Freehof,* Union of
American Hebrew Congregations.

THE RELIGION OF ISRAEL, *Yecheskel Kaufman,* University of
Chicago Press.

THE GROWTH OF THE OLD TESTAMENT, *H. H. Rowley,*
Hutchinson's University Library, London.

THE LIVING BIBLE, *Sylvan D. Schwartzman* and *Jack D. Spiro,*
Union of American Hebrew Congregations.

DEVELOPMENTS IN THE HEBREW LANGUAGE

by Edward Horowitz

EDWARD HOROWITZ: Chairman, Hebrew Department, Thomas Jefferson H. S., N. Y.; a graduate of the Teacher's Institute and Rabbinical Department of the Jewish Theological Seminary, he received the doctorate degree in Religious Education at the Teacher's Institute; author of **SIPPURIM KALIM** and of **HOW THE HEBREW LANGUAGE GREW.**

ASSYRIA was for centuries an enormous empire, extending over a million square miles and having great power and wealth. Not a line, not a sentence, hardly a word of what they said or wrote in ancient times impinges upon the consciousness of man in our day and age.

Egypt, too, was a great empire for many thousands of years, and again, hardly a sentence, hardly a line of what they wrote is part of the intellectual or emotional tradition of our day. Some will recall the phrase "Book of the Dead" or the pyramids, those gigantic monuments to vain pharaohs that reflected their intense preoccupation with life after death.

The day Franklin Delano Roosevelt died was our most stunning national tragedy since 1865, when Lincoln was assassinated. Time stood still and for days after people gathered in churches, synagogues and schools to seek comfort for the sorrow that had come upon them. Wherever they gathered, it was to the writings of the ancient Hebrews that they turned: "The Lord is my shepherd, I shall not want"—"Oh Lord, what is man that Thou takest account of him?"

When tribute was paid to John F. Kennedy at St. Matthew's Cathedral in Washington before the eyes of over 150 million TV viewers, almost all words spoken in his honor were from the ancient Hebrew writings he so loved and that were an intimate part of his life and thought.

By a universal assent no words seemed to be more perfect, more beautiful than those put together in ancient days by the Hebrew people. It is strange and bewildering that from the tiny little country of Israel has come forth the world's greatest literature, for from the Hebrew Bible have come expressions greater even than the writings of

111

Shakespeare in English, of Voltaire in French or of Goethe in German.

Hebrew was the spoken language of the Hebrew people for about 1700 years of their life on the soil of Palestine. But after the year 70 C.E. when the Romans destroyed the Temple and the Jews were driven to many different lands of the world, they had to learn to speak the various languages of the people among whom they lived. Thus Hebrew, in time, ceased to be their spoken everyday language.

However, Hebrew lived on in many other ways. It was the language of prayers that were recited daily and on the Sabbath and festivals. They read and studied the *Torah* in Hebrew. It was an actual requirement of Jewish law that every parent teach his child to read and write at least the Hebrew language. The literacy among Jews, even up to modern times, was by far the highest of any group anywhere in the world. In the Middle Ages in an average village of 1,000 perhaps three or four would be able to read and write—the priest, the village clerk and perhaps one or two others.

The Jews carried on an extensive correspondence in Hebrew, and in the course of the centuries since the destruction of the Temple, they wrote some 20,000 books in the Hebrew language.

THE CHAMPION OF LIVING HEBREW

In the 1870's a number of small countries in the Balkan peninsula were gaining their independence from Turkey. A young man, Eliezer Ben Yehudah, observed these events with a certain amount of envy. All these Balkan peoples were tiny and really unimportant, he told himself. What, after all, had they contributed to the welfare of the world compared to the Hebrews? Nevertheless, all of them had their own little land, their own government, and above all, their own language. And we Jews, what did we have?

One morning he awoke and told his perfectly astounded wife that from that day on they were to speak only Hebrew in their home. When their son, Ittamar, was born, he became the world's first Hebrew-speaking baby in 1,800 years. Ben Yehudah began speaking Hebrew to his colleagues, also scholars and writers, and they looked at him with utter amazement.

"Ben Yehudah," they said to him, "you are *meshugah* (out of your mind). A language is a living thing; once it has died, it can never come back to life."

Ben Yehudah said something equivalent to "We'll see about that," and left Europe with his little family in 1882 to go to live in Jerusalem in Palestine.

At that time there was a community of 50,000 Jews in Jerusalem, speaking in a babel of a dozen different languages, largely the native tongues of the countries from which they or their ancestors had come. Yet they all knew Hebrew to some extent, and it was with these Jews that Ben Yehudah began his heroic efforts to get people to use Hebrew in their daily speech. The sheer logic of Ben Yehudah's insistence on speaking Hebrew dawned on them finally, and it became clear to all how despairingly difficult it would be to have a Jewish "people" if they went on speaking everybody else's language.

Within a fairly short time practically all the Jews in Palestine began to use Hebrew in everyday speech, and from there the speaking of Hebrew spread to all the Jewish centers in the world. One of the greatest miracles of all time had come to pass: a language that had ceased to be spoken in ancient times had come back to the lips of men and women and little children. This had not happened before.

HEBREW AS A LANGUAGE

Hebrew belongs to a family of languages called Semitic. There was a very ancient Semitic language, now long lost, from which have come a large group of closely related tongues—Aramaic, Assyrian, Phoenician, Ethiopic, Arabic, and others. A more familiar family of languages is the

Indo-European, which includes English, German, French, Spanish, Italian, etc.

Before looking into Hebrew as a language, it is important to be clear about one thing: scholars do not know exactly how language began. Very possibly the first words were the names of animals and were simply imitations of the sounds made by them. A lion was something like ra-ra, a snake—sss, a bird—tsip tsip. This simple way of naming may have suggested to man in very ancient days the idea of giving names to all the other things their eyes could see, but we are not really certain. In one way or another, however, and in a manner unknown to us, ancient man arrived at some agreement as to what to call certain things. But from that point on, our knowledge of how language grew is quite extensive.

Once basic essential words called roots were established, a kind of pattern developed that kept each language rolling along. The way in which Hebrew grew does not vary widely from the way in which English evolved.

For example, take the root "port," meaning "to carry." We can with the utmost ease create export, import, report, reporter, deport, support, etc.

Or "pose," meaning "to place" or "put." Again, we can very easily create impose, expose, exposition, compose, composer, depose, suppose, etc.

There is a similar pattern of word building in Hebrew. For example, from the root *katav,* meaning "to write," we can create the following words:

(*ktivah*)	כְּתִיבָה	writing
(*michtav*)	מִכְתָּב	letter
(*ktav*)	כְּתָב	document
(*ketubah*)	כְּתֻבָּה	marriage contract
(*ktiv*)	כְּתִיב	spelling
(*ktovet*)	כְּתֹבֶת	address
(*machtayvah*)	מַכְתֵּבָה	desk

In every case it is easy to see that the words coming from בָּתַב *(katav)* are related in some important way to the idea of writing.

The great central theme of all word building in Hebrew is essentially this, that practically all words go back to a root containing three consonants. You can do almost anything you want with a root. You can use it for any verb form or tense. You can turn it into any one of ten, twenty or more nouns. No matter what you do, you will always see the three consonants of the root, just as in the examples given for the English roots "port" and "pose."

Hebrew has an enormous flexibility. There are over a hundred ways in which the root can be changed by prefixes, suffixes or infixes in order to create new words. Actually, as in English, only about twenty or so are commonly used. But when the Hebrew alphabet passed over to the Greeks, a very striking and interesting difference between Hebrew and European languages showed up, a difference which is important to understand.

VOWELS MAKE A DIFFERENCE

About the year 900 B.C.E. Phoenician merchants dropping anchor in a Greek port and busily trading with their Greek hosts suddenly became aware that the Greeks, who spoke a language of great beauty and complexity (if you think Hebrew grammar is hard, stay away from Greek), could not write a single syllable of what they spoke. So the Phoenicians set about teaching them the 22 pictures (we now call these pictures the letters of the alphabet) with which they wrote the sounds and words of their language.

The Greeks eagerly began to play this utterly fascinating new game of putting down on paper the thoughts that passed through their minds. However, the Greeks felt that the Phoenician system lacked something; there were no pictures for the sounds of *a, e, i, o, u.*

The Phoenicians claimed that these were really not very

important. In their language the vowels hardly counted, since they really didn't change the meaning of the word too much.

It was not the same for the Greeks, however. They had to have pictures for the vowel sounds, else they would not know what their written words were saying. For in Greek, as in other European languages, the meaning of the word depended upon the vowels as well as upon the consonants. Different vowels, when used with the very same consonants, would create entirely different words having altogether unrelated meanings. This can easily be illustrated in English, using the consonants R and D but changing the vowel between them:

By changing the vowels between these two consonants, we can get many, and for the most part unrelated words. There is a world of difference between *reed, red* and *road,* and it would be impossible or extremely difficult to read in English words made up only of consonants, in which the vowel letters were omitted. The Greeks, too, simply had to have vowel letters or they would not know what word the consonants were intended to communicate.

In Hebrew, it is true, a change in vowels will also change the reading of a word, just as the change in the vowel between R and D did. The difference is, however, that all these Hebrew words will be related in meaning. Take as an example the root קָדֹשׁ *(kadosh),* meaning "holy." By changing the vowels we get:

(kadosh)   קָדֹושׁ   a holy person

(kodesh,	קֹדֶשׁ	holiness
kedushah)	קְדֻשָׁה	
(kadish)	קַדִּישׁ	a prayer for the dead
(kidush)	קִדּוּשׁ	a prayer over wine, making holy the Sabbath or festival
(kidushin)	קִדּוּשִׁין	the marriage ceremony
(mikdash)	מִקְדָּשׁ	Temple

The words are pronounced differently, but they all contain a sense of *holiness* in them.

It is for this reason that it is quite possible, in fact easy, for a person with a fair knowledge of Hebrew to read it without vowel signs. In fact, Hebrew got along without vowel signs for many centuries. But it is quite impossible to read words without vowels in Greek or English. So the ancient Greeks made symbols for the vowels they needed by borrowing letters from the Hebrew-Phoenician alphabet that stood for sounds the Greeks did not need. For instance, the Hebrew consonant ע (*ayin*) had a deep gutteral sound in ancient times. The Greeks had no use for it because they had no such sound in their language. They therefore took the *ayin* but made it stand for the vowel sound "o." They didn't need the ancient *aleph* א either, so they turned it into the vowel "a."

The word "turned" is a very apt one to use in this connection, for it graphically describes exactly what the Greeks did with the ancient Hebrew-Phoenician letters. In the beginning the Greeks wrote in Semitic style, from right to left, like Hebrew. Later on they decided to change the system and began to write from left to right, as in English and other languages that derived from the Indo-European tongues. As they made the change they "turned" and swung the letters they had taken from the Phoenicians into new positions and appearances.

In the chart below you will find some of these letters and the manner of their "turning." A few moments of study will produce some startling insights into a linguistic process that actually influenced our own English language.

◀ —is old Hebrew א *(aleph).* Set it up straight by turning it clockwise and it is our very own "A."

◁ —is old Hebrew ד *(dalet).* Turn it clockwise a little and make a curve of the two lines extending to the right and it is a "D."

ঽ —is old Hebrew ה *(hay).* Swing it to the right on its vertical (or turn it mirrorwise) and we have the "E."

ɪ S —is old Hebrew ז *(za-yin).* Pivot it to the right, mirrorwise, and it is a "Z."

✗✝ —is old Hebrew ט *(tet).* There evidently was little change in the turning. It was practically the "T" then as now.

O —is old Hebrew ע *(ayin).* Without any change except in sound this became the sound "O."

The Greeks adapted a great many Hebrew-Phoenician letters, and the process turned out to be a momentous forward step in the development of language in general. With it the alphabet passed from the exclusive possession of the Semitic group and became an instrument for the writing of the Indo-European languages. In a certain sense the Greeks can be regarded as co-creators of the alphabet as used at present.

ASPECTS OF THE HEBREW ROOT

Usually the road from the root to the word is simple and direct, but sometimes you have to think hard to see the connection between the root and the word that was made from it.

Take the common root חָבַר *chavar.* Now look at the strange group of apparently unrelated words that come from it:

(chaver)	חָבֵר	a friend
(chibur)	חִבּוּר	a composition
(chever)	חֶבֶר	a group

(*chavurah*)	חֲבוּרָה	an association
(*chevrah*)	חֶבְרָה	congregation
(*machberet*)	מַחְבֶּרֶת	a copy book
(*mechaber*)	מְחַבֵּר	an author

A *friend* seems to have little do with a *composition* or a *copy book*, nor does an *author* seem to be related to a *group* of people. And yet, without too much intellectual exertion it should be possible to work out the basic meaning of the root חָבַר (*chavar*). Its fundamental meaning, *joined together*, leads easily and clearly to every word listed above.

Thus חִבּוּר (*chibur*), meaning *a composition*, implies the joining or putting of words and thoughts together. The words *chevrah*, *chavurah* and *chever* refer to a group of people joined together for one or another reason. And *machberet*, meaning a *copy book*, is made up of pages joined together, while *mechaber*, an *author*, is a person who joins together thoughts, stories, etc.

Another fascinating root is קֶרֶן (*keren*), which means a horn. Many thousands of years ago, as the ancient Hebrews looked up at the rays of the setting sun, it seemed to them that they resembled gigantic horns coming off the sun, and so they called the rays *karney hashemesh*, "the horns of the sun."

But they weren't horns. They were rays of light, and so *keren* got to mean a ray of light. From it, the Hebrews created the word *karan*, "to shine." The Bible uses *karan* in a very beautiful verse (Ex. 34:30) to describe Moses coming down from Mt. Sinai carrying the two tablets of stone on which the Ten Commandments were engraved. The Hebrew Bible says that after Moses's encounter with God קָרַן עוֹר פָּנָיו (*karan or panav*) meaning "the skin of his face shone."

I once took a group of high school Hebrew students on a study trip to Israel. On the way back we stopped in Rome, where the guides took us to the Church of St.

Peter in Chains. There we saw what is probably one of the most beautiful single sculptures ever made by the hands of a human being, the famous sculpture of *Moshe Rabenu*, "Our Master Moses," by Michelangelo.

We stared at it with a certain awe and then with a growing sense of wonder. From Moses' head came forth two horns. Why did the artist portray Moses in so strange a fashion?

The answer takes us back to one of the greatest linguistic blunders of all times.

Around the year 400 C.E. there lived in the land of Israel a Christian monk named Jerome. He was a grown man and literally did not know the difference between an *aleph* and a *bet* so far as Hebrew was concerned. But there had grown upon him a very profound conviction that God wanted him, His servant Jerome, to make a translation of the Bible directly from Hebrew into Latin. Such a translation had never before been made.

He set himself then to study Hebrew. Year after year he worked from early morning until late at night and after about ten years he knew enough Hebrew to make his translation, which he called the Vulgate. It has been used in all Catholic churches the world over all these centuries since.

It is a great literary masterpiece. But St. Jerome did make one really fascinating error when he came to the verse, *karan or panav*. Since the word *karan* came from the root *keren,* meaning "a horn," he mistranslated the verse in this way: "Horns formed on Moses's head."

A thousand years later the error had not been corrected. When Michelangelo prepared himself for the making of his great masterpiece, he went to the Bible and there he read in the Vulgate, "Horns formed on Moses's head."

And that is why this majestic sculpture of Moses was made with two horns coming from his forehead.

The word *keren* has still another meaning, "a fund." You may know *Keren Ami*, "the fund for my people," or *Keren Kayemet,* "the Jewish National Fund." How did *keren* get this meaning of "fund"?

Today we throw out as rubbish all kinds of containers such as boxes and jars; in days of old, however, anything that could serve as a container was precious. The horn of an animal, for instance, could be used as a sort of box. The ladies of ancient Israel used them to store their eye paint. In the Middle Ages they were used to store ink, and were called ink horns. In more modern times American frontiersmen used animal horns as storage places for their gunpowder and called them powder horns.

Once you think of a horn as a container, then you can accept a "fund" as a place where you store up money for a certain purpose.

Translating the Hebrew Bible

Men on this earth have spoken in thousands of languages and used millions of different words. Yet of all of these words one, and only one, has entered twelve hundred different languages unchanged. It is the Hebrew word אָמֵן (*amen*). How did this one little word leave ancient Israel and travel so widely through all the lands of the world?

In the year 250 B.C.E. there lived in the city of Alexandria, in the land of Egypt, a very large Jewish community of perhaps 250,000 Jews. The *Talmud* tells us that the synagogue in Alexandria was so enormous that a man had to stand beside the cantor and wave a flag so that the people in the back would know that the cantor had finished, and that it was time for them to make responses to the prayers.

The king of Egypt at that time was Ptolemy Philadelphus and, as kings go, he was an unusually learned and literate man. He had what was then the world's largest library, and hearing that the Jews had a very important book containing history, wise laws and great poetry, he informed the heads of the Jewish community at Alexandria that he wanted a copy of this Bible for his library.

The Jews were pleased that the king was interested in their Bible and told him that they would arrange for

scribes to prepare a very exact and beautiful copy of the
Hebrew Bible for him. But he did not want it in Hebrew,
for it would not mean anything to him. He wanted it in
Greek, so that he would be able to read and enjoy it.

The Jews were startled. To turn the Hebrew Bible into
Greek! No translation had ever been made of it into any
other language, and it did not seem right. But they finally
decided it would be worthwhile to make this translation.
And so, according to the tradition that has come down to us,
they sent to Israel for 72 scholars who knew both Hebrew
and Greek well. These men worked many months, and met
up with many problems.

What were they to do about a word like *Elohim,* meaning "God"? The Greek language had words for idols of all
kinds, but not a word that meant exactly the invisible God
who created the whole universe. It did not seem right or
proper to take the Hebrew name for God and put it into
the Greek language, so they took the Greek word *kurios,*
which meant "lord, master," and declared that whenever
it appeared in the Bible it would mean the Creator and
Ruler of the universe.

Another problem word was *Shabbat.* Where in the
Greek language could they find a word which would mean
a day when all men, women, children, slaves, animals, etc.
were to have their rest? To the Greeks who saw Jews rest-
ing one whole day each week, the Jews appeared to be a
lazy people. Unable to find a suitable Greek word the Jewish scholars made them a present of the Hebrew word
Shabbat, but since Greek had no "sh" sound the word had
to be written as *sabbat.* Since the English word for *Shabbat*
derived from the Greek, our famous rest day came to be
called Sabbath in English.

There were many such difficulties in making the Greek
translation, but the scholars managed in most cases to find
some Greek word that was close to the meaning they wanted. It was a different matter when they came to the word
אָמֵן (*amen*). This one little word means "may this prayer
come true." This was easily translatable into Greek, but it

required a whole sentence. Since the word *amen* occurs fairly often, the translation began to look rather cluttered up. The Greek line, where the word *amen* appeared, was always so much larger. This led one of the translators to suggest that they make a gift of the word *amen* to the Greek language. So they transliterated the word into Greek and let it have the same meaning in Greek as in Hebrew.

In this way, in the year 250 B.C.E., the word *amen* migrated from the Hebrew language and from Israel and turned up in Alexandria as a Greek word.

When Jerome translated the Bible into Latin, he also accepted this idea; he transliterated *amen* into Latin and it became a Latin word.

The Bible has now been translated into 1,200 different languages and in every single one of these the Hebrew word *amen* has been retained in its original form and has become an integral part of all these languages. Thus *amen* has become the most widespread and widely used word in all human speech.

HEBREW TODAY

Hebrew is one of the great languages of this world, not only the Hebrew from ancient times, but the Hebrew of our own day. The flexibility of the Hebrew root is such that there is simply no limit to the number of new words that can be created. There is a group in Israel, appointed by the Government, called the Academy for the Hebrew Language, whose responsibility it is to supply the words needed by the people of Israel today.

Hebrew did have a rich stock of roots when Ben Yehudah and his colleagues began the Hebrew renaissance. There was a tremendous literary and poetic vocabulary, but there was a vast gap between the words they had and the everyday needs of life in late nineteenth century Palestine.

Every modern language, of course, had had to face (only

more gradually) the same problems that Hebrew had to
solve, that of creating the words needed by the changing
times. Hebrew had to do this more quickly, but Ben Yehudah and his helpers were able to take some cues and hints
from the way other modern languages had developed.
They did this, for instance, in their search for a Hebrew
word for "newspaper."

If they had wanted to be mechanical and literal about it
they would have taken the word for "news"   חֲדָשׁוֹת
(chadashot) and   נְיָר (n'yar), meaning "paper" and put
them together, but they liked better what had been developed in German. The Germans created their word out of
what a newspaper does: it tells what is happening at the
time of its issue. Their word for "time" is *tzeit,* and their
word for newspaper is "tzeitung." So the Hebrew scholars took the word   עֵת *(ayt),* meaning "time" and created from it   עִתּוֹן *(iton),* meaning "newspaper."

In a similar fashion they made a large number of other
words. For instance, they produced the word   מִלּוֹן *(mi-
lon),* meaning "dictionary" from מִלָּה *(milah)* "word."
From   שָׁעָה *(sha-ah)* "hour," came   שָׁעוֹן *(sha-on)*
"watch," from   אֲוִיר *(avir)* "air" came   אֲוִירוֹן *(aviron)*
"airplane."

The Hebrew language builders matched meanings
wherever they could, but they resorted to different gram-
matical rules and constructions to make the new words
sound correct in Hebrew. Thus רָכַב *(rachav)* "to ride"
yielded   רַכֶּבֶת *(rakevet)* "a train,"   גָּפְרִית *(gafrit)* "sul-
phur" yielded גַּפְרוּר *(gafrur)* "a match," and out of
(barak) "lightning" came   מִבְרָק *(mivrak)* "a telegram."

They also did a very interesting thing that only Hebrew
could do. The Bible has a large number of obscure words
whose meanings are quite vague. And there are other
words that for various reasons have not been used for
thousands of years. The scholars dusted some of these off
or polished them up, giving them sharp and clear meanings so as to supply a much needed modern word. For example, מֶשֶׁק *(meshek)* has an uncertain meaning in the

Bible. Today it is the commonly used word for "a farm with all its livestock and equipment." Another biblical word חַשְׁמַל (chashmal) means "amber," but we use it today for the word "electricity."

But modern Hebrew does not insist on always creating words only from Hebrew roots. Like other modern languages, it also adopts international words, for there is a growing spirit in the world of cultural unity, at least in the field of linguistics. A few examples of such borrowings are: רַדְיוֹ (radio), סְפּוֹרְט (sport), טֶלֶפוֹן (telephone), טֶנִיס (tennis).

In these many ways has modern Hebrew evolved into an everyday language. Under the guidance of the Hebrew Language Academy, Hebrew scientists, scholars and philosophers have created for themselves the necessary technical and professional vocabulary of today. It is now possible to write in Hebrew clearly and exactly on any scientific or philosophic theme, however complex or abstruse.

Now in the twentieth century great contributions in science, biblical studies and philosophy are being made in the Hebrew language. It has become of sufficient importance to warrant the establishment of modern Hebrew departments in almost all great universities, and many scholars the world over are today mastering Hebrew so as to be able to read the scholarly works now being written in the language.

SUGGESTED READINGS

HOW THE HEBREW LANGUAGE GREW, Edward Horowitz, Jewish Education Committee Press.

HEBREW THE ETERNAL LANGUAGE, William Chomsky, Jewish Publication Soc.

HEBREW REBORN, Shalom Spiegel, Meridian Books.

THE NEW FUNCTIONAL HEBREW ENGLISH—ENGLISH HEBREW DICTIONARY, Nathan Goldberg, Ktav Publishing House, Inc.

DEVELOPMENTS IN JEWISH WORSHIP

by Herbert M. Baumgard

HERBERT M. BAUMGARD: Rabbi, Beth Am, South Miami, Florida; a graduate of University of Virginia, with graduate work at Columbia University; he was ordained at H.U.C.-J.I.R. in 1950; holds Doctorate in Hebrew Letters from H.U.C.; author of **JUDAISM AND PRAYER** and of pamphlets **WHAT IS LIBERAL JUDAISM, WHAT I BELIEVE AS A LIBERAL JEW;** frequent appearances on TV religious programs.

W HEN people speak of the "Judeo-Christian" tradition, they usually think of the Bible as its primary, if not its only, source. The Jewish aspect of this tradition is not by any means restricted to our *Tanach* (Bible). There are many other books in the vast Judaic treasury that are sacred to us. Among them is the *Siddur* (Prayerbook). The Jewish Prayerbook, in a way, is as meaningful to the modern world as the Bible itself, for in almost no other book are Jewish hopes and ideals more clearly revealed than in the *Siddur,* and nowhere else are Jewish attitudes and perspectives more fervently expressed.

THE PRAYERBOOK

Consider, for example, the heart of the prayer-service, the prayer generally called the *Sh'ma,* whereby the congregation proclaims, "Hear, oh Israel, the Lord thy God, the Lord is one." Every time the Jew participates in this part of the worship service, he is reminded that there is one Father for the entire brotherhood of mankind. Although the original source of this declaration is the *Torah,* it is from the Prayerbook that the Jew most often receives the reminder of this central tenet of his faith. The traditional Jew has for hundreds of years read large portions of the *Siddur* daily, as part of the morning, afternoon, and evening services. He has not read as often from the Bible, important as that book has been to him.

The Bible (Leviticus 19) is the original source for the Jewish belief that man has the obligation to try to imitate God in His holiness. The Prayerbook, however, has served as the Jew's most frequently used aid in understanding the nature of the God whom we are to try to imitate. The prayers repeatedly describe Him as a God who is *tov* (good), full of *rachum* (mercy), *ohav* (loving), *tzadik* (righteous), *rofe cholim* (a healer of the sick), a God of *s'lichah* (forgiveness), and a *some-ach noflim* (supporter of the lowly or falling).

In past eras Jews were more dependent on the Prayerbook than they were on the Bible. A great portion of the men were able to recite the prayers by heart. Through the Prayerbook Jews became sensitive to the splendor of life. They were encouraged not to despair because God's creative powers were constantly being manifested anew. Through the prayers the Jew was re-rooted in his history, and the struggles of the present took on new meaning. In the prayer service the faith of the Jew in a Messianic future of peace and justice was stirred and strengthened. In sum, the Prayerbook offered both emotional release and intellectual exercise to the exiled Jewish community. It was a firm anchor in the stormy ocean of daily experience.

Most people think of prayer as a request for something, and there are petitions, of course, in the Prayerbook; but it contains far more than poetic petitions addressed to God. You cannot read from it, even as a mere observer, without learning a great deal about what has motivated Jews through the centuries, for it contains a record of their hopes and aspirations, as well as a statement of their beliefs and some of their practices. Unlike the Bible, the *Siddur* was never canonized, never closed to future inspiration. In fact, it has received extensive additions over the centuries, so that it has become a virtual library in and of itself.

With the passage of time, it has come to include such diverse material as Haggadic discourses from the *Talmud* and detailed regulations concerning practices like lighting the Sabbath candles. (Examples of these can be found in any traditional *Siddur,* like the Hertz edition of the *Authorized Daily Prayerbook* (p. 391, 396).

Actually, one can read the Prayerbook and learn a great deal about the Bible. There are a host of Psalms reprinted in it in whole or in part; there are sections of the book of Proverbs, such as the famous passage concerning the *Eshet Cha-yil* (Woman of Valor, see Hertz, p. 405); and many of the familiar prayers come from the Bible, like the *Sh'ma* (Hear, O Israel), the *V'ahavta* (You shall love the Lord), *Mi Chamochah* (Who is like unto Thee), and *V'shamru* (And you shall keep the Sabbath).

Since the Prayerbook was also used on the Festivals, it contains material shedding light on the origin and meaning of the various holidays. There is the story of *Chanukah* (p. 63 ff. of the Singer edition of the *Standard Prayer Book*), for instance, and the story of *Purim* (p. 64 ff. Singer). There is even an entire tractate from the *Talmud* for recitation and study during the period from the Sabbath after Passover until the Sabbath before the New Year. This tractate, known as *Pirke Avot* (Sayings of the Fathers), is a collection of wise and ethical teachings by Talmudic rabbis.

Some prayerbooks also included special home services, such as the candle-lighting ritual for *Chanukah* (p. 420, Singer and p. 948, Hertz); Grace at meals, (p. 424 ff., Singer and 962 ff., Hertz); the Marriage Service (p. 443 ff., Singer and p. 1008 ff., Hertz), the Circumcision Service (p. 449 ff., Singer and p. 1024 ff., Hertz), etc. We are therefore justified in saying that the traditional Prayerbook was much more than a book of prayers; it was in actuality a blueprint for a way of life. It is difficult to see how Judaism could have survived without it.

REFORM AND OTHER PRAYERBOOKS

Thus far, we have spoken of "the" Prayerbook, by which we mean the traditional Prayerbook or *Siddur* that derives from the first known book of Jewish prayers, the one compiled by Amram *Gaon* about the year 850 C.E. A later, and slightly different, version was the *Machzor Vitry,* which became the basis of the Ashkenazi *Minhag* (ritual or custom) that the French rabbis introduced in 1208.

The core of the prayers in these ancient prayerbooks probably was in existence already in the time of the Babylonian exile. Many of them are precisely mentioned in the *Talmud,* while some of the prayers date from biblical times.

The tendency in modern times has been to prune the Prayerbook or to update it. Most prayerbooks in use in American synagogues are less voluminous than the older traditional ones, even though they have an English translation alongside the original Hebrew or Aramaic. The *Union Prayer Book* (Volume I for Sabbath, Daily and Festival Services, and Volume II for the High Holy Days) was created by the Central Conference of American Rabbis, the organization of the Reform Rabbis of our country. Published originally in 1895, it was a pioneering effort to bring the traditional prayers to American Jews in an English translation and in condensed form.

The Reform prayerbook sharply edits both the prayers and the length and order of the prayer service. It is an attempt to make the service appealing to modern Jews. It includes only a few of the Eighteen Benedictions *(Sh'moneh Esreh)* in each service. These prayers are also called the *Amidah* (standing), because in traditional synagogues worshipers stand while reciting them. The *Union Prayer Book* excludes references to the return to Zion. It was prepared in a time when many American Jews were convinced that America was the messianic or ideal land. In addition, it excludes prayers looking towards the rebuilding of the ancient Temple in Jerusalem and the restoration of animal sacrifices, which traditional prayerbooks still contain. References to the physical resurrection of the dead and to Satan have also been removed.

The *U.P.B.* is not simply an abbreviated version of the traditional prayerbook. It has added many new and truly beautiful prayers that modern Jews find meaningful. Nevertheless, the *Union Prayer Book* leans heavily upon the traditional *Siddur.* It seems to present no new concept of God, even though it does emphasize more the role of man in serving as a co-worker with God, and it does stress the fact that we should love rather than fear God.

Another *siddur*, the *Sabbath Prayer Book*, published by the Jewish Reconstructionist Foundation in 1946 is also an attempt to "update" the traditional prayerbook. This book excludes references to Israel as the "chosen people." While its authors are deeply interested in the return to Zion, they exclude references to an individual Messiah, since they believe that salvation comes through the group, rather than through an individual. This seems to follow the Reform view. The Reconstructionist Prayerbook, like its Reform predecessor, eliminates references to the restoration of the Temple, the sacrifices, and to the resurrection of the body. While this book does not edit the traditional prayerbook as closely as does the *Union Prayer Book*, it does try to make the service more brief and concise.

The Reconstructionists have also produced a number of new and pointed prayers designed for modern Jews. They, too, attempt to give man a stronger role in the determining of events. It would be fair to say, however, that the Reconstructionist notion of God is a naturalist conception, and as such, it is at odds with the basic traditional view.

The Conservative Movement in American Judaism has also published a *siddur*, the *Sabbath and Festival Prayerbook*, issued in 1946 by the Rabbinical Assembly of America and the United Synagogue of America. Compared to the *Union Prayer Book* and the Reconstructionist Prayerbook, the changes made in this book are slight. It retains the *Amidah* in its entirety but it leaves out certain less essential prayers. The Conservative *siddur* follows the traditional prayerbook more closely than the others, but all of the newer versions regard the older book as the source of their being and their foundation stone.

WORSHIP IN THE ANCIENT TEMPLE

Jews did not always worship according to a prayerbook.

In the ancient Temple, presumably built by Solomon around 950 B.C.E., Jews prayed by means of animal sacrifices. The Biblical book of Leviticus is filled with descriptions of techniques used by the priests in offering animals before the altar of God. No doubt, there were verbal prayers in ancient times also (they may have accompanied the sacrifices), but they were not considered as significant as the animal sacrifice itself.

All ancient peoples employed animals in their worship service, and the eating of the animals had religious overtones. Among the primitives, the god was considered to be invested in a totem animal, like the bull in Egypt. During primitive worship services the totem animal was killed and eaten by the worshiper. In this way, the god, that is to say, his spirit and power, was absorbed by the worshiper who hoped to be strengthened or, perhaps, cured of an illness by this ingestion.

It is interesting that in many Christian churches today Jesus is "eaten" symbolically by the worshipers. Christians, of course, do not use a totem animal to symbolize Jesus. They use, instead, the wine and the wafer, the one symbolic of his "blood," the other of his "body." the Hebrews, on the other hand, so far as we have been able to discover, never regarded the sacrificial animal as the totem image of God. They never participated in the process of "eating the god." (Some scholars say the Hebrews refused to eat the wild boar or pig (chazir) because that beast was the totem animal of the god of the ancient Semites.)

The Hebrew service for the Temple was borrowed, in large part, from contemporary peoples, most likely from the Canaanites, who inhabited the land when the Hebrews came there. The Hebrew priests, however, were charged with the responsibility of teaching the moral law (Torah), a fact which distinguished them from their pagan contemporaries. Nonetheless, the Hebrew priests did employ many of the ritualistic forms used by the pagans. One of these was the use of an animal as an atonement for the sins of one or of many people. The life of the animal was given in exchange for the "life" of the sinner.

We must understand, however, that the animal generally was not wasted, for it was cooked and eaten for food. Part of the animal was given as a gift to the priests who participated in the service. These gifts made possible the setting aside of a group of men who did not labor in the fields, but who worked exclusively in the Temple.

In ancient times, the act of eating together was one of the outer signs of a covenant or agreement between two parties. The story of Moses and his stay upon Mt. Sinai includes a description of how Moses and the Elders (the council of wise men who climbed Mt. Sinai with him) ate a "covenant" meal together. The story seems to imply that in some way God was involved in this ritual meal. The text reads, ". . . and they beheld God, and did eat and drink" (Ex. 24:11). Even today, among the Arabs in the Middle East, if you eat with someone you are deemed to be his "covenant" brother. It is believed that one of the reasons why ancient Hebrews were enjoined not to eat with strangers was that they were to be wary with whom they joined together in a covenant relationship.

The Hebrews adapted some of the ancient pagan practices but made sure not to treat God as a demon that could be controlled or manipulated by man through magic or witchcraft. When the Second Temple was destroyed in 70 C.E., the entire custom of animal sacrifice was abandoned. From that time on the Jews began to worship God by means of verbal prayer alone. This change in the method of worship represented a major ritualistic revolution. (It is interesting to note that the traditionally oriented prayerbooks used by Orthodox and Conservative congregations today still include prayers calling for the restoration of the Temple and its animal sacrifices.)

The Synagogue

There is some, but not conclusive, evidence in the Bible

of the existence of the Synagogue. It is possible that even while the First Temple was on Mount Zion, the Synagogue was gradually growing in importance. The prophet Jeremiah, who lived while the First Temple still stood, speaks of a *bet am* (house of the people). We also find mention of *mo-adey el* (meeting places of God) in Psalm 74:8.

The destruction of Solomon's Temple in 586 B.C.E., no doubt, gave great impetus to the development of some substitute worship procedure. In all likelihood, the Synagogue had a rapid development in Babylonia because the Exiles of the sixth century B.C.E. had to establish a substitute for the Temple worship. It was there, especially, that the synagogues became the centers of Jewish learning.

The conquering Babylonians took most of the important Hebrew religious leaders away with them, and it may be assumed that the Jews who were left in Judah were not as thorough in creating a Temple substitute. In fact, most of the energy of the Palestinian community was devoted to the reestablishing of the ancient Temple. When Ezra came to Judah from Babylonia (possibly around 450 B.C.E.), he introduced the custom of reading and interpreting the *Torah*. The custom may well be linked to the synagogue practice of the Babylonian Jewish community.

Synagogues also seem to have existed in Alexandria, Egypt, in the third century B.C.E. This city was one of the great Jewish centers at that time, and in spite of the absence of a sacrificial center like the Temple, and despite the great influence of Hellenism upon the people, Judaism was vital and strong there. It may be assumed that the Synagogue (the very name is Greek, meaning "place of assembly") had a great deal to do with the successful preservation of Jewish identity in Egypt.

In describing the content of the Prayerbook, we pointed out that beyond the liturgical prayers it also contains material for study. We are not surprised, then, to discover that the Synagogue was called not only a *bet ha-t'filah* (house of prayer), but also a *bet ha-midrash* (house of study). Since the subject matter of the books studied by Jews usually involved religious matters, such study was, indeed, closely akin to worship. The Temple, too, had been a kind of school, for fledgling priests were trained there to master the *Torah* and the priestly rites. The Synagogue, however, provided a school open to all. It was not the "house of the priests," but a *bet am* (house of the people).

With the building of the Second Temple, around 500 B.C.E., the Jews of Palestine returned to the Temple sacrificial system as the central act of worship, but the Synagogue apparently continued to operate as a religious center alongside of it. The communities outside of Palestine were especially dependent on the Synagogues.

AVODAH

The technical name for the sacrificial service in the Temple itself was *avodah* (worship). Only those who were priests by inheritance could administer this service at the sacred altar. Portions of the traditional prayer service as developed in the Prayerbook bear this same title, *avodah.* The service in the synagogue might be led by anyone who had the knowledge necessary for it, and all worshipers were invited to share in the reading of it. In this sense, the prayerbook represents a democratizing of the worship service; the sacred prayers were made available to the common man. They were no longer the private possession of an esoteric priesthood.

It is said that Mohammed envied the Jews because they were the *Am Hasefer* (People of the Book). The book to which he referred was the Bible, but the title could also refer to the vast heritage of religious books which the Jews had composed. Since the average Jew longed to pray to God, and since the appropriate prayers were contained in a book, there was an added incentive for him to become literate. The existence of the prayerbook provided a strong motivation for learning, and the Jewish community made such learning available to all the people.

Without some kind of prayerbook, Jews could not have made an orderly transition from Temple worship to Synagogue worship. The fact that the basic core of prayers was probably already in existence when the Temple fell made it possible for Judaism to survive what might otherwise have been a totally catastrophic event.

There have been attempts throughout the centuries to modify the core of traditional prayers. We learn from the *Talmud,* which represents the thought of Judaism from about 250 B.C.E. to about 500 C.E., that several rabbis suggested abbreviated prayers which might be said by the Jew who did not have time for the entire prayer service. Jesus, who seems to have been raised as a Jew, is quoted in the New Testament as suggesting such a brief prayer the famous "Lord's prayer" (beginning, "Our Father, who art in heaven"). Its content is not dissimilar from other Jewish prayers.

In the 18th century, the Chassidim, a group of Jews who ultimately dominated the religious life of the peasantry in Eastern Europe, developed some brilliant insights into the nature of prayer. They maintained that when God created the world, He placed a spark of Himself in every creature. Since the time of Creation, said the Chassidim, this spark within man has been longing to return to its Source. It is as if there were an electric magnetism at work in the universe. This longing which stirs the hearts of man is *prayer,* according to the Chassidim. "It is the Divine calling to the Divine."

The Chassidim would have us believe that men pray because they have no alternative. Thus, even illiterate people, who are unable to verbalize their prayers in a formal way, must pray, and their prayer is acceptable to God.

Part of the Chassidic heritage left to us is the story of the illiterate peasant who came to the synagogue on the High Holidays and who longed to pray, after the manner of those who were reading from the prayerbook. Finally, in desperation, the peasant arose, lifted his face heavenward and cried out, "Oh, Master of the Universe! Here are the letters of the alphabet, *aleph, bet, gimmel, dalet.* Make yourself such prayers as you will, and to them I will say, *amen!"*

Derived from the same kind of orientation towards prayer is the Chassidic teaching, "There is a key to the gate of heaven, but God prefers that we break the lock with one heart-felt sigh." The "key" is the traditional prayers. The "heart-felt sigh" is a spontaneous, original feeling. The Chassidim did not attack traditional Judaism so much as they taught that there was also *another way* (perhaps even better, from their viewpoint) to be religious. They suggested that what God wanted most was something less formalistic than the *siddur.*

The Chassidim were more concerned with the natural outpouring of the heart. Indeed, when one disciple came to a famous *Tzadik* (Chassidic rabbi) and asked for the meaning of *avodah,* the *Tzadik* replied, "This is the *avodah* which God wants you to perform. He wants you to attain to three loves, the love of God, the love of *Torah,* and the love of Israel [the community of men]."

In Chassidism, we witness the final step in the evolution of the meaning of *avodah* (worship) from priestly animal sacrifice to the individual's expression of love towards man and God. The *Tzadik* would agree with the poet who wrote, "He prayeth best who loveth best, all things both great and small."

The Hebrew priestly ritual represented a broadening of pagan ritual, for the Hebrew Temple service was, at least, morally oriented. The rise of the Synagogue made every man who could read the prayerbook a "priest," in the sense that he, too, could stand before God and pray. The Chassidim reminded us that formal prayers can be helpful, but they are not the ultimate method of prayer. Ultimately, it is the deed of love which marks our prayerful link to the divine.

THE DEEPER MEANING OF PRAYER

Perhaps we can say that the Chassidim are in the tradition of the prophets who, long before the destruction of the Temple, attacked the hypocritical presentation of sacrifices in the Temple. "What does your God require of you," asked Micah, "but that you do justly, love mercy, and walk humbly with your God." The prophets were the first to teach that the basic test of religiosity is the way we treat our fellow men.

It has been argued effectively by many scholars that just as the Chassidim did not try to do away with formal prayer but, rather, tried to point the way to more profound prayer, so the prophets were not trying to do away with the Temple service in their day, but, rather, to point the way to the underlying purpose of the prayer service. In modern times there are some Jews who contend that we have outgrown the Synagogue and the formal prayer service. These are the advocates of the "Golden Rule" approach to religion. They apparently believe that if a man is good to his neighbor, he is "religious."

The High Holiday prayer-service teaches us that three things are required to insure a man's life. These are *prayer, repentance* and the *righteous deed.* Not prayer *alone,* not the righteous deed *alone,* but these two together plus "repentance" (really, "return" to the Torah-path). This wisdom seems more than we can refute. Those who think that the religious life consists merely of abstract prayer deceive themselves. True prayer in Judaism is part of a *process* that includes re-direction of one's life along the moral path and the active deed which binds man to man. Prayer is the preparation of the mind and the spirit for the righteous deed. It is the training of the soul that it might find its appropriate life-serving outlet.

Those who think themselves capable of living the righteous life without careful preparation (without prayer) are also deceiving themselves. Before the tree can produce good fruit for eating, the seed must be planted and the soil cultivated and enriched. Prayer involves the process of planting and cultivating, said the medieval Jewish philosopher, Bachya ibn Pakuda. Prayer involves reaching out, as high as we can, towards the living ideal that we call God. It involves reaching in, as deep as we can, towards the divine spark which God has placed within us. Investigation and introspection are part of the prayer-mood. Study and meditation are aspects of prayer. Respect for the past as well as respect for the unborn future is part of the prayerful approach to life.

We can find some answers only when we pray alone. Other answers are to be found only when we pray together. The "heart-felt sigh" has meaning in its special moment. Modern man has to learn both how to pray alone and how to pray with the congregation. He feels the need to assert his individualism, but he needs even more to reach out towards his fellow man. We need the private prayer, and we need the prayerbook, however streamlined and updated, for the prayerbook binds together the centuries and the living community.

In the end, there can be no such thing as a private religion, for religion has to do with community, with the union of many men in the one God. We say *Sh'ma Yisrael* (Hear, Oh Israel); perhaps we should say, "Hear, Oh Mankind," for unless we all hearken to the Voice that makes for unity, we shall create chaos. How can we make many voices into one voice? This is the question to which Judaism has addressed itself in its classical expressions. How can we make for the dominance of love over hate, of mercy over vindictiveness, of hope over despair? These are the questions for which prayer seeks, nay, demands, an answer.

In the ancient Temple service of animal sacrifice, the worshiper gave up something like a bird or an animal, in his plea for a gift from God. Ancient man thought that man had to give something of his own, before he could hope to receive something in return. Perhaps, there is no true prayer without this willingness to give of one's most precious gifts. The dearest thing one has to give dwells in the innermost recesses of one's heart and soul. Scripture teaches, "the sacrifices of God are a broken heart and a contrite spirit." Preconditions for profound prayer are the heart made heavy with attempts to offset the afflictions of mankind, and a spirit made humble by an awareness of the fact that God has many children as worthy as oneself.

When we come to the prayer moment prepared not only to receive but ready to give, we will find that the prayers will be more meaningful and will flow more readily.

SUGGESTED READINGS

JUDAISM AND PRAYER, *Herbert M. Baumgard,* Union of American Hebrew Congregations.

THE SMALL SANCTUARY, *Solomon Freehof,* Union of American Hebrew Congregations.

THE AUTHORIZED DAILY PRAYER BOOK, Edited by *Joseph H. Hertz,* Bloch Publishing Company.

SABBATH AND FESTIVAL PRAYER BOOK, edited by *Morris Silverman,* Rabbinical Assembly of America and United Synagogue of America.

UNION PRAYER BOOK, newly revised, Part I, Central Conference of American Rabbis.

BASIC JUDAISM, *Milton Steinberg,* Harcourt, Brace, World and Company.

TOWARD A MODERN
JEWISH THEOLOGY
by Jack Bemporad

JACK BEMPORAD: Rabbi, serving as Director of Worship at U.A.H.C.; a graduate of Tulane University, was ordained at H.U.C. in 1959; is a contributing editor to **DE HOMINE,** philosophical journal of University of Rome, and has written for **JEWISH SOCIAL STUDIES, AMERICAN JUDAISM, LA VOCE** (Italy) and others; has lectured at many universities.

THE TASK OF THEOLOGY

JEWISH theology, as contrasted with Jewish religious practice, is an attempt to think through systematically the various aspects of Jewish teaching and render them explicit, coherent, and theoretically consistent.

The theologian, in working to achieve a unity of what constitutes his religious world view, attempts to confront this world view with broader philosophical, scientific, ethical, and aesthetic viewpoints; that is, he attempts to integrate it with the various contributions that these disciplines make in dealing with their area of endeavor.

It is sometimes not clearly understood what particular problems are faced in the process of systematizing a religious tradition. First of all, a theology is a synthesis from a certain perspective. It is a mistake to think that one can see a religious tradition by itself as something apart from the historical-theological situation in which the systematizer finds himself. Second, the theologian will, of necessity, discard much in his tradition which he believes to be archaic and superseded. (And yet, in another time, these discarded elements may quite legitimately be reintroduced as essential.) He may also stress certain aspects as basic, while relegating others to the periphery.

The history of theology in general tends to illustrate the special interests of theologians in different periods, showing how they viewed and synthesized the tradition they were working on. It shows also how they contributed to the tradition, for in the act of synthesis they introduced numerous elements which in turn became part of Jewish teaching.

Jewish theology, however, is not purely relativistic. Each theological systematization had at its base a thesis

143

which unified the attempts at the clarification of Judaism that were made by theologians in different periods. To separate the permanent from the changing elements in Jewish theology, however, is a difficult task, one that contemporary theology must confront. All I wish to indicate at this point is that there are changing elements in Jewish theology and I believe that all branches of Judaism would in some form or other subscribe to this concept. Only a rigid fundamentalist would reject the idea of change altogether; the fundamentalist insists on identifying a particular theological synthesis, which had a specific setting and rationale in a definite period, as the sole criterion for all future syntheses in whatever other settings.

The problem being discussed here has been set forth cogently by Whitehead in his *Religion in the Making:* "You cannot claim absolute finality for a dogma without claiming a commensurate finality for the sphere of thought within which it arose." A theology must have the inherent freedom to modify and restate the application and extension of its basic ideas. Tillich makes a similar critique of fundamentalism in his *Systematic Theology:* "They (the Fundamentalists) confuse eternal truth with a temporal expression of this truth. . . . The theological truth of yesterday is defended as an unchangeable message against the theological truth of today and tomorrow. . . . It elevates something finite and transitory to infinite and eternal validity."

It is impossible to make a sharp distinction between the theological system as such and the standpoint or point of view from which the synthesis is made. In most cases the standpoint is in reference to a challenge to the continuation of tradition, and the work of systematization is an attempt to resolve or overcome such a challenge. From a strictly theological point of view, the basic problem or challenge derives from a current world view that is either partially or totally different from what one believes to be one's religious affirmation. The danger of overemphasizing the contemporary viewpoint is to make the tradition mute. The danger of overemphasizing the tradition is to refuse to face the contemporary challenge.

TRENDS IN THEOLOGY

There are numerous problems with which a contemporary Jewish theology must deal in its work of systematization. To begin with, it must address itself to the nature and meaning of the idea of God. Religion, furthermore, makes truth claims which transcend the sphere of religious practices, claims that have to be theologically justified.

The problem of evil is perhaps the most persistent problem of our time and we must strive to deal with it. Another problem, of what I shall call practical atheism, must also be met. The term "practical atheism" covers various meanings. It can refer to the discontinuity between religious and secular beliefs, or it can signify the distinction between affirming that God exists and letting that affirmation affect the pattern of one's life. In this essay, I will concentrate on the problem of evil since this seems to be the most urgent, and I will comment briefly on the others.

I. The Concept of God

It is fashionable nowadays to differentiate between the God of Abraham, Isaac, and Jacob and the God of the philosophers. The former, it is maintained, is the God of religious experience; the latter the God of a philosophical system. I personally believe that this differentiation is basically misleading. If anything, the two should reinforce one another and not be in conflict.

If we maintain that God is the God of religious experience, then we are limiting God to only those aspects that are directly derivable from such experience. We furthermore make certain claims as to the existence and nature of God within religious experience that cannot be vindicated solely by this experience. These claims can only be vindicated by viewing God as having cosmological and ethical functions. If we affirm that God is the creator, orderer and sustainer of the actual world, we are discussing God's cosmological function. If we affirm that God inspires man to ethical action, then we are concerned with His moral function. If, on the other hand, we speak of how God inspires in us a sense of awe or holiness, that He cleanses and purifies us, then we are speaking of God as revealed in religious experience.

These conceptualizations neither mean that there are several Gods nor that some functions of God are more important than others, but that God is vaster than any one systematization. We cannot restrict God solely to the realm of our religious experience, but we must affirm His influence on the world as creator, sustainer, etc., and we affirm His influence on man in terms of the ethical imperative. These claims to existence, and to His fulfilling cosmological and ethical functions, require a concept of God which is beyond the purely subjective realm. Whitehead somewhere makes a remark to the effect that God is too important to be used solely for religious functions. He has ethical and cosmological functions which are as important, if not more important.

II. The Truth Claims of Religion

No one would go about attempting to prove the existence of God unless he were certain that God is more than his subjective idea, and that the belief in God makes a certain truth claim which needs vindication. When one asserts that God exists, or is actual, or has being, we are immediately faced with the questions—in what sense, and how can we be sure? To answer these questions, so-called proofs are offered. For instance, the ontological proof asserts that God is "that than which nothing greater can exist or be conceived." Here God is identified as the most perfect being. Thus when we ask in what sense does God exist, the answer is in an eminent sense. This can then be rephrased as follows: Is there an entity, a being, that has quality x, y, z (perfection, goodness, power) in an eminent degree which other entities have only in a partial or derivative sense? If there is, then that entity is God.

The teleological argument argues from the order in the universe to an eminent ordering being. As Hartshorne has indicated, if each element contributed equally to the order of the universe what would result is chaos. Only if there is a preeminent ordering entity can there be any order and pattern worthy of the name.

These proofs make a claim which can only be vindicated within a philosophical context by maintaining that the goodness, power, and order of the universe require an eminent embodiment. I am not here attempting a proof for the existence of God. I am only trying to show what kind of concern a proof illustrates. The word "proof" may be somewhat forced, but what is at the base of the arguments is the belief that the derivative and finite is not self-explicative or self-subsistent but points to a transcendent. The arguments are successful to the degree that they illustrate how the world is not self-dependent or self-subsistent, but is rather dependent and derivative and thus points to something beyond. It is within this context (a philosophical context) that truth claims are made and vindications attempted.

III. The Problem of Evil

The problem of evil is an age-old question. It has been a stumbling block to faith and recently has been at the center of theological concern.

The problem is usually stated as follows: If God is all powerful and all good, then how can He allow evil? If God is omnipotent, then God by definition has the power to prevent any possible evil. If He is all good — absolute goodness — then He could not possibly desire any evil. Now, if God does not desire evil and has all the power necessary to prevent it, then why is there evil in the world?

It would follow from this argument that God is either *deficient in power or deficient in goodness,* otherwise the evil in the world has to be explained away as not really being evil at all. Most Jewish thinking on this question has denied the reality of evil. Medieval Jewish theology generally maintained that evil was merely the "absence of good." Some philosophers made evil necessary so that it could be overcome by the good.

If God is all powerful and all good, then the world can have no power or goodness. All power and goodness are His alone. But for the universe to contain evil it must have sufficient power to produce the good that evil destroyed. For evil to be real there must have been the possibility of genuine good in the world; but if we admit the possibility of genuine good in the world, then the world must possess sufficient power and goodness to bring it into being. In effect, it is impossible for the world to contain evil without its having at the same time the possibility of achieving good; yet in order for it to achieve good it must have power and goodness. It is, therefore, wrong to say that God is all powerful and all good, since in that case the world would have no power, goodness, or being.

What we must affirm is that God has the most power and goodness but *not all possible* power and goodness. The world must have *some* power and goodness in addition to God's power and goodness for the world to contain evil. And so, as traditionally stated, the question will not stand. If God has all power and goodness (all *possible* power and goodness) then creation cannot have *enough* power and goodness even to allow for the reality of evil.

It may seem at first as if this were a variation on the traditional solution with respect to man's freedom; that is, that man has freedom to choose evil. But this is not the case since the traditional view can in no way explain genuine choice, and hence in no way can explain man's freedom.

The problem of freedom concerns itself with an attempt to reconcile God's *omnipotence* with *human responsibility.* To say that God is omnipotent—in the traditional sense— means that God has all possible power. But if God has all possible power, and all possible knowledge, then God must not only *direct* all that happens but must *know* all that has happened, is happening, or ever will happen.

Such a view of God makes it impossible for man to have any genuine freedom or capacity to create. For how can he affect the process of creation at all—either positively or negatively—if God has all power?

God determines all. God knows all. God does all. If all that I am to do is already determined in God's mind, if the entire process of history is prewritten there, then how am I free?

If man has no power, then man can have no responsibility.

The solution lies in redefining God's attributes of *omnipotence, omniscience,* and *goodness* to mean that God is in *no sense* deficient in power, knowledge, and goodness. God is the most powerful being but not the being with all power, the most good but not the being with all goodness.

All the confusion in traditional theology, and the essence of the confusion concerning the problem of evil, stems from the Aristotelian dogma that God is to be identified with substance, and that substance needs nothing but itself in order to exist: that it contains everything, is complete, immutable and in splendid isolation. Once God is identified with the Aristotelian substance then the fullness of being, goodness and power is complete in God, and the world and man can add nothing to God. This means that God is exactly the same with or without creation.

But here is the basic problem. If creation really is, then God cannot be the same and have the same attributes and existence as if creation *were not.* By affirming that God is the sole being and sole reality, traditional theology denies the possibility of a multiplicity of real beings. In denying a genuine multiplicity of real beings it speaks in one context as if the world has being and thus, in some way or other, is additional to God, and in another context as if it has no genuine being and God is the sole reality.

In order to resolve these ambiguities, theology must affirm that there is genuine difference before and after creation. After creation man and nature have being and power, and all the attributes of God have to be redefined so as to account for the being and power of creation. Once we affirm that not only God but creation also has being, power and goodness, then one major consequence follows: God is not the sole cause of the continuing process of the world. He is the major cause in sustaining, ordering and actualizing the world but not the *only* cause, and hence cannot be *solely responsible* for actuality. Other beings make a genuine difference in the process. This allows for a genuine freedom. It vindicates both man's power and man's responsibility.

IV. Practical Atheism

The problem of what I have termed practical atheism is

an aspect of the increasing secularism of our day. Many would affirm that God exists, as the creator or even as a divine principle in the cosmos, and yet totally deny any sense in which the divine has a definite effect on their lives. It is the theoretical affirmation of God together with His practical rejection that constitutes practical atheism. One can assert that God has no practical effect on one's life by either maintaining that the belief in God has no implications in the way of behavior (i.e. ethical action or concern) or that there is no objectively valid (i.e. nondelusional) religious experience.

The first view mostly takes the form of Deism, which maintains that God may have gotten the universe started but takes no active role in the ongoing process of creation. The only answer to such a view is a metaphysics that illustrates how God is and is not involved in the ongoing processes of the universe.

The second view totally dismisses the validity of religious experience. It arises from prejudging what is admissible and what is inadmissible evidence. Usually one grants priority to so-called scientific experience (sense-data), relegating to the subjective realm aesthetic and ethical experience, and to the merely emotional realm any appeal to religious experience. This view has to be revised. Religious experience has to have the *same* (no more nor less) objective validity as any other experience, whether it is to be ethical, aesthetic or scientific. Religious intuitions, furthermore, have to be given their full due and integrated into a total philosophy of religion. They cannot be explained away either psychologically or sociologically. Once the validity and objective character of religious experience is vindicated, then man will have found a way towards genuine piety and worship and will be able to overcome this aspect of the problem of practical atheism.

Conclusion

What I have tried to indicate in this essay is the impossibility of separating theological questions from philosophical ones. Every major theological affirmation makes a claim which needs philosophical vindication. Both the need for, and philosophical character of, a modern theology can be attested from the purported conflict between science and religion. It is not the activities of science nor the rituals and ceremonies of religion that are in conflict. Such activities are perfectly consistent with one another. What raises the problem of the relation between science and religion is this: Are the philosophical presuppositions of science consistent with the philosophical presuppositions of religion? It is on this level that the conflict arises and on this level that it must be resolved.

Much that has been said above is tentative and suggestive. It is merely an attempt to clarify certain theological issues characteristic of our day. It is a first step—but a necessary one—if serious thinking in theology is to be carried on.

SUGGESTED READINGS

MEANING AND TRUTH IN RELIGION, *William Christian*, Princeton University Press.

RELIGION IN THE MAKING, *A. N. Whitehead*, Macmillan.

SYSTEMATIC THEOLOGY, Vol. I, *Paul Tillich*, University of Chicago Press.

ESSENCE OF JUDAISM, *Leo Baeck*, Schocken.

PHILOSOPHIES OF JUDAISM, *Julius Guttman*, Holt, Rinehart and Winston.

THE DIVINE RELATIVITY, *Charles Hartshorne*, Yale University Press.

ORIENTATION: CURRENTS IN AMERICAN JEWISH LIFE
by Benjamin Efron

BENJAMIN EFRON: Director of Union of American Hebrew Congregations' **COLLEGE OF JEWISH STUDIES** in Los Angeles; degrees from City College and Columbia University; author of **PATHWAYS THROUGH THE PRAYERBOOK, MESSAGE OF THE TORAH, STORY WITHOUT END** and other books.

THE material in Part One constitutes a study of modern Jewish religious thought; in Part Two the focus is on Jewish life in America.

A new Jewish community has been evolving in the United States, vastly different from the ghettos of Eastern Europe, and we want to place the activities and problems of this emerging community in proper perspective. The articles also provide historical background for understanding many of the changes that are occurring in the American Jewish community.

Jews are asking many questions today, basic questions about the old traditions and values and about the meaning of Jewishness for today. If integration within a democratic society is the goal, many want to know, college students in particular, is it not an act of separatism, a reactionary step, in fact, to insist on Jewishness?

Then again, what is Jewishness; what makes one a Jew in modern America? And this Jewishness (our grandparents from Eastern Europe used to refer to it as *Yiddishkeit*) —what role does it play in actual life; does it still have power to move Jews toward the traditional ideals of Judaism, to make the people Israel a light unto the nations?

Part Two opens with THE AMERICAN JEWISH COMMUNITY, an article which traces the development of the Jewish community in America. The author gives special attention to the manner in which our people organized themselves to meet new and continually changing conditions over the course of the years. This is followed by an account of the rise of another modern Jewish community, the people of the new State of Israel. ISRAEL AND THE JEWISH PEOPLE considers the impact of Israel on the Jews of America, and discusses not only the significance

153

of the rise of the new state, but also some of the problems
that exist in the relationship between the American and
the Israeli Jewish communities.

In democratic America more and more Jews grew up
with a feeling of belonging, with a sense of being part of
the American family. They were able to enter fully into
the cultural life of the country, and Jews early began to
contribute to it as fellow Americans. In THE PATHS OF
JEWISH LITERATURE the literary output of the Jews
is surveyed, and the influence of the Jewish tradition on
their writings is discussed.

For a long time Jewish men have had a reputation for
being "good providers" and good fathers, and the Jewish
family was held in high esteem as a stable unit. The statistics of some thirty or forty years ago show that among
Jews there was a significantly smaller proportion of divorces than in the general population, and a smaller percentage also of criminals, unwed mothers and abandoned
children. But a change is taking place as regards these
matters, a transition that is dealt with in A JEWISH VIEW
OF SEX AND THE FAMILY. The article explores the
reasons for the changes and examines present-day developments in the United States in this area.

The integration of the Jew into American life has
brought him into greater contact with Christians than had
been the case in ghetto times. Three articles deal with the
complex situations that have developed as a result. JUDA-
ISM AND CHRISTIANITY treats of the points of conflict
between the two faiths and of the growing friendly dialogue between their adherents. ANTISEMITISM IN
PERSPECTIVE discusses the nature and direction of antisemitism in America, while INTERMARRIAGE AND
THE JEWISH FUTURE makes some salient comments
about a development that is causing the Jewish community
considerable anxiety.

The final article in Part Two deals with the deeply felt
concern of the American Jew about his identity within the
mass American culture and about the continuing creativity
of the Jewish people as a whole. BEING A JEW IN

AMERICA aims at defining *Yiddishkeit* in the context of contemporary American life.

There are no pat answers to the questions being asked, and our authors do not give offhand replies. Instead, they bring creative thinking to bear on the problems. With their aid, we hope the reader can arrive at a better understanding of the direction Jewish life is taking and of the forces that are at work in the community.

THE AMERICAN JEWISH COMMUNITY

by Manheim S. Shapiro

MANHEIM S. SHAPIRO: Director, National Jewish Communal Affairs of the American Jewish Committee; educated at Brooklyn College, University of Michigan, the Rabbi Isaac Elchanan Yeshiva; he has written and lectured extensively on community relations, Jewish affairs, on prejudice and group identity.

OUR purpose in this article is to trace the development of the various forms through which Jews in America express their relationship to their own Jewishness and to other Jews.

When people say "the Jewish community" to mean the *organized* Jewish community, they include the Jews who express their identification with other Jews by joining or supporting or participating in some organized Jewish activity. This can be a temple or synagogue, a membership organization, or an agency to provide special services, such as a hospital or Jewish community center. While nobody would deny the Jewishness of those who don't do these things, many might refer to these non-participants by saying, "They are Jews, but they are not part of the Jewish community." In other words, "Jewish community" in this sense refers to all those organized activities which Jews conduct together.

To some the "organized" Jewish community means the special network of national, international and local Jewish groups that provide the special machinery for raising and distributing the money contributed by Jews for Jewish purposes. Certain Jewish institutions, like temples and synagogues, are often not considered as part of this specialized Jewish community because they do not share in the general funds, even though their members and leaders usually contribute to these funds and participate in raising them.

Still another tendency, current today, is to regard the Jewish federation or organization which raises, distributes and plans for the use of funds contributed by Jews as being itself "the organized Jewish community" of a particular area. Since the agencies which receive funds from the federated campaigns are dependent for most of their support on the money received from the federation, they are considered as subsidiary to it. This is further reinforced by the fact that in planning for the distribution of funds, federation leaders tend to make their decisions on the basis of what they perceive as best for the *whole* community. Because the federation usually tends to have leaders with a variety of Jewish viewpoints, it is often regarded as the place where a "Jewish community" consensus is reached for the services the federation supports.

THE EARLY JEWISH SETTLERS IN AMERICA

The way in which the Jewish community of America grew, with different groups of Jews coming from many different countries at different times, made it certain that there would be variety rather than sameness in the kind of agencies, organizations and institutions that Jews would develop here. All American Jews, of course, were linked together in one way or another by their attachment to Judaism or to the Jewish people as a whole. But many of them had come from different places with varying customs, traditions and outlooks and so they developed many different patterns of organization. In addition, the circumstances in which they found themselves in different periods in America also affected them in different ways.

The first *group* of Jews arrived in this country at New Amsterdam in 1654. Other individual Jews may have arrived earlier but little is known about them. The landing in 1654 was the first occasion when a number of Jews arrived together as a group. These 23 men, women and children had been living in the Dutch colony of Recife, in Brazil, when it was captured by the Portuguese in January 1654. The Jewish community of several hundred were forced to leave and they set sail on 16 ships bound for various Dutch colonies in the West Indies. As a result of naval battles, one ship carrying the 23 Jews arrived at New Amsterdam. The captain of the ship sold their possessions to pay for their passage and left.

It may have been a good omen for the prospects of Jews in America that the burghers of New Amsterdam bought the goods belonging to these Jews and then returned all they had purchased to the Jewish owners. The Jews repaid this debt later with money received from other Jews in Holland.

This first group of Jews, as well as most of those who trickled into America until about 1800, were mostly descendants of Sephardic Jews who had lived in Spain for many hundreds of years, until they were expelled in 1492. (The word "Sephardic" is merely an Anglicized form of the Hebrew word *Sepharad* meaning "Spanish.") They therefore had some common historical and cultural characteristics.

It was the tendency in the early years of the American colonies for groups of people who were similar in religion and nationality to settle in the same locality, with the result that they usually established patterns reflecting their old country backgrounds. Thus, Massachusetts was settled mostly by English Puritans, whose life and government were shaped by their religious outlook. Parts of Pennsylvania were settled by German colonists who spoke German and who established churches of the particular German sects to which they had belonged in the old country. Louisiana, originally settled by Frenchmen, to this day reflects French culture and institutions.

The Jews of colonial times established such settlements in the cities of New York, Newport, R.I., Charleston, S.C. and Savannah, Ga. The main Jewish bodies that they organized were synagogues, because the early Sephardic settlers thought of themselves as a religious group and because the countries from which they came had had an "established" church (that is, a church authorized by and related to the government). As a result, it was the synagogue that became the principal communal body for the Jews in these communities.

These synagogues served their congregants not only as

a house of worship, the center for various ceremonies and the institution which maintained a Jewish cemetery, they were also the places where Jews suffering hard times could come for temporary help from their co-religionists. In the 1800's, Jews of a different background began to arrive in gradually increasing numbers. These were Jews from German states who had found the many restrictions established by their governments very difficult to live with. They could not earn a living in their accustomed occupations, and America seemed to offer an opportunity for a new life.

GROWTH OF A GERMAN JEWISH COMMUNITY IN AMERICA

Many of the German Jews who arrived in the early part of the 19th century settled in the cities where Jewish congregations had already been established. They soon joined these congregations, often married the daughters of the Sephardic Jewish families and became absorbed into the Jewish group life of these communities. By the 1840's and 1850's, however, the *German* Jewish community had become large enough and economically independent enough to establish its own cultural and religious patterns.

A large part of the German Jewish immigrants started their new lives in America as peddlers. They acquired a stock of merchandise and headed for the newly opened areas of the West and South as traders. Some set out on foot with only as much as they could carry in a pack on their backs, bringing such merchandise as needles, thread, buttons and other hard to obtain items to the settlers in the frontier areas. Those with more capital traveled with a horse and a wagon loaded with cloth, household goods and farm implements.

Many of the peddlers, once they had sold their stock, returned to the major cities with furs purchased from the Indians, and with other products of the South and West. Many soon established themselves as large-scale traders, transporting raw material from the western lands and bringing back manufactured products from the East. Those who accumulated sufficient capital would open a dry goods or general store in a new town or village. Since the period in which Jews were following these patterns was also the period when the large proportion of American cities west of the Atlantic seaboard were being established, these Jewish merchants grew with the cities, and to this day many of the leading stores in cities all over the South and West are those that had been established by these early Jewish traders.

Most of the Germans of the first part of the 19th century were single men, who, when they settled in the new towns, were usually the only Jews in the community. They were not numerous enough to establish Jewish congregations or organizations. Many of them married non-Jewish women and lost all contact with their Jewish origins. But most of those who came in the second half of the century, after the Revolution of 1848, arrived with their families, and settled in groups in many of the cities where the earlier German Jewish immigrants had established themselves. They did so because they were related to these earlier settlers and because other non-Jewish Germans had also settled there, so they could establish their new lives among people with the same language and similar cultural traits.

Although some proportion of these arrivals also began as peddlers, many of them brought to the new towns the skills they had acquired as doctors and lawyers, merchants, managers, bankers and editors. They were the products of the emancipation of Jews that had begun with the French Revolution. They had become part of the German society of that period, and had been trained in many of the professions and skills of the German cities of that time.

As one result of their emancipation, there had emerged among these Jews in Germany the new Reform Judaism. In addition to the religious changes introduced by Reform leaders, perhaps most important for its later effect was their commitment to the idea that Jews were not different from other citizens except in the matter of their faith.

Thus, when these groups of German Jews came to organize themselves, they tended to establish Reform congregations. Their most important religious leader, Rabbi Isaac Mayer Wise, not only formed an important Reform congregation in Cincinnati, he also helped to establish Reform temples in other cities, and to persuade existing congregations to become part of the new Reform movement. The Hebrew Union College, the first American seminary for the training of rabbis, was established in Cincinnati. Ultimately, there was formed the Union of American Hebrew Congregations, an association of the various Reform congregations; as well as the Central Conference of American Rabbis, an association of Reform rabbis.

Meanwhile, Jewish immigration kept increasing and the settled Jews began to organize agencies and societies to help needier Jews. Hebrew Free Loan Societies were set up and institutions were built to care for Jewish orphans and destitute old people; and in some places schools were organized to provide free religious education to the children of poor Jewish families.

This was also the period when the B'nai B'rith was founded as a society to discuss and act on problems facing Jews as a group. During this time, as well, the first Jewish newspapers appeared, generally weeklies for the reporting of events and activities of interest to Jews.

At the time of the American Revolution, there were about 2,000 Jews in the country. By 1820, this had risen to about 5,000. In 1880, there were close to 250,000, mostly of German-Jewish origin, and scattered in cities all across the country. But around 1880, a new wave of Jewish immigration began to reach the United States, part of a great population movement from Eastern Europe.

JEWISH IMMIGRATION FROM EASTERN EUROPE

During the 19th century the strong democratic spirit that had arisen in the west, and the Industrial Revolution stimulated social and economic unrest in the East European countries. Their monarchs and rulers began to impose severe restrictive measures to stamp out any liberal sentiments and movements among their peoples. One method that they used for distracting the aroused peasantry and city workmen was to turn their general feelings of anger toward the Jews.

Life was hard for the common people in general of Eastern Europe, but it became increasingly intolerable for the Jews of that area. The restrictions upon where they could live, upon the occupations they could enter and upon the kinds of education they could obtain, made making a living difficult for the vast majority. In addition, they were often in actual danger of their lives from *pogroms,* organized attacks upon Jewish residents by bands of peasants or by official military contingents, in which Jews were killed and their homes and property pillaged or set afire.

A massive migration of Jews took place from Eastern (and Southern) Europe. Substantial numbers settled in Germany, France, the Netherlands and England, but for the great majority the goal was America, the land of freedom and opportunity.

But these were a different kind of immigrant from the earlier Jews who had arrived here. First of all, they came in much larger numbers. In the years from 1880 to 1920, as many as 100,000 to 150,000 would arrive in a single year. Most were poor (on the average, they arrived here with about $9.00 each), and had always been poor. In the countries they came from they had lived their lives almost totally isolated from the surrounding population. They had grown up accustomed to living among other Jews, speaking Yiddish as their mother tongue, and maintaining their own communal life and institutions. Furthermore, their customs and habits, formed by Orthodox religious practice over centuries and by the conditions imposed upon them by a hostile environment, made them feel and seem strange in their new country.

They tended, therefore, to settle in the major cities along

the Eastern seaboard, such as New York, Boston, Phila-
delphia and Baltimore, clustered together in crowded
neighborhoods, like the East Side of New York, where
rents were cheap. Many of them found employment in the
factories and sweatshops of the ready-to-wear garment industry that was beginning to spring up in America. And
they began to establish communal institutions that would
continue some of the important religious and cultural elements of their old way of life.

One of the important organizations the new immigrants
started was the *landsmanschaft* (association of fellow-
countrymen), composed of people from the same region or
town. Thus there were societies of people who came from
the city of Bialystok or Minsk; from Latvia or Bessarabia.
These groupings enabled the newcomers to come into contact with others who spoke the same language, knew the
same people, followed the same customs. Many of them
established mutual-assistance societies to provide loans to
members who needed help, and burial societies to provide
for the costs of a funeral and a cemetery plot for a member
who had died.

In the same way, groups of people who had come from
the same place formed Orthodox synagogues of their own;
the older American temples and synagogues seemed to
them different and alien. The synagogue, too, enabled
them to maintain what was familiar: the same order of
prayer, the same pronunciation, the familiar melody of the
prayers and hymns, the same pattern of organization. They
also established *talmud torahs,* schools in which their children could be taught Hebrew, *Tanach* (Bible), *Talmud,*
and worship. Sometimes the synagogue provided education
for children, but often the schooling was provided by independent *rebbes* (teachers) who established small afternoon schools in their homes or in a rented room. Many of
the *talmud torahs* were established independently by people who banded together for this purpose and who secured
funds from the parents of the pupils and from voluntary
contributions.

A large part of the East European immigrants had been influenced by a movement called the *Haskalah* (scholarship), which had sought to modernize Jewish life in Eastern Europe by reviving Hebrew as a language for communication and literature, and by encouraging Jews to study all that had been developed in Western culture including science, literature and mathematics. They centered attention also upon the scientific study of Jewish history and thought, and the use of Yiddish as a literary and cultural language.

One result of this intellectual activity was the development among the immigrants of a whole network of cultural undertakings: Yiddish daily newspapers, a substantial number of Yiddish theaters presenting plays and musicals, many literary and dramatic societies, discussion and study groups, journals and research publications and societies and associations of writers, actors and musicians.

Another organized movement that was brought to America by the East Europeans was Zionism. This development had come about as a result of many influences: the eternal commitment of Judaism to the "return to Zion" as ordained by God's covenant with the Jews, the nationalist spirit of the times which moved Jews also to want to establish a nation of their own, and the reaction to the active antisemitism Jews had experienced in various European countries. For these and other reasons Zionism had stirred the feelings of many East European Jews, but they differed as to how the Zionist goals could be achieved. Each point of view, whether general Zionist, labor Zionist or cultural Zionist, usually had its own organization with its own activities, journals and leaders.

Again, many East European Jews had been influenced by the labor and radical movements of the late 19th century and were therefore often anti-religious. However, they felt themselves deeply Jewish and organized socialist-minded societies like the Workmen's Circle (which also provided insurance, death benefits, and Yiddish, non-religious, Jewish schools for children). Largely workers, the early East

European Jews organized Jewish trade unions, or set up Jewish locals in the craft unions of industries where Jews were working in substantial numbers.

THE REACTION OF THE OLDER JEWISH COMMUNITY

The reaction and feeling of the older-established American Jews to these new immigrants was mixed. In part, they were apprehensive. In the period of the large-scale immigration from Eastern and Southern Europe, there was a rising anti-foreign movement in America, directed against both Jews and non-Jews. Almost all of the immigrants coming from that part of the world were poor and strange in their dress and ways, and different in their language and customs. For the Jews there was hostility not only because of the general anti-foreign sentiment, they encountered also a rise in antisemitism which flared among some American groups at this time. This made the older established Jews fearful lest Americans develop an intense anti-Jewish feeling, which would endanger all Jews, including the many already Americanized Jewish families.

On the other hand, many of the older Jewish families were also moved by sympathy for these East European Jews, who were after all their co-religionists, and who had suffered such fearful disabilities in their countries of origin. They wanted to help them over the difficulties they were having in making their way in the new land.

The net result of these feelings was a multiplication of efforts to assist Jews in need, and to help them in the process of adjustment to America. Old charitable institutions and welfare programs were expanded, and new ones were created. Jewish hospitals, free loan societies, orphanages, homes for the aged, educational aid societies and free schools grew and multiplied. In addition, classes in English and citizenship were instituted. Family aid agencies were developed. YMHA's were established to provide wholesome recreation for the children and young people from the immigrant families and to make available health, civic, recreational and cultural training for the older people.

Each of these activities required drives for funds to support them. At the same time, the East European immigrants themselves were also raising funds for similar programs that they wanted to conduct under their own auspices. There were so many fund drives and charity collections in the Jewish communities that the leaders began to develop united or federated campaigns for entire cities.

In this process, too, there were mixed forces at work. For some, the important factor was that a single annual fund-raising campaign for all the various charities would make it simpler for the giver to make a decision about how and where his philanthropic contributions should be made. For others, the important element was that it would make the work of fund-raising easier and its administration less expensive. For still others, the significant point was that the use of charity funds could be planned better.

For some years, there was a conflict between the federations established by the "uptown" Jews (the older residents), and the organizations of the "downtown" Jews, those from the more recent immigrants. In some cities, there were actually two separate federations operating simultaneously for as much as fifteen years. Ultimately, however, as these two groups became more similar in outlook and activity, the federations merged. Now, in almost every American city where there are substantial numbers of Jews, there is a single Jewish federation, or its equivalent.

The large stream of Jewish immigration slowed down to a virtual standstill in 1924, when, after World War I, the United States adopted restrictive immigration laws. Over the years since then, with the exception of such groups as the Chassidim, who prefer like the Amish and Mennonites to cling to "old world" ways, the vast majority of American Jews have adapted to American life, language and ways of living. In 1964, it is estimated that around 85% of all American Jews were born and educated in this country.

In this period there were many historic events, each of which had its effect upon the feelings of Jews and on the programs of Jewish organizations. The need to help Jews overseas in the early years of the 20th century led to the creation of organizations like the American Jewish Committee and the Joint Distribution Committee. The discrimination in different fields in America led to programs to combat restrictions against Jews in employment, education, housing and other areas. The rise of Hitler and Nazi propaganda which seemed to encourage antisemitic activity in the United States, led to organizations and movements to combat such teachings.

At the same time, as it became apparent that the Jews of Germany and indeed of all Europe would need assistance and a place of refuge, American Jews began to work vigorously for the establishment of a homeland for Jews in Palestine. This was intensified after World War II, when the remaining Jews who had survived Hitler's attempts to destroy all the Jews were without any means of subsistence and had almost no place to go, for the doors to many countries were closed. Nor did the eventual establishment in 1948 of the State of Israel put an end to assistance to Israel by American Jews, since Israel continued to be threatened by its Arab neighbors. Also, the vast problem of providing for the immigration and settlement of Jews in Israel required massive financial resources.

This was, in short, a period of vast and important change, in which the ways of expressing Jewish identification and interest in America have taken on new forms.

CATEGORIES OF JEWISH ORGANIZATIONS

A look at the current patterns of Jewish activity and organization, and their development from the beginnings described above, presents the following picture. Jewish institutions in America fall into these categories: religious; civic and community relations; Zionist and Israel-related; educational, recreational and cultural; health, welfare and social service; coordinating and servicing; and professional associations. Sometimes these overlap; for example, a religious body may also act in community relations; a Zionist body or a community relations organization may also conduct educational and cultural activities, etc.

For the most part, each of these types of activity has its own particular supporters, generally members of an organization which emphasizes a particular outlook or interest. The funds for most of the activities of these various groups come from federated campaigns in all the various communities where Jews live, from their own members or from unorganized contributors.

The religious bodies consist of the various congregations, Orthodox, Conservative and Reform, with their affiliated groups: boards of directors and trustees; brotherhoods and sisterhoods; religious school committees and parent-teacher associations; and youth groups. For each branch of Judaism, the congregations are usually banded together in national associations to provide for exchange of information and experience, and to perform services which would be too difficult or costly for any single congregation to conduct alone. Examples are the publication of prayerbooks or religious-school textbooks, the development of school curricula, or the planning of adult education or social action activities. The principal national bodies of this kind are the Union of Orthodox Jewish Congregations, the United Synagogue of America (Conservative) and the Union of American Hebrew Congregations (Reform).

Each of the branches of Judaism has institutions for the training of rabbis and of other religious and educational personnel. There are numerous Orthodox institutions of this kind but perhaps the most prominent of them are the Rabbinical Seminary and Teacher's Seminary of Yeshiva University. The central Conservative institution of this kind is the Jewish Theological Seminary. The Reform seminary is the Hebrew Union College–Jewish Institute of Religion.

ORGANIZATIONS IN THE CIVIL RIGHTS FIELD

The national community relations and civic organizations grew up in response to the need to protect the civic and religious rights of Jews, to combat antisemitism and discrimination and to express viewpoints of Jewish organizations on various civic issues. Most of the organizations which have concentrated upon this kind of activity have generally found that antisemitism was related to other kinds of prejudice and to general social conditions. Thus, they have tended to become involved in efforts to make a better society in which the rights of *all* individuals would be respected, and in which men would treat each other as equals. They have thus tried to have general anti-discrimination laws enacted and put into practice, to maintain civil rights and civil liberties for all people, to assure the separation of church and state, to guarantee to all access to public facilities, to secure equal opportunity for all Americans in employment, housing, education, and to eliminate all types of prejudice.

The major national bodies of this type are: the Anti-Defamation League of B'nai B'rith, which has conducted campaigns to overcome various types of prejudice and discrimination and to foster mutual understanding between Jews and other Americans; the American Jewish Committee, which has been active in helping to protect Jews abroad, in fighting prejudice and discrimination in America, and in evolving an American-Jewish outlook to encompass full participation in the American society and maintenance of the distinctive Jewish heritage; and the American Jewish Congress, an outgrowth of a coordinated effort of American Jews to protect Jewish interests before the Peace Conference following World War I, and a pioneer in the development of legal and legislative efforts to overcome patterns of discrimination.

Other national organizations active in the community relations field are the Synagogue Council of America, a body representing the congregational and the rabbinic associations of all three branches of Judaism; the Jewish Labor Committee, representing Jews associated with the trade-union movement; and the Jewish War Veterans.

In the local communities, community relations activities are conducted primarily by local Jewish community councils, community relations councils and community relations committees. Most of these include individuals who also belong to the local branches of the various national community relations organizations, as well as to other local groups interested in community relations.

The National Community Relations Advisory Council is a coordinating body, composed of representatives from both the local community relations councils and many of the national organizations active in this field. It seeks to provide for an exchange of ideas and for development of effective program goals and methods.

The Zionist and Israel-related organizations are too numerous and varied to describe fully. In general, they are of two types, those which seek to spread Zionist ideas of various types (though since the actual establishment of the state of Israel, this function has declined), and those which seek to obtain support for Israel generally or for particular aspects of Israel's needs. The first type is best represented by organizations such as the Zionist Organization of America or the Labor Zionist Organization of America. The second type can be illustrated by the Jewish National Fund (to reclaim the land in Israel), Hadassah (to establish and maintain various health and welfare institutions in Israel), Histadrut (to secure support for activities of Israel's labor federation), the American Friends of the Hebrew University (to obtain support for the Hebrew University in Jerusalem) and many others. Virtually every kind of project for the health, welfare, education, culture and general well-being and security of Jews in Israel has an organization in America to secure funds to support it.

In addition, almost every Jewish organization in America considers it as part of its outlook, policy or program to support the maintenance and progress of Israel.

EDUCATIONAL AND CULTURAL GROUPS

Educational and cultural bodies are also of many different types. The Jewish education of children has now become almost exclusively a function of individual congregations, which run their own schools. Each of these is autonomous and determines its own program, though each is influenced to some degree by the national bodies of its particular branch of Judaism.

Most of the larger communities have bureaus of Jewish education, supported by the local federations, which sponsor higher Jewish education and teacher training programs, provide advice to individual schools, attempt to improve standards of Jewish education and seek to obtain wider support and understanding of the goals of Jewish education.

The American Association for Jewish Education, a national organization, conducts research on matters pertaining to Jewish education, and publishes materials intended to assist and improve Jewish education throughout the country.

However, the general category of "education and culture" includes many other kinds of activity: institutions of higher learning in which scholarship in Jewish matters may be developed, publication of books and journals on subjects of Jewish interest, research and archives in Jewish affairs, fostering of interest and activity in Jewish literature, music, art, dance and drama, and many more. In recent years, the National Foundation for Jewish Culture was established with the help of some of the larger federations to secure additional support for the institutions which conduct these various activities, and to foster special projects to stimulate increased interest and activity in this field.

Every community in which a substantial number of Jews lives tends to have a variety of health and welfare activities: Jewish hospitals, family and child service associations, day nurseries, homes for the aged and many more. Most of them also have Jewish Community Centers, which provide a variety of social, cultural and recreational activities for the Jewish residents of the community. The National Jewish Welfare Board, an association of all the YMHA's and Jewish Community Centers, provides guidance and services to assist in the programs and activities of these institutions. It also serves as the agency which provides for the Jewish members of the armed forces special chaplaincy and USO services.

In recent years, there has grown a tendency to establish or extend Jewish-supported institutions to serve the general community. Typical examples are Brandeis University, a Jewish-sponsored nonsectarian institution of higher learning; City of Hope, a medical institution which serves all who need its services; and the Albert Einstein School of Medicine of Yeshiva University. Increasingly, services established originally to serve the needs of Jews alone have accepted requests for service from any who sought it, Jewish or not.

RAISING AND DISTRIBUTING FUNDS

Two special aspects of all these developments must be described to complete the picture.

The first is the elaborate machinery to raise and distribute the funds to support all this activity. Most of this fund raising is conducted by a local Jewish federation (which now generally includes the welfare fund, originally a separate body to raise money for national and overseas needs). The federation generally conducts an annual campaign which solicits contributions from all the Jews in the community. The moneys collected in this way are then allocated to three types of agencies: those which provide assistance to needy Jews overseas and to Israel (through the United Jewish Appeal, which supports both the Joint Distribution Committee providing relief and rehabilitation for Jews abroad and the United Israel Appeal, to help in the maintenance and development of Israel as a haven and home for Jews); those national agencies in America serving purposes described earlier; and the various agencies and institutions serving Jews in the local community.

In 1948, these federations all together raised $200,-000,000. In the last fifteen years, they have been raising a national total of about $125,000,000 annually. In addition, an approximately equal amount of money has been raised by those institutions and agencies which raise their funds separately from the federated campaigns.

The second noteworthy aspect is the development of a corps of professional workers who carry forward the activities of these various expressions of Jewish commitment. The congregations are served by trained rabbis, cantors and educators, and by executive directors. The community relations agencies employ trained human relations specialists, lawyers, community organizers and social engineers. The health and welfare agencies utilize administrators, social workers, recreation specialists, psychologists and medical personnel. And so with all the various specialties, including those professional workers who raise the funds and plan for their most effective use.

The picture of the functioning of the Jewish community should make clear that it operates to fulfill the needs and interests of American Jews and that these needs and interests are shaped by developments in America and in the world. These activities are purely voluntary and some Jews remain aloof. However, most American Jews are touched in some way by these various organized Jewish efforts.

As the lives and interests of Jews change, their organizations must also change. Each of us who feels a relationship to the past, present and future of Jews has both an opportunity and a responsibility to help shape the organized expressions of our Jewish interests and commitments.

SUGGESTED READINGS

JEWISH LIFE IN AMERICA, *P. Friedman* and *Robert Gordis*, Horizon Press.

THE AMERICAN JEW: A REAPPRAISAL, edited by *Oscar I. Janowsky*, Jewish Publication Society.

A HERITAGE AFFIRMED: THE JEWISH FEDERATION MOVEMENT IN AMERICA, *Harry Lurie*, Jewish Publication Society.

THE JEW WITHIN AMERICAN SOCIETY: A STUDY IN ETHNIC INDIVIDUALITY, *Charles B. Sherman*, Wayne University Press.

THE JEWS: SOCIAL PATTERNS OF AN AMERICAN GROUP, edited by *Marshall Sklare*, The Free Press.

ISRAEL AND THE JEWISH PEOPLE

by Myron Fenster

MYRON M. FENSTER: Rabbi, Jewish Center of Jackson Heights, N.Y.; visiting Rabbi, Moria Congregation in Haifa, Israel in 1963; has contributed articles to **MIDSTREAM, CONGRESS WEEKLY, HADASSAH NEWSLETTER,** etc.

THE date of May 14, 1948 represents a high moment of fulfillment in modern Jewish history. On that Friday afternoon, in a small hall of the Tel Aviv Museum, David Ben Gurion, in the presence of 37 members of the National Council and 50 other guests, read the proclamation establishing a Jewish state. Standing under a stern and sad-eyed portrait of Theodore Herzl, the founder of the modern movement of political Zionism, Ben Gurion declared: "We, the members of the National Council, representing the Jewish people in Palestine and the Zionist movement of the world, met together in solemn assembly today, the day of termination of the British Mandate for Palestine, and by virtue of the national and historic right of the Jewish people and of the resolution of the General Assembly of the United Nations, hereby proclaim the establishment of the Jewish State in Palestine to be called Israel."

A few hours later the Sabbath began, only to be disrupted on the morrow by Egyptian bombers raining destruction from the sky. But the Jewish people had waited a long time for their return, and now that the British had withdrawn and the United Nations had declared their right to the land, they were not likely to retreat.

Immediately the new government issued its first ordinance to the effect that all laws enacted under the British government, and specifically the White Paper of 1939 which restricted Jewish immigration to Palestine, "are hereby declared null and void." Two days later Chaim Weizmann was elected the first president of Israel.

An observer, who at the time was living in embattled Jerusalem, wrote: "The lamp snuffed out nearly 2,000 years ago was relighted today. . . . The war may only be starting, but we are our own masters, in our own land."

The predictions of war proved to be correct. A bloody battle for independence was fought against an invading army of six Arab nations. Poorly-equipped and hastily-summoned, the Israeli forces fought with pluck and determination, but often with little else. The invasion continued for more than half a year until an armistice was signed. At the end, the Arab onslaught had been repelled and the people of Israel had defended their land and established their sovereignty. Although only a shaky peace existed, Israel was an historic fact.

PROBLEMS OF STATEHOOD

Among the statements Ben Gurion read to his colleagues on that fateful Friday in Tel Aviv was the promise that "the State of Israel will be open to the immigration of Jews from all countries of their dispersion; and will uphold the full social and political equality of all of its citizens, without distinction of race, creed or sex; will safeguard the sanctity and inviolability of the shrines and holy places of all religions; and will dedicate itself to the principles of the Charter of the United Nations." Despite the guarantee to uphold full equality for all citizens, a half million Arabs fled the country to live in discontent in border camps, becoming voluntary refugees from their own home.

Additional problems were to arise with the state's establishment. Among them was the relationship between the Jews in Israel and those outside of it. The securing of the State had been a joint enterprise on the part of people from all areas of the world. Now, a new and thorny issue arose. The Israelis had given "a call to the Jewish people all over the world to rally to their side in the task of immigration and development and to stand by us in the great struggle for the fulfillment of the dreams of generations: the redemption of Israel." This call was understood by most Jews not in terms of personal immigration to Israel—

known in Hebrew as *Aliyah*—but in the less direct albeit
necessary ways of economic, political, and moral support.
The participation of Jews outside of Israel in the building
of the State then became a source of discussion and at times
of heated debate. Certain Israelis proclaimed it the duty of
all Zionists to come personally to Israel to settle. Others
maintained that one could be a good Jew and a builder
of Israel anywhere.

Another pressing problem was that those who did come
were primarily from North Africa and the impoverished
countries of Tunisia, Algeria, Morocco, and Yemen. These
immigrants often arrived penniless and had to be absorbed
into the older segment of the community with whom they
differed in culture and mores, in customs and world-out-
look. Often there were conflicts of a religious nature, as
even educational horizons were not the same. Even such
mundane things as the daily menu, clothing styles, and
types of housing presented difficulties. A decade after the
State, it had become obvious that the integration of these
two communities would be one of the most formidable
hurdles that Israel faced.

However these and other difficulties may be resolved,
the events of May 1948 were a considerable achievement.
They were, however, not isolated moments in Jewish history. Rather, they were determined by the entire history
of the people prior to that date. In order to understand
these factors, it is necessary to sketch briefly some of the
outstanding events that preceded this high moment.

THE JEWISH ATTACHMENT TO ZION

The Jews' attachment to the land of the Eastern Medi-
terranean and to the values and literature that sprang
from its soil, goes to their very beginnings as a people.
The earliest memories of the Patriarch Abraham are tied
up with the Promised Land. Deeply embedded in the
consciousness of the people is God's promise to Abraham
in Canaan, "I will give this land to your offspring" (Gen.

12:7). The Jews' attachment to the land proceeded continuously thereafter, and became especially pronounced
in modern times after the soaring promises of the Balfour
Declaration issued by the British government in 1917, but
it always summoned up the biblical settlement and promise. Abraham purchased his first plot of land in Canaan
(Genesis, Chapter 23) and thus paved the way for the
future acquisition of the soil.

In retrospect, what may be considered most remarkable
is the strong desire to dwell on the land, a desire that survived centuries of homelessness and exile. For a long time
Jews were a minority in Palestine; the land was barren
and desolate and spiritual creativity appeared to be dried
up. For a long time the dream of a return was sustained
by little more than prayer and memory.

Carried into Babylonia by their captors in the sixth century before the Common Era the exiled Hebrews "wept
when we remembered Zion. . . . How shall we sing the
song of the Lord in a foreign land?" (Psalm 137). Half
a century later, a few thousand of those who had been de-
ported returned to rebuild and to try to recapture some
of the past glory. Many of those living outside of Palestine
had already sunk roots into the soil of their new homes.
The Jewish community of Babylon lived and flourished
creatively, foreshadowing a process that was later repeated
in many centuries and countries. No longer was Judaism
dependent on any one country. The Jews had become a
world-people. When, however, they experienced hostility
from their neighbors they were forced to take the wander-
er's staff in hand. Zion thus never completely left their
thoughts.

In all the lands of their dispersion, pious Jews turned
eastward three times daily toward "Jerusalem, The Holy
City," in the prayer that "God would return there with
compassion and mercy." And the prayer entered the peoples' consciousness, as did the observance each year of
Tisha B'av, the ninth day of the Hebrew month of Av,

a day of mourning over the loss of Zion and separation from the home land.

The land of Palestine lay desolate, but the memory of it burned brightly. It was especially bright in the heart and mind of Judah Halevi, one of Zion's sweetest singers in the 11th century in Christian Spain. First in Toledo, later in Cordova, Judah was seized with a longing for Palestine, a longing which became a consuming passion. Jewish legend has it that when Halevi finally arrived in the Holy Land after a long and dangerous trip, he was killed by an Arab at the gates of Jerusalem. But his famous ode to Zion, overflowing his loving soul and written before his ill-fated trip, lived on to inspire the generations:

> My heart is in the East
> But I am in the ends of the West;
> How can I taste what I eat
> And how can food to me be sweet?

THE RISE OF ZIONISM

These romantic and at times vague yearnings began to take on form and substance with the rise of the movement of modern nationalistic Zionism in the late 19th century. That movement culminated in success fifty years after its formal founding in Basle, Switzerland in 1897. But it is a matter of speculation whether Zionism would ever have been fulfilled had it not been for the incomprehensible and unbelievably tragic events in Europe in the years 1939 to 1945. It is conceivable that it would have remained the dream of individual Jews rather than the demand of the many.

The 1930's and '40's were years of anguish for humanity; history witnessed in those years the destruction of one third of the Jewish population. Shocked and dazed by the barbarity of the Nazis and their willing conspirators and silent bystandars, a troubled world at war's end recognized that as a matter of fundamental justice the Jews were at last entitled to a home of their own. Even on this there was no

universal agreement, and so dramatic steps had to be taken
to bring the plight of the Jews to world attention. There
is no doubt, however, that the conscience of civilized men
everywhere had been stirred. Quite contrary to their pronounced goal, Nazi Germany had inadvertently contributed to the survival of the Jewish people. The State of
Israel is as much a memorial to the Six Million whose death
brought it into being as it is a tribute to those who fought
for its establishment.

Decades before, Theodor Herzl anticipated these tragic
events of the 1930's. He saw clearly that antisemitism
would persist and that therefore "the Jews must look for
a country of their own." This, others had sensed before
him. But none had brought to it the passion, the unflagging
dedication and the persistent energy of the black-bearded
Herzl, who bore himself like a prince and whose vision
penetrated the heart of the Jewish masses.

Before him Moses Hess of Germany had written: "Every
Jew, whether he likes it or not, is bound to his people in
a bond of solidarity." Most of Hess's fellow Jews in Germany considered their status not as part of a worldwide
people, nor as a nationality of which a segment aspired
to nationhood. Rather, they thought of themselves as
being of the "Mosaic persuasion," tied only to a specific set
of Jewish rituals and universal ethics, but without any
relation to a historic homeland or language or people
(Jews) everywhere. They were Germans above all. Hess's
now classic "Rome and Jerusalem" appeared in 1862.
Its influence on his fellow Jews was minimal.

After him Rabbi Zevi Hirsch Kalischer in Prussia succeeded in stirring the longing for Zion in some select
circles. A small group started what later grew to large
and important proportions. They called themselves *Cho-
vevei Tziyon* (the Lovers of Zion). Kalischer's book appeared at almost the same time as Hess's, and with the
same negligible immediate results.

A third Zionist whose writings influenced the elite of
Europe was Leon Pinsker, whose book "Auto-Emancipa-

tion" in the 1880's and whose visits to European capitals helped pave the way for the new settlement in Palestine. His call has a distinctly modern tone, for he urged a program of self-help: "The international Jewish question must receive a national solution. We must take the first step towards national regeneration—help yourselves and God will help you!"

Years later, after Herzl had published his own work on the Jewish State without first having read Pinsker, the latter's work was brought to his attention. Herzl confessed that had he known of "Auto-Emancipation," he would not have found his own pamphlet necessary.

Although the thoughts of Hess, Kalischer, and Pinsker did not immediately strike root, they were part of a much larger movement of nationalistic aspirations of the 19th century in Europe. Such people as the Poles and the Hungarians broke away in that period from larger empires and formed their own independent countries. The Jews, these early Zionists reasoned, should likewise establish an independent homeland through systematic colonization and settlement in Palestine. Such was their dream and their announced goal; but only the devoted few proceeded to act upon it.

Herzl was unaware of these devoted few and of those who preceded him. In the beginning a Viennese journalist who was removed from Jewish thoughts and aspirations, his indignation was aroused when he witnessed the Dreyfus trial in France while on an assignment for his newspaper. During the trial and its subsequent events Herzl witnessed antisemitism in its most primitive form, made more frightening by the fact that it was occurring in France, the citadel of democracy in Europe. Stirred by the experience, Herzl thought long and deeply about the Jewish problem. Then suddenly in a state of heightened activity he set down the substance of his thinking. The result was a pamphlet called "The Jewish State," which changed the history of the Jewish people.

Herzl was personally aware of the economic discrimination that the Jews suffered in Europe in those days. Though financially secure by virtue of his family's wealth, Herzl, a lawyer by training, knew that certain professions were closed to the Jew. He was denied the right to be a judge; others were kept from becoming physicians or university professors. In some areas business restrictions were imposed, and altogether the Jew was always at the mercy of the majority.

Said Herzl: "We are a people—one people, regardless of where we live—whether we like it or not—it is our common enemy that makes us a people as it has been through history. In the hour of crisis we stick together and we suddenly discover our strength. Yes, we have the strength to create a state, and a model state at that." Left unresolved by Herzl was a clear way in which the land would be colonized, by whom, and what the status of the Jews outside of the land would be to those who dwelled upon it. Herzl thought of a mass migration. But he was not able to stimulate such a migration and the settlement in Palestine proceeded very slowly. He envisioned that all the Jews in Europe would seize the opportunity of going to Palestine if it were to be a Jewish state. It was inconceivable to him that a Jew would remain in Europe when he could live among his own people. He did not forsee the possibility of coexistence of a Jewish state alongside many organized Jewish communities outside of it. Nor did this problem disturb any of the early Zionist efforts.

Herzl was primarily concerned, in his pamphlet and in the first Zionist Congress in 1897, with securing the land—and this in itself was a formidable task. It occupied all of his considerable talent and devotion, in the end consuming him in untimely death. He is considered the founder of political Zionism, not because the theory was new, but rather because of his ability and practicality at proceeding to act upon his great dream. After the first Congress concluded, Herzl wrote: "I shall beware of saying this in public, but in Basle I founded the Jewish State. In five years perhaps and certainly in fifty, everyone shall see it." In its time the statement was considered romantic and even insane by some. For Herzl it was an article of unshakable faith. Fifty-one years after he uttered it, the Jewish State was born.

The Nature of the Jewish State

One who did concern himself with the long range goals of Zionism was Asher Ginsberg, who adopted the pen name Ahad Ha-Am (one of the people). His approach differed from that of Herzl. First, a national feeling would have to be created among Jews; then colonization would come, not the other way around. Ahad Ha-Am theorized that Palestine must be the spiritual center for all Jews. This would require no large scale physical *aliyah* (immigration), but only truly Jewish (and therefore human) achievement in terms of cultural and ethical activity and exemplary life. Colonizing alone, he emphatically declared, was not the way.

But Zionism could ill afford the luxury of debate over the nature of a Jewish state which as yet had not come into being. More concrete problems demanded immediate concern. In 1903 a pogrom took place in Kishinev, Russia, in which Jews were wantonly killed and their property destroyed, not by isolated individuals, but by officials of the government. A wave of protest spread throughout the world. Subsequently Herzl himself saw Jews beaten by Russian police in Vilna, for nothing more than wishing to greet him as his carriage passed through the streets of the city. It was obvious that some substantial program had to be undertaken to relieve the Jews' lack of status as a people.

Finally, a breakthrough appeared, or so it seemed at first. The British Colonial Secretary, Joseph Chamberlain, told Herzl, "I have a land for you—Uganda, on the coast of Africa." In 1904 the Zionist Congress convened to consider Uganda. Herzl and his friend, Max Nordau, favored the proposal, but it was decidedly rejected by the delegates, for whom a haven had to be more than a physical place of rest. In his concluding address to the Congress, Herzl recognized defeat on the matter of Uganda and said: "I wanted to suggest to you an expediency of emergency. In the meantime I have come to know your hearts, so let me tell you a word of comfort in the language of our fathers—and it is an expression of commitment for me: *Im eshkachech Y'rushalayim tishkach y'mini* [If I forget thee, oh Jerusalem, let my right hand lose its cunning]."

Years later the plan was revived. This time Arthur James Balfour, later to be Foreign Secretary of Britain, suggested it to Chaim Weizmann, then a scientist at the University of Manchester. Balfour could not understand why the Jews did not grasp at Uganda. "Supposing," it is reported Weizmann asked, "I would offer you Paris, instead of London, would you take it?" "But we have London," Balfour shot back. "Yes," Weizmann retorted, "that is true, but we had Jerusalem when London was a marsh."

The only resolution that had been arrived at by the Jewish people was that, if there was to be a Jewish homeland it would have to fulfill the biblical promise. Jerusalem remained the city eternal.

However, the return to the land was not accomplished in the political arena alone. Other forces were at work as well. In 1909 a group of young men and women, filled with social idealism for a better way of life than that which they had known in their native Russia, came to an insect-infested marsh land alongside Lake Tiberius in northern Palestine. Working with unflagging devotion they proceeded to transform the land and themselves. They called it Degania, and it became known as the mother of the *Kevutzot* (collective settlements), where the property is leased by the Jewish National Fund and is worked in common. In this and other settlements like it, the land is owned by the Jewish people. The young settlers of Degania were inspired by the presence of a grey-beard in their midst. A. D. Gordon, the Jewish Tolstoy, became the father of the pioneering movement.

Gordon spoke of the "holiness of labor." He had turned his back on purely intellectual activity to come and work on the land, saying, "the Jewish people has been completely cut off from nature and imprisoned within city walls for 2,000 years. We have become accustomed to every form of living except to a life of labor—of labor done for its own sake. In Palestine we must ourselves do all the work—from the cleanest to the dirtiest and most difficult. If we desire life we must establish new relationships with nature, we must open a new account with it." By example, Gordon helped to open that new account. Modest colonization followed, but with it a crucial growth of settlements and *kibbutzim* (collectives).

The Hebrew language also was reborn. The effort this entailed is associated with the single-minded devotion of Eliezer Ben Yehudah, who insisted that Hebrew, the tongue of the prophets, be heard in his home and in the community at large. With fanatic devotion he proceeded to create a modern Hebrew to meet the needs of a new and dynamic society. It was for him a magnificent obsession, and he is remembered alongside Herzl and Weizmann and Ben Gurion, as one who dared to dream of a new life for an ancient people. Ben Yehudah's dictionary, in which the modern terms are built on classic roots, has become a marker on the road to Jewish rebirth.

The same may be said for the poetry of Chaim Nachman Bialik. His poetry flowed in faultless Hebrew as he sang not only of religion but of nature, of the old synagogue and the new hope, of Jewish aspirations and desperation. At times his muse was a stinging rebuke but always with the sense of identification and love for his people. Hebrew began to be a language of communication in all forms of art and science.

Though by now the stage had been set, the high moment of drama was still a long way off. The Jewish people had to become accustomed once more to patient waiting. The great ideological battles of Zionism, of the nature of the State and of the ideal relationship of the Jews living in

Palestine to those outside of it, were again deferred, for on the political side progress was tortuously slow.

THE ESTABLISHMENT OF THE STATE

As the First World War drew to a close, a series of far-reaching events occurred. On November 2nd, 1917 the British issued the Balfour Declaration with its assurance "that His Majesty's government views with favor the establishment in Palestine of a national home for the Jewish people." Again, Jewish hopes soared. Chaim Weizmann's influence in Britain and his contribution to the war effort had been decisive. Five weeks after the Declaration, the British forces under General Allenby rode into Jerusalem, liberating Palestine from Turkish domination. Jewish joy knew no bounds; Britain had Palestine and the Jews had the Balfour Declaration!

Many Zionists had combined their efforts to bring that moment about. In the United States, Rabbi Stephen S. Wise, Felix Frankfurter, Louis Brandeis, and others had spared no efforts on its behalf. President Woodrow Wilson's support had also been effective. The Zionist heavens are dotted as well with the brightness of other faithful luminaries, such as S. Levin, M. Ussishkin and Nahum Sokoloff. At last it appeared as if the efforts of many people in diverse parts of the world was approaching fulfillment.

But again many long delays were in store; many commissions of inquiry, pressures from the outside, restrictive quotas of entry lay ahead. Initial British enthusiasm waned. In May 1939 an infamous White Paper appeared, casting a dark shadow over the hearts of the Jewish people. By its provision a maximum of 75,000 Jews would be admitted to Palestine over a five year period, after which all Jewish immigration was to cease. And so, during the darkest days of Hitler tyranny, many thousands of Jews were denied legal entry into the Promised Land. Many perished for lack of a place to go and for those who did survive, the port of Haifa too often remained officially closed as a legal entry into the land where they longed to rebuild their lives.

By war's end Jewish suffering had reached its outer limits. Indignation ran high when it became known to what maniacal extent Hitler and his hooligans had gone and how well they had succeeded in "the final solution to the Jewish problem." But more tragedy was yet to come as those who managed to reach Palestine were turned back by the British policy of restrictive immigration. The harbor of Haifa became the gateway of despair and disillusionment, and not of hope.

So desperate had some of the displaced Jews become at being denied entry into Palestine, that 265 of them blew up their own ship and perished aboard the "Patria" rather than return to the concentration camps of Europe. The "Struma" sank with a loss of 765 refugees who had also been barred from entering the land, the hope for which had sustained them in the long hours of trial while awaiting liberation.

But the most tragic of all was the fate of the "Exodus 1947" whose tragedy struck a deep blow to all decent-minded people everywhere. Unlike the later fictionalized account, the 4,500 passengers, inhumanly packed aboard the ill-fated ship, never were allowed to set foot on the soil of Palestine. The British first rammed the "Exodus," then turned it around and sent it back to France and from there to Germany. Those who refused to disembark onto German soil were dragged and shoved down the gangplank. Once removed, they were again placed into the same camps from which they had just come. And this, two years after the war's end!

The situation had obviously become intolerable. Jewish terrorist activity broke out in Palestine against the British. It was the fruit of despair and frustration. Its climax was the wanton blowing up of Jerusalem's King David Hotel with the loss of 100 lives, 40 of them Jews. Britain's Palestine policy, under Foreign Secretary Ernest Bevin, was

in a state of collapse. American President Harry Truman
had already intervened on behalf of the refugees. As
world criticism mounted, Britain finally turned the problem over to the United Nations, meeting then in Flushing
Meadows, New York, with the hope that they would be
able to find a solution.

By August of 1947, the United Nations' investigation
committee had collected its information and made its
unanimous recommendation, that the British Mandate
should come to an end. The partition of Palestine into
Jewish and Arab states was suggested. At the United
Nations hearings the Jewish cause had been eloquently
presented by Rabbi Abba Hillel Silver of Cleveland, a
long-time Zionist who reflected the deepest feeling of a
passionate people when he agreed to the partition plan.
After breathtaking delays, frantic negotiations and a long,
tense roll call of votes, in which both Russia and the
United States voted for partition and Britain abstained,
while hundreds of thousands of Jews sat glued to the
radio's broadcast straight from the United Nations, the
plan was finally adopted. Then there was light and joy,
happiness and rejoicing for Jews everywhere.

But in Palestine cooler heads were restrained because
they knew the turmoil that awaited them around the corner. During the United Nations discussions the Arabs
had continued their threats and intimidations to the point
where they would almost have to embark on a campaign
to reverse the decision, if for no other reason than to
save face. But in any case, the long wait was over as Jews
officially returned to form their own sovereign state, which
was officially proclaimed on the 5th of Iyar, 5708, the
Hebrew date which corresponded to the 14th of May,
1948, one day before the British Mandate was to expire.

Again, the tangled events had not made it possible for
a long-range discussion of goals and theories to take place.
Israel announced the Law of the Return, whereby any
Jew wishing Israeli citizenship was entitled to it upon
arrival. Jews proceeded to come from 52 countries, but

only a small percentage came from the Western democratic world. And it was this immigration that was most sorely needed.

With the State's establishment, democratic institutions were immediately set into motion. A *Knesset* (parliament) was established in which minority groups, including the Arabs, were represented. A compulsory education law for all youngsters was enforced. A military draft law—even for women—was adopted. President Truman immediately recognized Israel and a year later it was admitted to the United Nations, to take its place among the families of nations. A promising beginning had been made but much remained to be done.

Not the least of these tasks was the working out of a bridge of communication and influence between Israel and the Jews of the free world. The Zionist movement in the United States, Great Britain, Canada, France, and elsewhere had succeeded in helping Israel to become a fact. But what was their goal to be now? Could they survive victory as well as they had been sustained by frustrating defeat, and would they find a purpose now that the State had been accomplished? During the period of stress thousands had rallied to the side of their brethren. Now that a home had been found, would they stay or drift away?

Israel had many accomplishments to show the interested the first years of existence. Ringed by hostile neighbors on all its borders, with only the sea an untroubled entrance and exit to the world, Israel continued to receive "the tired and the tempest-tossed, those yearning to breathe free" and thousands of other visitors annually. Fully half of its budget, however, had to be spent on the needs of military preparedness and, unfortunately it had to be taken from the necessities of education, housing and other activities that could raise the standard of living.

Yet the work of human and territorial salvage continued. The 600,000 hardy souls who established the State by placing their bodies on the line in its defense, had grown to two and a half million in a decade and a half.

Despite Israel's internal needs, technicians and experts had been spared to help the developing nations of Africa and Asia, countries less politically and economically mature than Israel. Pipe lines carrying precious water to the south had been laid and the Negev had begun to grow again. Land that had not seen habitation since biblical days now knew settlement and creativity as well. Whole cities grew up—Dimona, Arad, Eilat—on spots where for centuries the wind had howled and the jackals yelped.

But basic questions remain unresolved. Herzl's hope of a haven of refuge for those who wished it has been established. But the emergency tempo of Israel's existence has deferred the solution of many continuing, knotty problems. Among these is the tangled issue of religion, which in Israel is supported by the State. This carryover from Mandate days invests the Chief Rabbinate with final authority in all matters concerning marriage, divorce, Jewish status and inheritance, and a host of other laws that in effect give the Chief Rabbinate absolute control in most situations involving personal status. The problem is complicated by the fact that the religious forces in Israel make up a political party as well, which is part of the government coalition in the *Knesset*. The "official" religion is Orthodoxy; this denies status to other forms of Jewish religious observance, on the theory that to do so would complicate the legal structure.

The failure to resolve some of these long-deferred issues has caused consternation to many of Israel's closest friends and supporters. A complete sense of harmony and understanding between Jews in Israel and those outside of it is still in the future. For the last 60 years, ideology has been shunted aside for the more important task of saving and restoring life. Israel is still concerned and occupied with that task. Yet it is hoped that future years will see the bonds between Israel and the Jewish People elsewhere grow more intimate and their links become stronger.

SUGGESTED READINGS

FULFILLMENT: THE EPIC STORY OF ZIONISM, *Rufus Learsi,*
World Publishing Company.

ISRAEL—IDEA AND REALITY, *Emil Lehman,* United Synagogue.

EVERYONE'S GUIDE TO ISRAEL, *Joan Comay,* Doubleday.

THE WILD GOATS OF EIN GEDI, *Herbert Weiner,* Meridian
Books.

THE PATHS OF
JEWISH LITERATURE

by Charles E. Shulman

CHARLES E. SHULMAN: Rabbi, Riverdale Temple in N. Y. C.; a graduate of Ohio Northern University Law School, with graduate degree from University of Chicago; he was ordained at the H.U.C.; author of **PROBLEMS OF THE JEWS IN THE CONTEMPORARY WORLD, EUROPE'S CONSCIENCE IN DECLINE, WHAT IT MEANS TO BE A JEW;** has had several sermons in **WORLD'S BEST SERMONS,** and lectured widely.

JEWISH literature covers a long span of more than three thousand years and a variety of subjects immense in scope. But the theme of Jewish literature is not hard to identify because it concerns itself generally with man's relationship to God, and man's relationship to man. The first aspect of it makes man something of a philosopher, the second a humanitarian. Combined they educate the human being toward an understanding of justice, humility and peace.

Basically all Jewish literature might possibly be condensed in the famous Biblical statement of the prophet Micah: "What does the Lord require of you, O man, but this: to do justly, to love mercy and to walk humbly with your God." All phases of Jewish literature are in one way or another associated with this prophetic ideal.

JEWISH LITERATURE IN ANCIENT TIMES

Ancient Jewish literature, from the beginnings of Jewish history until the time of the Maccabees (165 B.C.E.), is mainly concerned with the development of the books of the Bible. The great devotion of the Jewish people to the Bible made them, in the words of Mohammed, "The people of the Book." Among no other people in history has the written word exerted such influence upon the daily life of the common man as it did in ancient Israel.

In time the influence of the Bible traveled beyond the small territory of Palestine to reach into every corner of the earth. It was, and still remains, the guide book of western civilization. Its stories are familiar to every child and its Psalms are often better known than the national anthems. The King James translation of its majestic Hebrew lines set the standard of the English language in the 17th century, and phrases and verses from it are proverbs and household sayings everywhere. In addition to contributing to the heart of Christian education, the biblical concepts exerted a powerful influence on the religion of Islam. Almost half the population of the present day world thus learns from this basic book of Jewish literature.

We know today that Israel was not as old a culture group as the Egyptians or Babylonians. Archaeological discoveries indicate, moreover, that the Israelites learned a great deal from their older neighbors. There is a Genesis-like story of creation in Babylonian lore, but it was the Jewish genius to adapt and weave that story into the background of the Sabbath. Many centuries after the Jewish people first recorded the statement that God rested on the Sabbath day, and the fourth of the Ten Commandments ordered the special observance of it, a great Jewish philosopher, Ahad Ha-Am, was to say that more than the Jews kept the Sabbath it was the Sabbath that kept the Jews.

The most important parts of the Bible, such as the books of the Prophets, the Psalms, the Book of Job and others are unique among the ancient literatures of the Near East. The monotheism and social morality of the Hebrew prophets, who propounded their message over twenty five hundred years ago, have never been equalled by the literatures which followed. We have only to recall Isaiah's exalted dream of nations, "beating their swords into plowshares and their spears into pruning hooks" as the inspiration of the United Nations of today to realize the continuing power of the Bible down the centuries.

The biblical authors originally *spoke* their messages, and most of the oldest songs and stories were transmitted by word of mouth for a very long time before they were finally committed to writing. Even in the days of the Second Temple, when the art of reading was generally known, oral means of teaching Judaism were common and widespread. This we know from the *Torah she-b'al peh* (the oral *Torah*) of the Pharisees which, by its commentary on the Bible, preserved many of the old religious teachings and folk traditions. However, writing was well known in Israel from the earliest times and was often employed for literary purposes as we note in the book of Isaiah: "Now, go," the prophet is commanded, "write it before them on a tablet and inscribe it in a book, that it may be for the time to come forever and ever" (Isa. 30:8).

In no other people's social life has the idea of holiness held so high a place as in Israel. It dominates all the thoughts and feelings of the Biblical authors. The famous holiness code in the Book of Leviticus (Chapter 19) contains the sentence: "You shall be holy for I the Lord your God am holy." But the concept of holiness in human relationships is also stressed in Jewish literature. According to the teachings of this literature all our obligations, laws and agreements derive their legal and moral authority from God's holy word, from the Covenant at Sinai.

From the standpoint of cultural and literary history the Bible codes are of special interest since they are not only legal, but social and psychological in scope. They developed in the Jewish people what the German language calls a "weltanschaung," an attitude toward life. The Hebrew word *Torah* means more than law. It also means teaching, and religious guidance and knowledge generally. It is this two-fold character of *Torah* that distinguishes Jewish law, both in biblical and post biblical times, from the literature of the neighboring peoples.

The Fourth Commandment in the Book of Deuteronomy, for example, dealing with the keeping of the Sabbath day, takes pains to explain the reason in most humane terms, saying: "Observe the Sabbath day to keep it holy as the Lord your God commanded you. . . . Six days shall you labor and do all your work but the seventh day is a Sabbath unto the Lord your God; in it you shall do no manner of work, neither you nor your son nor your daughter, nor your manservant nor your maidservant nor your ox nor your ass nor any of your cattle, nor your stranger that

is within your gates, that your manservant and your maidservant may rest as well as you, and you shall remember
that you were a servant in the land of Egypt and the Lord
your God brought you out from thence by a mighty hand
and by an outstretched arm; therefore the Lord your God
commanded you to keep the Sabbath day."

The historical writings in the Bible form the backbone
of biblical literature and constitute almost half of the
Bible. This unusual concern with history is an important
characteristic of ancient Hebrew literature and finds expression in such books as the Prophets and the Psalms, as
well as in other biblical poems. Bible history has no equal
in the ancient world. This is due primarily to the artistry
which the Jews developed in expressing themselves, and
the fact that biblical literature is essentially national in
character. The prophets, the religious poets and the writers
of the historical books are concerned with the people as a
whole. The appeal "Hear O Israel" is directed to the nation, as well as to the individual. Concern for the fate of
the people, interest in the national past and a sense of
national responsibility permeate biblical literature to such
an extent that the nation as such is frequently spoken of
not as an abstract concept but as a living personality. The
prophets called the nation "Daughter of Zion," "Daughter
of Israel" and similar names. Hosea and Jeremiah compared the relations between the people of Israel and God
in terms of relations between man and wife.

There is hardly a page in the Bible that does not arrest
attention. If you want drama look for it in the famous story
of David and Bathsheba in the second Book of Samuel, or
in the encounter of Elijah and Ahab in the first Book of
Kings. If you desire beautiful poetry read such Psalms
as the eighth or the nineteenth. If you seek wisdom it can
be discovered in the Book of Proverbs. And if you wish to
discover early evidence of the fear of the unlike see the
Book of Esther, in which Haman complains to King Aha-
suerus that there was a people (he meant the Jews but
did not name them) living in the kingdom whose laws

were different, which was cause enough for them to be destroyed. Or if you desire to know the humanity of the Jews in ancient times and their tolerance of strangers, read the Book of Ruth and see how Ruth, a poor Moabite girl, is accepted into the Jewish ranks and becomes the great grandmother of Israel's greatest king, David.

JEWISH LITERATURE IN THE HELLENISTIC AGE

Jewish literature of the Hellenistic period was created during a span of five hundred years, from about 330 B.C.E. to about the year 200 C.E. Much of this literature is contained in a collection called the Apocrypha (a Greek word meaning hidden). While these books were written by Jews, and evidently studied by Jews, the rabbis of about 100 C.E. declared them to be unsuitable for inclusion in the Bible. They were to be, in fact, hidden from sight. They were preserved, however, as part of Christian Scriptural writings; nevertheless, they are considered to be part of the literature created by Jews during the Hellenistic Age.

Some of these books were written originally in Greek, while others were translations from Hebrew or Aramaic writings that date from the Greek and Roman period. The Hellenistic Jewish literature indicates the way certain sections of ancient Jewry adapted to Greek and Roman life. Dr. Ralph Marcus, a noted authority in this field, tells us that the Hellenistic Jews who composed historical works were less interested in writing objective and carefully documented accounts of the nation's past than in producing books that might foster Jewish national pride, or impress Gentiles with the cultural achievements of Israel.

Of all the Hellenistic Jewish writers, Josephus was the most widely read. He is actually the only source for the greater part of the history of the Jews in Palestine and the Diaspora during the late Hellenistic and early Roman periods. Josephus was born in Jerusalem in the year 38 C.E. In 64 he went to Rome and helped to obtain the release from prison of some Jewish priests. Two years later the Jews of Palestine rebelled against Rome, a rebellion Josephus did not favor because he felt the Jews had no chance to win. Nevertheless, he was made a commander of the Jewish troops in Galilee. But unlike his fellow-Jews who fought to the death, Josephus surrendered to the Romans after the fall of Jotapata, an important Galilean stronghold. He lived well under the Romans and wrote important Jewish histories to establish Jewish worth in the eyes of non-Jewish readers. One of his famous books is called *Against Apion,* an antidefamation type of work, which answered the antisemitic libels of his time.

Another writer of this period, Philo, has been called by Dr. Harry Wolfson, the noted scholar of Harvard, one of the founders of the whole religious philosophy that existed in Western Europe from the first to the seventeenth century. His writings are of great importance for the understanding of Christian theology. It is interesting to note in this connection that Philo's influence on Christian thinking was far greater than on Jewish thinking. There is hardly a reference to him in Jewish literature before the 16th century.

THE LITERATURE OF THE TALMUD

Hellenistic literature emphasizes the historical development of the Jews during and shortly after the biblical period, but the heart of the writings produced in that era was the Bible, the textbook of the Jewish faith. Every verse, practically every word of the Bible underwent close study and discussion, and in time a vast body of *midrashim* (interpretations or explanations) accumulated. Rabbis and scholars also fashioned new laws and regulations from the Bible's commandments, as they sought to make the old laws applicable to the new times. Finally, about the year 200 C.E., a large part of these extensions of the teachings of the Bible were brought together into a collection called the *Mishnah.*

Although it grew out of discussions in study circles and academies, the *Mishnah* itself came to have a status as sacred as the Bible, and its law code was in turn carefully studied and interpreted. The new interpretations, when finally collected about the year 500, were given the name *Gemara.* The combination of the *Gemara* and *Mishnah* makes up the *Talmud,* and comprises a substantial number of volumes. In the minds of most Jews in times past the *Talmud* was a holy work, an extension of the Bible itself.

The greater part of the discussions in the *Talmud* are in the form of dialogue. The compilers of the *Talmud* were extremely successful in creating the illusion of unity of time and space within the books, but the fact is that many of the rabbis who are quoted within a single book of the *Talmud* lived centuries and hundreds of miles apart. The dialogue form made it possible to pose questions and to probe for the whys and wherefores.

The rabbis were always alert to question ideas and hypotheses. They questioned the questioner himself. If someone asked when was the right time to say the *Shema,* the Talmudic rabbi would probably counter with the question why the *Shema* should be read at all; only after that was settled would he tackle the original question. And not always did the rabbis accept the answer given by the previous respected rabbi. If they had another answer they would include theirs too. The result was that when the various oral records were brought together, a question was answered in a number of ways. For example, here is how a question dealing with the time of the creation of man was answered: "Our rabbis taught: Adam was created last of all beings on the eve of the Sabbath. And why? Lest the Sadducees say: The Holy One Blessed be He had a partner (Adam) in His work of creation. Another answer is: In order that if a man's mind becomes too proud, he may be reminded that the gnats preceded him in the order of creation. Another answer is that he might immediately enter upon the fulfillment of a precept (the hallowing of the Sabbath)."

The subject matter of the *Talmud* consists of two parts, *halachah* and *agadah*. The term *halachah* stems from the Hebrew word *halach* (to go), and is suggested by Exodus 18:20, "And you shall teach them ordinances and laws and shall show them the way wherein they must *walk* and the work they must do." It embraces all the rules of religion and civil law which may be enforced by appropriate sanctions. *Agadah* consists of everything excluded from the domain of *halachah*. Together they represent the sum total of Jewish law and literature of the Talmudic age.

The *Talmud,* through its extensive interpretations of the Bible, brought it beyond its original range and furnished the people with an entire Jewish way of living and thinking, including manners, morals, hygiene and etiquette. It thus underlay every expression of the Jewish spirit. The following excerpts from one of the Talmudic books, *Pirke Avot,* illustrate some of the facets of this spirit:

Rabbi Judah Ha-Nasi said: "Never look at the pitcher but what it contains; there may be a new pitcher that is full of old wine and there may be an old pitcher that does not even contain new wine."

Rabbi Simeon said: "There are three crowns, the crown of the *Torah,* the crown of the priesthood and the crown of royalty; but the crown of a good name excels them all."

Rabbi Chanina, an assistant to the High Priest said: "Pray for the welfare of the government for were it not for the fear thereof men would swallow each other alive."

Rabbi Tarphon said: "The day is short, the work is great, the workers are lazy, the reward is great and the master (God) is urgent." He also used to say: "You are not obliged to complete the task, but neither are you permitted to desist from it entirely."

PHILOSOPHERS AND COMMENTATORS

Renowned scholars called *Geonim* continued the process

of elucidation and modification of the *Talmud* throughout the period of the 6th to the 11th century. The *Geonim* of Babylonia sought to develop the principles of Jewish religious and civil practice. They helped to create a considerable body of literature consisting of poetry and philosophy, and of responses to questions sent to them from Jewish communities the world over seeking interpretations of the *halachah*. The greatest of these *Geonim*, Saadiah ben Joseph (882-942 C.E.), wrote many *responsa* on Jewish law and was the author of a celebrated book called *Emunot ve-Deot* (on doctrines and beliefs), in which he formulated a comprehensive system of Jewish religious philosophy which exercised a great influence on Jewish scholars in the field of philosophy and religion.

With the appearance in the 11th century of Rabbi Solomon ben Isaac, popularly known as Rashi, a new epoch began in the study of the Bible and the *Talmud*. Rashi's great gifts were lucidity and simplicity. He made the *Talmud* easily understood by the clarity of his commentaries. No Jewish child in future ages would study the Bible without Rashi, and no Talmudic student could do without his remarkably helpful commentary.

The greatest formulation of the entire Jewish law, however, was made by Moses Maimonides in the 12th century. His *Mishneh Torah* is considered the greatest single achievement in the whole field of rabbinic literature. He compressed all of Jewish ritual and legal institutions into a single volume. He aimed, and to a large extent succeeded, at a complete formulation of the entire Jewish law.

There is a road that Jewish literature of those ancient days followed: from the Bible to discussions and interpretations of it, and to discussion and modification of the interpretations, and discussion again and revision if necessary—and all of it for the sake of realizing, if possible, the exalted visions of the Bible, of achieving a nobler humanity on earth under the reign of one God. Israel Zangwill expressed it in the terms: unity, sanity and sanctity.

The yearning to be holy and worthy of God's love had
its impact also on the development of the *Siddur* (which is
treated in detail elsewhere in this volume). The moving
poems of praise and petition that found their way into the
prayerbook, are in a sense, another way of interpreting the
Bible and the laws of the *Talmud;* they also reveal the
love and loyalty of the people toward God and Judaism.
While it is primarily a book for public prayer, the *Siddur*
is thus also a part of Jewish literature.

Although most of Jewish poetry was devotional, there
were some Jewish poets who also wrote secular poetry.
Among the most famous medieval Hebrew poets are three
great philosophical minds, Solomon Ibn Gabirol (born
1021), Moses ibn Ezra (1060), and Judah Halevi (1081).
The quality of their poetry was so great as to be incorporated in the Jewish prayer book. Gabirol's famous *Shachar
Avakeshcha* (At Dawn I seek Thee) is familiar to readers
of traditional Jewish literature:

> At the dawn I seek Thee
>   Refuge, Rock, sublime;
> Set my prayer before Thee in the morning
>   And my prayer at even time.
> And, withal, what is it
>   Heart and tongue can do?
> What is this my strength and what is even
>   This, the spirit in me, too?
> But indeed man's singing
>   May seem good to Thee;
> So I praise Thee singing, while there dwelleth
>   Yet the breath of God in me.

No poet in Jewish history ever equalled the power of
Judah Halevi in writing of Zion. His feelings have carried
magically into the generations of the Jewish experience
and he is remembered by such poems as "Ode to Zion,"
containing such stirring lines as these:

Art thou not hungry for thy children, Zion—
Thy sons far-scattered through an alien world?
From earth's four corners over land and sea
The heavy-hearted remnant of Thy flock
Now send Thee greeting . . .

MODERN JEWISH LITERATURE

The world of modern Jewish literature begins with the
Haskalah (enlightenment) movement about the year
1750. It is, as Professor Meyer Waxman has pointed out,
modern in that it reflects in varying ways and degrees
characteristically modern attitudes toward life, man and
nature. And it is a modern *Jewish* literature in the sense
that it is largely a record of movements which aimed to
adjust Jewish life to the changing environments of the
modern world. One offshoot of *Haskalah* in Western Europe, particularly in Germany, led to Reform Judaism.
The other offshoot, in Eastern Europe, led to Zionism.

The *Haskalah* movement arose in Germany and spread
to neighboring countries. It aimed to elevate and enrich
the Jewish community with the values of the then current
world culture (denied to Jews forcibly cooped up in the
ghettos), so that Jewish life could more closely approximate the life of the outside world. Education was considered the means for this adjustment, literature the principal
means of education, and Hebrew the proper vehicle for
the literary expression of the new aims and values. It was
thus that modern Hebrew literature gradually came into
being.

Moses Mendelssohn (1729-1786), philosopher and fore-
most German Jewish intellectual of his time, was the central figure in the *Haskalah* movement. He undertook the
German translation of the Pentateuch in collaboration
with other scholars, and the Hebrew commentaries with
which the translation was provided contributed to the revival of Hebrew. He also started a Hebrew monthly magazine *Hameassef* (the gatherer), which became the rally-

ing point for a group of writers and a vehicle for learned essays on current problems.

The *Haskalah* in Galicia and Russia was tempered by the intense character of Jewish life in eastern Europe. Poetry, fiction and essays on a variety of themes characterized its influences. The outstanding novelists of this period (the early 19th century) were such well known writers as Abraham Mapu and Peretz Smolenskin. This was a time when many periodicals were published, and with the appearance of the essayists on Eastern European Jewish life the age of modernism set in. They were critics of the Jewish scene and were able to point to new directions and thus exercise considerable influence on later trends. Their writings were contained in Hebrew periodicals like *Hamelitz, Hatzephirah,* and *Hashachar;* but a very considerable literature in Yiddish, the mother tongue of most East European Jews, was also produced.

It was in this period, too, that Jewish nationalism found expression among Jewish writers in Eastern Europe. This was due to a variety of factors, one of them being the rise of nationalism in Europe. Secondly, *Haskalah* dealt with secular matters and nationalism was a more immediate goal to be envisaged than the messianism of religious Jewry. Thirdly, the outbreak of pogroms in Russia in the eighties and the promulgation of the notorious May laws of 1882 not only caused the great migration of Russian Jews to the United States but turned Jewish thinking toward Palestine. The appearance of Herzl and the launching of the world-wide Zionist movement added strength and confidence to the national aspirations. One important result of the growth of Zionism was the secularization of Jewish life. Much of the modern Jewish literature laid stress upon the political aims and types of action, and the solving of the economic difficulties of the Jewish people.

Two tendencies struggled for expression in the literary endeavors of this time. On the one hand there was a secularizing tendency that in its extreme form sought to minimize the uniqueness of Jewish life, to sort of homogenize it with the life of the larger environment. On the other hand there was developing an intensified feeling of Jewish uniqueness which stressed the values of the Jewish tradition and sought to establish a distinction between the peculiarly religious in Jewish life and the non-religious character of Jewish literature. These conflicting tendencies were embodied in Zionism and account for the great variety in the works of the new literature, ranging from the extremes of naturalistic fiction to the poetry of veneration of past Jewish life.

The dominant tendency during most of the period was one of romantic idealization of the past. This may have been due to the fact that the contemporary Jewish scene was marked by conflict, tension and crisis, and the fixed past offered better material for writing. The important aspects of the modern literature of this era were a new interest in Palestine, a positive attitude toward Hebrew as language and literature, and an emphasis on Jewish survival regardless of contemporary challenges. These elements in Jewish life were clearly portrayed by such writers as David Frishman (1865-1922), Mordecai Zeev Feierberg (1874-1899) and Judah Steinberg (1861-1908). They combined the capacity to analyze current Jewish life, with reverence for the Jewish tradition and a sense of sorrow at its passing. Frishman's stories, for example, contain two motifs—the tragedy brought to parents by the apostasy of children attracted by the glamor of the non-Jewish world, and the struggle to maintain Jewish integrity within. Feierberg portrays the inner struggle of the young Jew of the post-*Haskalah* period between two worlds, that of the ghetto and that of the outside. Both attract and repel. The solution, it is suggested, will come only with Jewish rebirth in Palestine.

LEADERS IN HEBREW AND YIDDISH LITERATURE

The later years marked the advent of such influential writers in modern Jewish literature as Mendele Mocher

Seforim, the grandfather of Yiddish literature, Yitzchok
Leibush Peretz, Sholom Aleichem, Sholom Asch, Chaim
Nachman Bialik, Saul Tchernichovsky, Zalman Shneour,
Nachum Sokolow, Hillel Zeitlin and many others. Each of
these personalities deserves a complete essay by himself.
Mendele, Sholom Aleichem, Peretz and Asch adorned the
field of Yiddish literature and their works are still very
widely read.

The greatest Hebrew poet since Judah Halevi was Bialik (1873-1934), who was acclaimed in his lifetime as the
poet laureate of his people. He mirrored better than any
other writer the soul of the Jewish people, gave voice to
their joys and sorrow, their hopes and disappointments,
and he held out for them the vision of the greater beings
they could be. His poem *The City of Slaughter,* written
after the Kishinev pogrom of 1903, stirred the heart of
Jewry and aroused the ghetto people to form their own
self-defense groups. He was the national Jewish poet par
excellence.

Influential as Bialik was as a poet, so was Achad Ha'am
in his time (1865-1923) as an essayist. His impress is
still strongly felt in Jewish life. Throughout his career he
emphasized the spiritual aspects of Zionism. He was critical of Herzl and other Zionist leaders for accentuating
the idea of political Zionism to the exclusion of the cultural phases of the movement. His ideas received wide circu-
lation and he has been the teacher and guide of two generations of Hebrew thinkers, poets and political leaders. One
of his famous essays *The Revival of the Spirit* shows the
continuity of the moral theme in Jewish literature century
after century. In it he wrote:

It is not necessary to prove the existence of an original
Hebrew culture. As long as the Bible exists no one will
deny the original creative power which lies within the
spirit of our people, and even they who deny the existence
of the Jewish people in the present are forced to admit that
this people was creative when it did exist and that the cultural legacy which it left behind bears the ineradicable

stamp of its original spirit . . . The fruit of a tree planted
on its home soil differs from the fruit of the same tree
planted on strange soil and preserved in an artificial manner. The tree, however, is the same wherever it may be as
long as its trunk has not died. It produces fruit after its
kind. It erected cultural structures in an original manner
peculiar to it, not only while it dwelt upon its own soil,
but also at the time when it dwelt in all the lands of the
Diaspora, as long as the conditions of its existence allowed
it some freedom to do its work and to employ all of its
inner powers to this end.

In the Palestine settlement *(Yishuv)* there was great
literary activity even before the reestablishment of the
State of Israel. Eliezer ben Yehudah, known as the father
of modern Hebrew, had already completed his monumen-
tal Hebrew dictionary. Joseph Klausner's historic studies
on Jesus and Paul had won world-wide attention by the
time of independence, and his numerous essays in the literary field already filled several volumes. In fiction there
were already established such writers as Abraham Abba
Kabak, Samuel Joseph Agnon, Judah Burla and Moshe
Smilansky, who had won world wide recognition. Among
the poets there were new stars in the firmament including
such names as David Shimoni, Abraham Shlonsky, Uri Zvi
Greenberg and Nathan Alterman. Since the rise of the new
State, Moshe Shamir has been acclaimed as outstanding
among the Hebrew novelists.

Yiddish literature began almost a thousand years ago,
and from its rise in South Germany to the middle of the
Eighteenth century in Eastern Europe, two main currents
were dominant. The first had its source in tradition and
helped to bring about a religious and traditional literature
in this tongue. The second had its source in the surround-
ing non-Jewish literatures, German and later also Italian.
Gradually it achieved its own individual character, dealing with both religious and secular themes. Among the
first books published in Yiddish in its earliest stage were
the *Maasebucher* (story books), which were collections of

folk tales, legends and parables associated with Bible, Talmudic, and medieval Jewish personalities. From this beginning Yiddish developed into such a universally spoken
and written language that in the nineteenth century it was
the most widely used language among the Jews of the
world.

AMERICAN AND ENGLISH JEWISH WRITERS

England's greatest Jewish writer was Israel Zangwill
(1864-1926), who dominated the Anglo-Jewish literary
scene in the nineteenth and twentieth centuries. He was a
master of English prose and in addition to novels and short
stories, wrote superb essays. His volume *The Voice of Jerusalem* contains sentiments on the position of the Jew in
the modern world that have not been matched by any writer in the English language. He also made some of the finest
translations into English of the medieval Hebrew poetry
which we possess. His most important fiction works are
Children of the Ghetto, Dreamers of the Ghetto and *King
of the Schnorrers.*

The importance of Zangwill lies in the fact that he was
the first to present the image of the Jew to a non-Jewish
English speaking world, and he was famous in the times
of such great writers as Shaw, Wells, Kipling and Gals-
worthy. *Dreamers of the Ghetto,* a book of short pieces
based on the lives of such notable personalities as Spinoza,
the *Baal Shem,* Heinrich Heine and Theodor Herzl, is a
model of essay writing as well as a brilliant portrayal of
character. Holbrook Jackson, a noted British literary critic
characterized Zangwill's contribution to literature in these
terms:

"By writing in English, Israel Zangwill has not only
revealed the tragedy and comedy of Jewry to the English
speaking members of his race, he has also revealed them to
a nation which still takes its knowledge of the Jew from
the naivete of Shakespeare's Shylock and the buffoonery
of the comic papers . . . Zangwill is adapted by birth, ex-

perience, gifts and temperament to communicate between ineradicable Israel and absorbing England."

England has not produced a Jewish writer of Zangwill's stature since he died in 1926.

A recent publication edited by Dr. Oscar Janowsky, dealing with a reappraisal of American Jewry, states in a chapter on literature contributed by Marie Syrkin of Brandeis University that by the middle of the 20th century Jewish writers were winning recognition in American letters in impressive numbers, and that what distinguishes the latter day American Jewish writers from their predecessors is not so much the subject matter as the status they now hold as writers. A list of distinguished American writers of the 1960's would include a high proportion of second and third generation American Jews.

To a large degree, Miss Syrkin notes, the American Jewish novelist reflects the historical experiences of the Jew in America. From the immigrant Abe Cahan to the American born Saul Bellow or Philip Roth, there is to be noted the process of taking root and alienation, of adaptation and recoil which mark the general life of the American Jewish community. Abraham Cahan's novel *The Rise of David Levinsky,* published in 1917, was the first notable work of fiction dealing with the American Jew. It was the first Jewish novel to make an impact on the non-Jewish as well as the Jewish world. This novel, like many others in earlier years, was concerned with Jewish adjustment to the American way of life, the struggle for economic security, intermarriage and the problem of maintaining Jewish traditions in a changing social order.

The novels which have followed this one have not always portrayed Jewish life in a favorable light. Some showed Jewish self-hate and some like Milton Steinberg's *As a Driven Leaf* and Irving Fineman's *Hear Ye Sons* displayed beautifully the Jewish character and moral fibre of the past centuries. Among the writers who have written positively on the American scene was Ludwig Lewisohn, whose books *Israel, The Island Within* and *The Last Days of Shylock* are moving portrayals of Jewish adjustment to changing environments.

Maurice Samuel ranks among the best of the Jewish essayists and nonfiction writers in America. His primary interests are directly associated with Jewish life and problems. He is a brilliant polemical writer who has dealt extensively with questions of nationalism, antisemitism, and Zionism. In addition, his studies of Yiddish writers, among them Sholom Aleichem and Peretz, have served to bring the vanished *shtetl* (the European Jewish small town) to the English speaking world. In essays, novels, prose and verse translations he has devoted his talents with great energy to the study and illumination of contemporary Jewish life.

In analyzing Jewish cultural life in the United States in the contemporary period, we note Jewish literary figures who are involved in American life but not necessarily possessed of a deep awareness of Jewish identity. They do portray disenchantment and alienation, characteristics of the modern intellectual outlook on the world. Many of the most gifted of the younger Jewish intellectuals have also shown estrangement as well as belligerency toward their origin to accentuate their sense of alienation. They thus contribute to the puzzlement over the directions of the Jewish future in America.

Ludwig Lewisohn once defined a Jewish book as one written by a man who knows he is a Jew. This definition has aptly characterized Jewish literature throughout the unbroken centuries of Jewish existence. Lewisohn added a few thoughts on the continuity of Jewish literature which reflect the spirit of this essay. His words, written in the introduction to the volume *Great Jewish Books,* edited by Caplan and Ribalow, deserve recording:

"Among us the Book never became rigid or doctrinal or dispensable or capable of substitution by credal or other formulae. On the contrary, the *Torah* in the original sense became by expansion and penetration, by comment and enlargement, *Torah* in the broader sense. It broadened

into *Mishnah* and *Gemara* and *Midrash,* it soared strange-
ly into Zohar; it was defended in Yehuda Halevi's *Kitab
al Khazari.* Age after age it was reexamined under the aspect of the world's philosophies. Maimonides reestablished
it under the aspect of Aristotle; long before that Philo of
Alexandria had sought a reinterpretation under the aspect
of the Platonists. In our own day Herman Cohen sought
confirmation in the philosophy of Kant. From it sprang
the liturgy—*siddur* and *machzor;* based upon it were the
mighty compendia of Joseph Caro, the *Shulchan Aruch*
and the unrivalled intellectual powers of Rashi were used
in commentaries upon it. Yet—and this is of ultimate import—the original text never lost life and freshness. It
was never submerged in the seas of interpretation and
commentary. Its original words remained words of life to
all men and a light to all peoples, so that in our own
generation a supremely great artist from among the Gentiles, Thomas Mann, wrote a great creative super-midrash
upon a few chapters of the *Torah* in the tetralogy of novels, *Joseph and His Brethren.*

. . . And so it is clear that Ahad Ha-Am, the 19th
century rationalist, and Bialik as well as Herzl, the Viennese man of letters in whose diaries the word *Torah* does
not occur, all wrote, all proclaimed, as it were, from within the spirit and destiny of Israel and so added to and expanded *Torah* and deepened and broadened that immortal
stream. In that last sentence the relation of the authentic
Jewish writer to the Book, to literature, has been defined.
He writes from within the spirit and destiny of Israel. In
some sense and in whatever language he adds, however
humbly, to *Torah*."

This *Torah* of which Lewisohn speaks represents the
spiritual effort of man to live the good and noble life on
earth. Jewish literature in every age has dealt with this
problem in one form or another. Modern Jewish writers
are engaged in the same struggle, to validate in our time
the worth of the message proclaimed in the Bible by the
Jewish people, and treasured by so many countless millions

throughout the world today. The Hebrew poet Chaim Nachman Bialik caught the significance and meaning of the constancy of the message to be found in Jewish literature in his words spoken in the year 1925 at the Dedication of the Hebrew University in Jerusalem: "The Books of the Chronicles," he said, "the last of the Scriptures, are not the last in the history of Israel. To these small books there will be added a third, perhaps more important than the first two. And if the first two books of Chronicles begin with "Adam, Seth, Noah" and end with the proclamation of Cyrus which three hundred years later brought the gospel of redemption to the heathen of old, the third will undoubtedly begin with the proclamation of Balfour and end with a new gospel of redemption to the whole of humanity."

SUGGESTED READINGS

THE HISTORY OF JEWISH LITERATURE, *Meyer Waxman,* Thomas Yoseloff.

CHAPTERS ON JEWISH LITERATURE, *Israel Abrahams,* Jewish Publication Society.

POST-BIBLICAL LITERATURE, *B. Halper,* Jewish Publication Society.

MODERN HEBREW LITERATURE, *Simon Halkin,* Schocken.

A JEWISH VIEW OF
SEX AND THE FAMILY

by Henry Enoch Kagan

HENRY ENOCH KAGAN: Rabbi, Sinai Temple, Mount Vernon, N. Y.; a graduate of Columbia University, he was ordained at Hebrew Union College; he is also a licensed psychologist, and the author of **SIX WHO CHANGED THE WORLD, CHANGING THE ATTITUDE OF CHRISTIAN TOWARD JEW,** and co-author of **JUDAISM AND PSYCHIATRY.**

THE way in which the human race has satisfied the sexual urge has had a long history of development. The attitudes of people toward what is right and what is wrong in the area of sexual relations have changed through the ages. Even in the biblical period, which people mistakenly view as an undifferentiated era of time, there are marked differences in the rules that were supposed to govern the sexual behavior of people.

In the laws that Moses taught the Hebrews during the Wilderness Years there were many that dealt specifically with the ethics of sexual relations. Most of those laws on sex reflect the accent on virginity in the female at the time of marriage. There were laws, too, against wantonness and whoredom (Leviticus 19 and 21; Deuteronomy 22 and 23). However, one also reads in the Bible, specifically in the books of the great prophets Hosea, Jeremiah and Ezekiel, about the way the Hebrews of Canaan assimilated the ways of the pagan people of that land. They engaged in sexual orgies as part of the agricultural festivals, and even adopted the custom of the Temple harlot (*kedeshah* in Hebrew).

Because the sex urge is instinctual, it does not follow that sex is to be satisfied without let or hindrance, any more than man is permitted to satisfy his hunger without consideration for the rights of others, or without recognition of the natural limitations of the human body. One doesn't eat gobs of food simply because it is at hand and will fill up the stomach. There have always been rules to govern sexual relations, but they have had varying effects upon people in different periods. In our own time the inherited sex laws seem to be having less impact upon a substantial portion of the people.

217

SOME EARLY CONCEPTS ABOUT SEX

An odd note concerning sex was sounded recently by the rector of a village church in England, whose words would probably have gone completely unnoticed except for the fact that among some teen-age girls from a private school who were attending the Sunday service at his church was Princess Anne, daughter of Queen Elizabeth. To these teen-agers the rector said: "You cannot read or hear anything, or go to any of the cinemas or other programs, without sex being brought in. Forget it. It is only a trifle."

Sex was not regarded as a trifling matter in the early centuries of the race, and certainly no such ostrich-like avoidance of the subject was advocated by the early codes. In biblical Judaism sex was a vital activity; on it depended the propagation of the race and the stability of the family.

The Bible's account of the first human couple has left us with a heritage of differing interpretations that have influenced people's attitudes toward sex. According to the Bible, the first man was fashioned by God. Adam himself was, therefore, not the product of sexual intercourse. After God gave Adam a wife as a "helpmate," no mention is made of sexual relations between them until after the incident of the eating of the forbidden fruit. It is then that Adam and Eve became aware of their nakedness; it was then, says the Bible, that they "knew" one another.

The sex life of Adam and Eve has had an all pervading influence on the attitude of Western civilization toward sex and the family. On the surface, it would appear that Adam and Eve were happy in the Garden of Eden until they ate of the fruit of the Tree of Knowledge and learned of sex. Their expulsion from Paradise followed. They were also punished by being introduced to pain; for woman, the pain of giving birth to a child, for man, the pain of toiling for his bread. And both Adam and Eve were subjected to death.

Was the sin of Adam and Eve sexual? The answer to this question is very important because in the answer we will find the roots of a historic difference between Judaism and Christianity toward sex. Christianity says that because the first man and woman disobeyed God by eating the fruit and indulging in sex, their children were born in sin and as a result the entire human race inherited this sexual sin. In contrast, Judaism says Adam and Eve disobeyed God but not because they experienced sex. The Bible explicitly says about Adam and Eve that "they were not ashamed" of their nakedness, by which is understood sexual relations.

It was not until the rise of Christianity that sex became a sin, that relations between a man and a woman came to be considered as inferior to celibacy. This view is to be found in the New Testament; nowhere does it appear in the books of our Bible, the so-called Old Testament. The very first commandment in the Bible is "be fruitful and multiply" (Genesis 1:28). Throughout the 39 books of the Bible, from Genesis through Chronicles, covering over 1000 years of Jewish civilization, there is frank discussion of sex as being normal and healthy so long as it takes into consideration not only respect for the family but also respect for the person of the sexual partner.

To some it may seem impossible that such a modern view of sex can be extracted from the Bible. After all, are there not severe puritanical restrictions on various forms of sexual activities in the Bible? Are not women put into an inferior position since the polygymous society of biblical times permitted a man to have more than one wife?

There are restrictions against certain sexual expressions in the Bible. In fact, it treats incest, adultery and homosexuality as capital crimes punishable by death. And the laws of the Bible do permit man to have more than one wife, but it is a mistake to conclude from this that women were regarded as inferior beings. Abraham, the first Hebrew, had the approval of his wife, whom he loved, before he took a concubine so that he might have a son, at the time that Sarah, his wife, was barren. When Sarah later gave birth to her son, Abraham sent the concubine away. The Bible is filled with accounts of romantic love such as the devotion of Abraham for Sarah, Isaac for Rebecca, and Jacob for Rachel.

In the main, the Bible has a very high opinion of women. The Bible's first man could have had the world all to himself, but God said, "It is not good that man should be alone; I will make a helper for him." And when Eve was created Adam was so pleased that he said, "This is now bone of my bone, flesh of my flesh." The Bible concludes this episode with the following remark: "Therefore shall a man leave his father and his mother, and shall cleave unto his wife, and they shall be one flesh. And they were both naked, the man and his wife, and were not ashamed" (Gen. 2:23-25).

LOVE IN THE BIBLE

The language in these and other parts of the Bible about sex shows an awareness that there is more than physical need involved in the sexual relations of a man and a woman. In Hebraic thinking, a man's need for a woman is not merely sexual. It is a psychological and even an intellectual need as well. Wisdom in Hebrew is itself associated with the feminine gender. The Book of Proverbs speaks of wisdom as if she were a woman to be wooed: "Get wisdom, get understanding . . . Forsake her not and she shall preserve thee; love her and she shall keep thee . . . Extol her and she shall exalt thee; she shall bring thee to honor when thou dost embrace her" (Prov. 4:5-8).

This glorification of the female was counteracted, however, by a warning against the wiles of unscrupulous women, in another part of that book. "Hold to wisdom and understanding," it says, "that they may keep thee from the strange woman, from the alien woman that maketh smooth her words . . . Now she is in the streets, now in the broad places, and lieth in wait at every corner" (Prov. 7:5-12).

Where the love of a man and a woman is true and

honest, such love is accompanied by the divine blessing of God. The prophets of Israel thought so highly of this kind of love between a man and a woman that they used this human relationship for a simile to describe the love of God the people of Israel. When Hosea, Jeremiah and Ezekiel criticized the people for worshipping idols, they accused Israel of running after false lovers instead of God, whom these prophets called Israel's true husband. Isaiah charged Israel with trying to divorce herself from God, when the people followed other gods. "For thy Maker is thy Husband," Isaiah told his people. In this poetic description of the bond between God and Israel in terms of the relation of two lovers, one can see that the Bible by no means has a low opinion of the love of a man and a woman.

The most exalted view of such a love is found in the biblical book, The Song of Songs, a lyrical drama involving a maid, her shepherd lover, King Solomon, and the women of his royal harem acting as a chorus. Once, on a summer excursion Solomon and his court came upon a beautiful sunburned peasant girl, Shulamith, working in her vineyard. The king, more than middle-aged at the time, tried to win her affection and finally compelled her to give up her rustic home for the harem in Jerusalem. However, Shulamith had already pledged her heart to a young shepherd and against this love the king's enticements were powerless. In the end Shulamith was permitted to return to her home. At the close of the poem the lovers appear together and sing this duet: "Set me as a seal upon thy heart, as a seal upon thine arm, for love is strong as death. Jealousy is cruel as the grave; the flashes thereof are flashes of fire; a very flame of the Lord. Many waters cannot quench love, neither can the floods drown it; if a man would give all the substance of his house for love, he would utterly be condemned."

The Song of Songs glorifies love in this poetic manner but does not describe it as some unreal, imaginary fantasy. The physical and sexual aspects of love are realistically described: "My beloved is unto me as a bag of myrrh that lieth betwixt my breast (6:13) . . . Let his left hand be under my head and his right hand embrace me (2:6) . . . By night on my bed I sought him whom my soul loveth (3:1) . . . Thy lips are like a thread of scarlet and thy mouth is comely (4:3) . . . Thy lips, O my bride, drop honey—honey and milk are under thy tongue (4:11) . . . Thy navel is like a round goblet wherein no mingled wine is wanting; thy belly is like a heap of wheat set about with lilies (7:3) . . . Let thy breasts be as clusters of vine and the smell of thy countenance like apples; and the roof of thy mouth like the best wine that glideth down smoothly for my beloved (7:9-10) . . . How fair and how pleasant are thou, O love, for delights" (7:7).

It is significant to observe that in this oriental imagery, love and sex are not separated; sex is not treated as a muscular reflex, not as simply an expression of body chemistry. In The Song of Songs love is both sexual and sanctified.

TALMUDIC ATTITUDES TOWARD SEX

Unfortunately, this positive attitude towards sexual love was not carried over into the New Testament, largely because Paul, a bachelor, had an anti-feminine bias. "Women," he said, "are created for men and not men for women . . . It is good for a man not to touch a woman, but if they cannot contain let them marry . . . He that is unmarried careth for the things of the Lord while he that is married careth for the things that are of this world." Paul depreciated both sex and marriage, placing them on a lower level of living. It was he who was mainly responsible for the idea that Adam's sin consisted of sex relations with Eve.

The rabbis of the *Talmud,* especially those who were contemporaries of Paul, took great pains to refute early Christianity's negative idea about sex and marriage. Of course, the Talmudic rabbis did not endorse unbridled sexual license, but they were remarkably frank in pointing out the importance of sex for a successful marriage. They said, "Were it not for the sex drive no man would build a house or marry a woman or engage in any occupation." They looked upon sexuality not only as a normal act of healthy living, but as a gift of God; sex was a virtue to enjoy and a sin to deny. Thus the rabbis opposed Christian asceticism, going so far as to say that "in the world to come every man will be called to account for the *legitimate* pleasures which he has not enjoyed."

However, to them the pleasures of sex were "legitimate" only in marriage. On the other hand, the sexual pleasure of a husband and a wife, Talmudic rabbis declared, did not require the birth of a child to justify itself. This liberal view of 2000 years ago has only lately been adopted by some branches of Christianity.

There are many sections in the *Talmud* in which rights of the wife to sexual satisfaction are dealt with; there are discussions also on sexual play, on positions of sexual intercourse, and on the use of contraceptives to prevent a childbirth that might endanger the health of the wife or to avoid impregnating a nursing mother, a form of planned parenthood. These discussions are surprisingly modern but consistent with the rabbinic attitude toward the pleasure of marriage.

To guard youth against sexual experimenting, the *Talmud* recommended early marriage. A young man was to be married at the age of 18 and girls even younger, and dowries were provided for these teen-age marriages. Parenthetically, it can be noted that in the agricultural society of those days there was a place for young people as responsible workers; they could therefore marry earlier.

The rabbis of the Talmudic period were quite concerned about the selection of a proper spouse. They advised that an extremely tall man should not marry an extremely tall woman, lest the children be gawky. Nor should an extremely short man marry an extremely short woman, lest their children be midgets. Their ideas on eugenics were not quite scientific, but they strongly advised against marriage into a family with hereditary taints. They also considered cultural factors, cautioning the scholar against marrying the daughter of an illiterate, and the daughter of a scholar not to marry an illiterate man.

The Talmudic rabbis even had psychological reservations about impulsive, romantic marriages. They held that a young man should not marry a girl before he knows all about her immediate family, especially about her brothers, for "sons usually inherit the traits of their mother's brothers." We do not today accept the idea that such traits are inherited, but most people do agree that people's character and personality are conditioned by their respective families, so that it can be of some value to know the family before marrying one of its members.

Significance of the Jewish Family

The Jewish people have always been profoundly concerned about achieving good marriages, not only for the welfare of the two persons involved, but also because of the supreme importance of the family for the survival of Judaism itself.

An outstanding characteristic of the Jewish people has always been its mobility. The Jewish people began as nomads and have been more or less on the move throughout history. Perhaps it is this continuous, widespreading movement that made the family unit so important in the religious life of the Jews. Close-knit family life helped provide roots for people ever on the move. Whatever the reasons, Judaism has incorporated into Jewish family life a whole set of ceremonies and rituals, so that the family unit became a *mikdash m'at* (a little sanctuary) wherever it happened to be. In this family sanctuary the father and mother acted as the priest and priestess. In a sense they served God at an altar of love when they presided over the ceremonies of the Sabbath evening meal at home. Their duty to educate their children was a sacred obligation. Everything in the Jewish family had a religious motive, including sex.

The preservation of the Jewish family became a great challenge when the ever-moving Jew came into contact with different cultures. One such famous confrontation came about during the Hellenic period of our history, when the Jews were a subject people within the Grecian world. Greek customs and practices threatened to undermine the stability of the Jewish family. The Greeks worshipped a variety of gods and goddesses, and could, in the name of religious expression, indulge in public sex orgies.

Greek ideas had some impact upon the Jews too, for they produced great philosophers and thinkers. It is important to note, therefore, that Aristotle had a low opinion of women, and Plato glorified homosexuality. Even the distinguished medieval Jewish philosopher, Moses Maimonides, seemed to have been influenced by some Greek notions about sex. He said: "We ought to limit sexual intercourse altogether, hold it in contempt and desire it only rarely . . . the act is too base to be performed except when needed." Fortunately, Maimonides was directly challenged by Nachmanides, another medieval Jewish authority, who declared: "It is not true, as our master, Maimonides, has said in his *Guide for the Perplexed,* praising Aristotle for teaching that the sexual urge is a source of shame to us. God forbid that the truth should be in accordance with the teachings of the Greeks! . . . The act of sexual union is holy and pure . . . The Lord created all things in accordance with His wisdom and whatever He created cannot possibly be shameful or ugly . . . When a man is in union with his wife in a spirit of holiness and purity, the Divine Presence is with them."

Jewish survival power through the family can be seen especially when we examine the home life of the Jewish immigrants who came to America by the hundreds of thousands annually from 1880 to 1914. This includes the grandparents or great-grandparents of most of the readers of this essay. From Eastern Europe they had brought their own philosophy of family living, which had been developing over centuries and which had been protected against outside influences because they had lived in isolated ghettos. When they arrived in the New World, they brought with them certain positive and healthy characteristics of Jewish family life. But it was not easy to transplant these values and ways of life to the new conditions they found in the United States.

The widely read Yiddish newspaper, *The Jewish Daily Forward,* used to print a family column called the *Bintl Briv* (bundle of letters) containing many complaints from husbands and wives and children. A Christian sociologist, Professor W. T. Thomas, learned Yiddish in order to make a study of these letters so as to analyze why the Jewish immigrant family was able to stay together despite economic and social forces that tended to break other immigrant families apart. From the Thomas collection of 3,000 letters to the family complaint column, between the years 1920 and 1945, and from an excellent book entitled *Life Is With People* which describes life in the *shtetl,* that is, the Eastern European Jewish village, one is able to recapture the mood of the home life that the Jewish immigrants to America brought with them.

One striking quality among them was the strong feeling of *mishpachah* (family or kinfolk). This meant that a Jewish family was not an independent, individualistic unit made up of parents and one or two children separated from all relatives. There was, instead, a sense of responsibility for relatives of varying degree. Because they were strangers in a strange land, they had a feeling of closeness to every newly arriving cousin, whom they willingly put up in their crowded tenement until the newcomer could start out on his own.

Their ideal was a home in which *Sholom Bayis* (peace in the house) prevailed. Much of their waking time was devoted to the marrying off of children, for they placed a high value on marriage. Even the Sabbath was referred to in wedding terms, being called a bride, a day to be enjoyed, in other words. And when the infant boy was circumcised he was dedicated to *Chuppa* (marriage). The matchmaker or *schadchan* was a familiar figure in the community, trying to arrange marriages in which the factor of *Yichus* (family background) was kept in mind.

The parents were often referred to as a dual authority, by the phrase *der tateh-mameh* (the father-mother). The Swedish mother so popularized in the play "I Remember Mama" had her counterpart in the Yiddish *mameh* who also had her *Knippl* (a knot in a handkerchief), in which she kept coins for family emergencies. The parents' greatest happiness was to *Kleib nachas fun kinder* (gather happiness from children). And *machen menschen fun kinder* (making people out of children) was a parent's sacred obligation.

The immigrant Jewish parent was not afraid to punish the child, and among phrases of remonstrance that were frequently heard were *mit derech eretz* (with some respect) and *es past nit* (it doesn't look right). For being an *azzus ponim* (impertinent child) one could receive a *potch* (slap) from one or both parents. And they did not fear that their punishment would be regarded by the child as a rejection of him, for the withdrawal of love from a Jewish child was simply unthinkable to these parents. On the other hand, the child's obedience to the parent did not render him quiet and passive. They were expected to question things as they do at the Passover *Seder* in the Four Questions, and to be active members of the household. But the Fifth Commandment was to be taken seriously throughout the years.

The peaceful household Jews hoped for was not always easy to attain. In the immigrant period there might be at least three generations in a small apartment: grandparents, parents and children. There were, as the family column in the *Jewish Daily Forward* indicated, many arguments between one generation and the other. Arguments, however, were not considered to be incompatible with family stability. People seemed to act on the principle that it was better to say what was on one's mind than to remain silent, for the quarrel could be an outlet for pent-up feelings, after which the family could go on living together. This reminds us of the poem by Blake:

> I was angry with my friend,
> I told my wrath, my wrath did end.
> I was angry with my foe,
> I told it not, my wrath did grow.

The Family in Contemporary America

The culture of the American Jewish family of East European background is no longer based on the customs of traditions of the *shtetl*. Most of the readers of this article are third and fourth generation Americans. They probably do not know the Yiddish language, and are in all likelihood unaware of the *shtetl* values that have just been discussed. In most respects contemporary Jewish youths are more accustomed to the values and mores of the "typical" American than of the specifically Jewish family.

The American family today is preponderantly middle class, living mostly in urban metropolitan communities, that is, in large cities and their ever increasing suburbs. The old, large stationary farm family has been replaced by the smaller, mobile city family. A very large percentage of these city families move to a different location every five years. The first characteristic of this modern urbanized American family is, therefore, its rootlessness.

There is a significant difference in the size of the American family in relation to the religion of the partners. Roman Catholic couples have more children than non-Catholics, partly because they are restricted by their church in the use of birth control methods and partly because they seem to want more children. Roman Catholic families have an average of three to four children, Protestant families between two and three, and Jewish families average two children. A study by the Office of Population Research of Princeton University showed that the wealthier and better educated Jewish couples are beginning to desire larger families. On the other hand, there are Jewish couples who want their children to have more than they received in their own childhood, and therefore plan to have smaller families. Some recent studies have aroused alarm as to whether Jews are reproducing themselves proportionately with the growth in the general population in America. The Jewish population as of 1964 represents 3% of the total American population, but as other groups reproduce themselves more rapidly this percentage may fall to less than 2% in another generation or so.

In addition to being rootless, smaller and mobile, the American middle class family is also less stable, which is dramatized by the fact that there are 400,000 divorces annually in the United States compared to approximately 2,000,000 marriages per year. In comparison with other religious groups the percentage of Jewish divorces is the lowest, despite the fact that Judaism has always been more liberal than Christianity in the variety of grounds it accepts for divorce. The Christian tradition of forbidding divorce except for adultery still influences modern law. Many states in the country insist that unless one of the unhappy couple proves that the other committed adultery or some domestic crime like it, a divorce will not be granted. In contrast, Rabbinic law long ago accepted even incompatibility of temperament as legal grounds for divorce. (Unfortunately, that same Orthodox Jewish law gives a Jewish husband superior rights over his wife in the cases of divorce, with which Conservative Judaism is struggling and which, happily, Reform Judaism has abrogated). In any case, no Jew feels condemned religiously if he or she turns to divorce for release from an intolerably unhappy marriage. And yet, the Jewish divorce rate, while rising, is still considerably lower than that of the general population.

The high rate of divorce does not necessarily mean that a large number of Americans are sick or neurotic. It may be, says Martin B. Hunt in a book entitled *The Natural History of Love,* because Americans, more than others in the past, seek love in marriage. Mr. Hunt, after studying the marital behavior of nine historical eras, from the time of Pericles to the Twentieth Century, comes to the optimistic conclusion that marriage is better today than ever before because Americans are romantic and marry for love. He claims that the high rate of divorce "reflects not so much the failure of love as the determination of people not to live without it."

The ultimate test of the stability of a marriage depends on whether the partners are capable of loving. Many experts are of the opinion that the main problem in marriage is whether the individual has the capacity to love, which is a learned response, not an automatic instinct. Love is learned from loving parents. Therefore, the best qualification for marriage is to have the good fortune of having loving parents. (But it is true, nevertheless, that many learn to love even though they were not so fortunate in the "choice" of parents).

IS MODERN MAN DIFFERENT

A quality that is key to stability in marriage is a feeling of confidence in oneself. Many marriage counselors believe that a major cause for marital trouble in our day is a widespread loss of people's confidence in themselves. A number of developments in recent centuries seem to have undermined man's self esteem. The Bible had let man glorify himself with the idea that his earth was the center of the universe, but Copernicus and Galileo shook him loose from that thought. The Bible also presented man as the being God made to have dominion over all life on land, in the seas and in the air. But Darwin and others weakened this concept and even permitted the thought that evolution may eventually produce a higher form of life. And as if this were not enough, along came Freud and removed from man the feeling that he had free will to determine his own destiny, for his actions were controlled by a libido and subconscious formed within him at a time when he had little power to do anything about it.

There have been other "upheavals" that have left man somehow diminished in individuality or stature in modern times. The industrial revolution made the machine so great that it tended to make the work of man less important certainly, the product was far removed from any individual craft or skill that one could recognize and feel proud to have contributed to the making of it. Even the increase in man's knowledge seems less substantial today. The scientific revolution has altered many of our previously held concepts of physics and other sciences. And, to boot, we now have atomic bombs that threaten the annihiliation of whole geographic areas of the human race.

The net effect of all these revolutions has been to reduce man in stature and significance. To this, as if the others were not enough, must be added still another: the sexual revolution, that is, the radical change in the status of woman in modern times.

CHANGES IN THE STATUS OF WOMEN

The modern emancipation of women, which is going on all over the world, is a rebellion against the doctrine of the superiority of the male over the female. Women have always been workers in the home and in the field, but more and more in modern times they have entered into gainful employment in factory, shop, store and office, and increased educational opportunities have brought them in larger numbers into the professions.

And now, with the concern over the population explosion placing greater emphasis upon planned parenthood, a new element is being added. Through the practice of birth control, women are asserting their independence from being limited to the biological birth-giving function. The widening area of occupation and independence for women, which today includes such "male" preserves as politics, has led women to try to counteract what some consider the "frightening" failures of man. Some view with disgust the ads that manipulate the sex image, that expose the female body to sell cars, cigars, mouthwash and cream to groom the male's hair. They believe there is more to a woman than her sexual attraction. Many women are today writing books to appeal to their own sex not to confine themselves to the home or to their children but to come out into the world and help resolve its difficulties.

From what was said in an earlier section, it is clear that a person should be mature before becoming a husband or a wife. However, young people are marrying earlier today than ever before. A large proportion of college girls actually drop out of school to be married. Judging by the high incidence of divorce among these early marriages many of them are proving to be premature.

Too often, the women who interrupt their schooling for marriage and children feel themselves, after some years, to be unfulfilled. Such feelings are a difficult burden upon the marriage relationship. It is not young women alone who feel this way; young men who become fathers, with all the responsibilities that this entails, often feel trapped, unprepared to give what is required. They have little spontaneous fun.

Changing Sexual Mores

Newspaper and magazine articles have been saying for some time that there has been a decline in chastity and an increase in promiscuity among young people. Many reasons are given: greater numbers are attending schools away from home, there is greater availability of contraceptives, the general atmosphere we live in is freer, etc. It is also claimed from the psychological point of view that many young people use sex as a way of expressing their independence, or perhaps their rebellion against taboos or restrictions.

When sex is used to prove some point, or to respond to a need arising from childhood experiences, it is transformed into something that it is not; a disembodied impersonal act. It is often resorted to, for instance, as a measure of the potency of a man or woman. The noted writer, Eric Fromm, has wisely demonstrated, however, that potency has two meanings; power over someone else, or power to do something. Some people, feeling themselves impotent in the sense of being unable to do things in other activities of life, may try to compensate by dominating another person sadistically, in a form of sexual revenge. On the other hand, a person who is really potent both in sexual and other aspects of living does not need to seek a feeling of power through sexual "attack" upon another. In such situations sex is a weapon, not an expression of love.

It is a tragic mistake to think that one can achieve happiness merely by sexual activity. The zoologist, Dr. Kinsey, and his staff, wrote two books on the sexual behavior of men and women in America, which seemed to indicate that a person would have a more successful marriage if he or she had sexual activities and experimentations with different partners before marriage. The measurement of human happiness seemed to be the number of orgasms that a person achieved. In the Kinsey study, the tenderness of love does not appear.

Poets and novelists, by and large, are more sensitive in articulating ideas about love. They write affirmatively about love, when they believe that life has meaning and purpose. But when writers are disillusioned about life, and nothing has any meaning, they write bitterly as though love were nothing but an obscene sex joke. The Victorian Age was prudish about sex, but it was an age of hope in the future of a better world, so Robert Browning could write in his poem *Love Among the Ruins:* "Oh heart, oh blood that freezes, blood that burns, earth's return for whole centuries of folly, noise and sin, shut them in, with their triumphs, and their glories and the rest—love is best!" However, in our Age of Anxiety which knows so much about sex but seems to have lost its faith in its own future, the men and women who seek love in T. S. Elliot's poem *Wasteland* are ridiculed and rejected. In his *Cocktail Party* love is described as "the noise of an insect, dry, endless, meaningless" and the "aftermath of love is tedium not the residue of ecstasy." When there is confidence that life itself has meaning and purpose, love between a man and a woman can be experienced as something more than mere detached sex.

A happy marriage requires that the husband and the wife believe that each has a future as a man and as a woman. Marriage between a man and a woman sexually in love with each other is a commitment to this belief. Such a marriage is fulfilled by children whom one should bring into the world not as an accident but as a sign of their own hope in tomorrow. This requires courage and "the bravest are the tenderest, the loving are the daring." The indispensability of tender love is the struggle to overcome the destructive forces in our day, and the role that sex plays in such love, is the theme of *Lady Chatterly's Lover*. While frustrated, prurient adolescents of whatever age thumb through its pages for what they foolishly think are pornographic delights, Lawrence's novel is a book with a serious message.

Prophetically, Lawrence has his man tell the woman that because they must realistically face the world, including the possible doom of the human race, he must offer her in their proposed marriage something more than his body. He says: "A man must offer a woman some meaning in life if she is a genuine woman. I just can't be your male concubine and just give you a child. Bad times are coming, but all the bad times that ever have been haven't been able to blow the crocus out, so long as we have each other . . . Our crying need is a bit of delicacy; a bit of tenderness, to come into tender touch with another without losing pride, dignity and integrity."

JUDAISM ON LOVE AND MARRIAGE

Judaism believes that a man and a woman must give each other tenderness of love, which alone can make sex meaningful. Judaism has such a high regard for the love of a man and a woman for each other that to describe their sexual relations the Bible uses the Hebrew word *yadah,* which means "to know" her. Accordingly, the Jewish idea of sexual love in marriage is not the abuse of, but the understanding of the total emotional needs of the other person for the sake of the maturity and stability of both.

To help young Jewish men and women understand this magnificent and healthy normal Jewish point of view about sex and love, modern rabbis receive some training in the field of counseling young people before marriage. Some rabbis will not perform a wedding ceremony without such a pre-marital conference.

Leaders of the Jewish faith believe, too, that the religious convictions of the mates are of considerable importance in the stability and health of a marriage. We know from studies that there are more unsuccessful marriages between those who leave their religion and intermarry, than in marriages within a faith. We also know from a very extensive study of the American home by Professor Terman that those families are the most unstable where religion is too strict, or where there is no religion at all. Those homes are the most stable where the father and mother join with their children in an intelligent, adventurous approach to religion.

Just being a Jew by name or birth—or a Christian for the same reasons—does not help to give one a religious philosophy of life. We mean not philosophy in general but a religious philosophy, which guides one toward meaning and purpose in life. When there is a feeling and understanding of this kind, there is greater likelihood that a person will be able to respond to love and marriage as a total being. When husband and wife can share such an outlook they can surely enjoy sex as an expression of their life together, rather than as a random physical encounter.

Our rabbis point out that the first four of the Ten Commandments deal with the belief in God and the last six speak of respect for man. The fifth, which calls for honoring one's parents, is the one that joins the first four with the last six. It was assigned that particular place, say the rabbis, because it is in the home that one learns to have a healthy attitude toward God and toward men. The home must have it in the first place, and that is why it is so important for the mates to see eye to eye religiously. Without a faith that God meant people to have confidence in themselves and in a future that they can help make, there will be little honor in any home.

The prophets of Israel compared the love of God for His people to marriage and they did so purposely. It was not only because they regarded marriage as a sacred relationship, but also because they wanted to teach our people that because of God's love, God wanted man to live and not die. This is a teaching that can still give heart today, in this Atomic Age of uncertainty and foreboding.

The family in Judaism has always been the heart of the faith. It is still the best place for making a human being out of an infant. The kind of human being it produces is, of course, the most important thing. The home can acquit itself honorably if it can instill within the children an acceptance of themselves as individuals with a touch of the sacred. The Jewish family today can still play the great role it did in the past, but only if the father and mother accept their lives as having meaning within the traditions of Judaism. Children growing up in such families could more readily develop the kind of maturity that would make marriage for them a union of two beings helping each other to find joy and fulfillment.

SUGGESTED READINGS

SIX WHO CHANGED THE WORLD, *Henry E. Kagan,* Thomas Yoseloff.

MARRIAGE AND THE JEWISH TRADITION, *Stanley R. Brav,* Philosophical Library.

MARRIAGE LAWS IN THE BIBLE AND TALMUD, *Louis M. Epstein,* Bloch Publishing Company.

HEBREW MARRIAGE: A SOCIOLOGICAL STUDY, *David R. Mace,* Philosophical Library.

SEX AND FAMILY IN THE BIBLE, *Raphael Patai,* Doubleday.

LIFE IS WITH PEOPLE, *Mark Zborowski* and *Elizabeth Herzog,* International University Press.

JUDAISM AND CHRISTIANITY:
Points of Contact and Conflict

by Arthur Gilbert

ARTHUR GILBERT: Staff Consultant and Director of Religious Freedom and Public Affairs of the National Conference of Christians and Jews; a graduate of N. Y. U., he was ordained at J.I.R. in 1955; has lectured widely and is author of **MEET THE AMERICAN PLURALISM,** and contributor of articles and essays to many publications.

DURING the dark days of 1938 when Nazi brutality threatened European Jewry and all of the world as well, Pope Pius XI, spiritual leader of Catholics, interrupted his reading from a prayerbook. A passage in the missal asked God to accept the prayers of the Catholics with the same delight with which He once accepted Abraham's willingness to sacrifice his son Isaac. The Pope declared to the Belgian pilgrims who had brought him the prayerbook: "Mark you, we call Abraham our father, our ancestor. Antisemitism is incompatible with the sublime thought and reality expressed in the text . . . through Christ and in Christ we are of the spiritual lineage of Abraham. Spiritually we are Semites."

By that declaration the Pope was suggesting that Christians are one in spirit with Jews, and that Christians were once all Jews. Jesus was Jewish, as were his mother and father and his earliest followers.

The teachings of Jesus draw upon and reflect his Jewish education. Christianity thinks of itself as sharing the promises God made to the people of Israel through the patriarchs Abraham, Isaac and Jacob, and through Moses and the prophets. The Jewish Bible is accepted as part of the Christian Bible. The psalms of the Jewish Bible are a major part of Christian prayer services. Many of the customs of Judaism are incorporated in Christian ritual.

The earliest Christians were all Jews. They observed Jewish holidays and made annual pilgrimages to the Temple in Jerusalem. They read and studied the *Torah* and the words of the prophets. They had their sons

239

circumcised, observed the Sabbath and ate food listed
as *kosher* in the *Torah*. But there was one important
difference: They believed that Jesus (in Hebrew: Joshua
or Jeshua) of Nazareth was the Messiah long promised
by the prophets.

A JEWISH CONCEPTION OF THE MESSIAH

According to traditional Jewish belief, God will some
day appoint a redeemer, a Messiah (in the Hebrew:
Moshiach, anointed one) who will restore the Hebrew
people to national independence, and bring men and
nations to recognize that the God of Abraham is Lord
over all the earth; then all men will live in tranquility
and God's law of justice will prevail. They believed then,
as some Jews still believe, that in the time of the Messiah
all the dead will be raised up to a restored life in order
to stand judgment before God, and that those whom God
favors will spend Eternity in the joy of God's Presence.

Such beliefs in an extraordinary change of circumstances once the Messiah appeared gave Jews hope and
courage during the period of the Roman occupation of
their country, for their lives were otherwise quite grim.

Even before the Roman conquest of Jerusalem in 63
B.C.E., the Jews of Judea had endured much suffering.
Their own Hebrew rulers, John Hyrcanus and his son
Aristobulus, had acted like oriental despots, and the people
led by Pharisee rabbis had rebelled against them. Civil
war had raged before the coming of the Romans, and
with them came plunder and more bloodshed. It is
estimated that about 100,000 Jews were killed in the
quarter century after Pompey took Jerusalem, and no
one knows how many were sold into slavery.

From about the year 6 C.E., Rome ruled Judea through
Roman procurators, who taxed the people grievously.
One of the most insenstitve and greedy of the procurators
was Pontius Pilate, in whose administration Jesus was
sentenced to death. Pilate, like other Roman rulers,
understood correctly that the Jewish concept of the

Messiah included the idea that the hated Roman rule
would be overthrown upon the coming of the *Moshiach*.
This explains why Pontius Pilate, along with the Sadducees and the corrupt Jewish priesthood who depended
upon the Roman governor for their power and wealth,
were alarmed at the claim made in the name of Jesus
that he was the Messiah or the King of the Jews.

THE MINISTRY OF JESUS

Jesus, as the Christian texts record, was deeply influenced by a zealous, ascetic preacher called John the
Baptist, whose style of living in the desert recalled that
of the prophet Elijah. Tradition had it that Elijah would
appear on earth to announce the coming of the Messiah,
and some Jews believed that John, who spoke eloquently
about the kingdom of heaven being near, was fulfilling
Elijah's role.

After the death of John, some of the disciples of Jesus
became convinced that great cataclysmic events were
about to take place. They began to regard the young
teacher from Galilee as the promised redeemer.

Jesus was a forceful and persuasive personality, and in
those dark and troubled days hundreds of Jews gathered
about him seeking inspiration and hope. He himself
evidently believed that God's Kingdom was soon to
appear, and in his teaching Jesus set the religious ideals
of Judaism above all other considerations. He called on
men to forsake their families if necessary, and to distribute all of their possessions to the poor as a way
of preparing themselves for God's imminent salvation.
Jesus called on his followers to love the enemy, return
good for evil, forego violence and to be pure in thought
as well as deed.

It happens that the teachings of Jesus were well within
the spirit of Judaism. Other Jewish teachers of the time
taught similar doctrines, especially members of the Jewish sect called the Essenes. There were Pharisee rabbis,
too, who urged the people to return to the traditional

prophetic ideals of Judaism. But in some matters Jesus did come into conflict with *some* of the Jewish religious leaders, and with the Roman authorities as well.

He often stated his interpretations of the Law as if his saying it made it so. But in Judaism no rabbi has the power to claim authority for a religious law simply because he thought it valid. There was a procedure in those days by which the requirements of the faith were defined and enacted. But we learn from the Gospels that Jesus frequently said to his followers, "Verily I say unto you," when he taught them the meaning of Judaism, an attitude that led some Jews to believe he was operating outside the established pattern. Even more irritating was the suggestion that Jesus was God-incarnate, that is, God become man. In Jewish tradition such a claim is a blasphemy, for we do not believe that a man can become God, or that God would become a man. The *Moshiach* in Jewish belief is to be a human leader.

The claim of Jesus and his disciples that he was the "Christ" (the Greek translation of the Hebrew word *Moshiach*) created trouble for him with the Roman procurator too, since this implied that Jesus was to be the King of the Jews, a redeemer and a savior of the nation. Credence was lent to that claim by an act of sensational boldness on the part of Jesus when he came to Jerusalem for the Passover: his driving the traders out of the Temple court and personally overturning the tables of the money-changers. Passover brought tremendous numbers of Jews to Jerusalem and the Roman procurator and his henchmen among the priests became worried over the stir and excitement that Jesus's acts engendered. Pontius Pilate evidently feared a possible outbreak of rebellion and ordered the "troublesome" Jewish leader to be arrested and executed in the usual Roman manner of being nailed to a crossbeam, with a sign over him mocking him as the "King of the Jews."

The death of Jesus caused a crisis among the followers of the Nazarene, for in Jewish tradition the coming of the Messiah was to change the circumstances of the national life in significant ways. But Roman rule went on, peace and brotherly love were only words, and the poor remained in poverty. Nevertheless, some Jews remained convinced that Jesus was the Christ. Trusting that he would soon appear again, they maintained their lives as Jews in close fellowship. They met regularly for prayer and instituted a special ritual meal for the first day of the week, Sunday, for according to their belief it was on that day that the resurrection of Jesus took place.

THE SEPARATION OF CHURCH AND SYNAGOGUE

It was chiefly through the organizational genius and missionary zeal of Saul of Tarsus, a Jew who had become convinced of the Messiahship of Jesus, that the Jewish Nazarenes became a separate church. Saul, better known by his Greek name Paul, had been one of the Jews who persecuted and harassed the Nazarene sect; but as a result of a sudden overwhelming vision Paul had accepted the crucified Jesus, and devoted the rest of a creative life to the spreading of the Gospel, that is, the "good tidings" that Jesus was the Messiah.

There was opposition to the Nazarenes within the Jewish community from the very start, but the hostility grew in intensity when the followers of Jesus began to accept converts among the gentiles and Samaritans without obliging them to obey Jewish religious law. One of these new converts, Stephen, was stoned to death after he had provocatively preached blasphemous sermons within the synagogue, thus becoming one of the first martyrs in the history of Jewish-Christian conflict. Paul himself recounted in his Epistles that he received lashes from Jews on five occasions, that he was beaten three times and stoned once, for preaching his doctrines in the synagogues and gathering places of the Jews.

To many Jews these doctrines were a departure from the norm of Jewish belief and practice of those days. Paul, finding himself repulsed by the Jews, began to concentrate on the conversion of the gentiles; however, what he offered them was a new religion, a faith based on belief in the crucified and resurrected Christ.

The New Testament, especially in the book "Acts of the Apostles," records a bitter quarrel between the leaders of the Nazarenes in Jerusalem and Paul over the idea that converts were required to be circumcised and to follow other laws set down by Moses. A compromise was reached finally that Jewish converts to the Nazarene sect were expected to observe Jewish practices, particularly circumcision and the dietary laws, while the converts among the gentiles were to be free of such obligations.

With the destruction of Jerusalem in 70 C.E. and the increased dispersion of the Jewish people, the gentiles in the new sect gained clear predominance. And Paul developed a theology that justified their independence from the synagogue.

He taught that Jesus had fulfilled Jewish law. Men were required now only to believe in Jesus. In fact, Paul asserted that the *Torah,* Jewish law, was no longer capable of assuring man's redemption from sinfulness, that only faith in Jesus achieved the Grace of God. God had made a new covenant with mankind through Jesus and Paul asserted that those who accepted the "New Testament" became the "New Israel," the chosen people of God. Paul believed that at some future time the people from whom Jesus descended, that is, the Jewish people themselves, would accept Jesus as the Christ.

In order to counter the claim of the Jews that the crucified Jesus could not have been the Messiah, the gentile Christians reinterpreted the traditional Hebraic understanding of the mission of the Messiah; they adopted instead the Greek notion of salvation, that is, that the Christ would save men from the instincts and inclinations of the flesh that lead to sin. Furthermore, Christians were assured that just as Jesus had conquered death through the resurrection, so the believer would obtain immortality. Finally, in some future time, Jesus would reappear and Life Eternal would be given to those who had faith in him.

The Christians established a calendar of their own holidays based upon events in the life of Jesus: December 25, a date made official in the 4th century, commemorated his birth; New Year's Day, his circumcision; Lent, his temptation in the wilderness; Good Friday, his crucifixion; and Easter, his resurrection. The break with the synagogue became even more evident when the New Testament was added to the *Tanach* (the Jewish Scriptures) to make up the Christian Bible. And a church organization based upon patterns established and authorized by Jesus was instituted in the new religion. It included a priesthood and bishops, and by the 3rd century the Bishop of Rome became the head of the church and was called Pope (from the Greek word *Pappas* and the Latin *Papa,* meaning father).

CHRISTIANITY BECOMES AN OFFICIAL RELIGION

For the first centuries of its existence the church was barely tolerated in the Roman world and frequently persecuted. But Emperor Constantine, about 312 C.E. embraced Christianity and gave it a preferred position in the empire, and in 380, Theodosius I named Christianity as the official religion of the Roman Empire.

During this period the leaders of the Church met in various ecumenical councils in order to formulate basic doctrine and establish authoritative organizational patterns. The bishops claimed for their Church that it was the living body of Christ in the world, and assigned to the Church a divinity and an authority quite in contrast to the synagogue, which is considered by Jews to be only another human agency in the continuous effort of man to know God and to serve Him.

Armed with the support of the state, the Church then engaged in a serious effort to unify all men within one faith, to root out heretics and to curb other competing faiths. The Jewish religion was particularly suppressed, since the refusal of the Jews to accept a savior, who had been one of them, was particularly embarrassing. The

early missionaries found it embarrassing, also, to teach
that Jewish prophets had foretold the coming of Jesus,
who was Jewish in all respects, when the vast majority
of the Jews did not recognize him as the Messiah. Furthermore, the Jews kept insisting that only they were Israel
and that the Church had distorted the religion of Judaism
which had been established by the God of Abraham.
Finally, the Jews were also active and effective as missionaries. The pious nature of their lives, their love of learning, their commitment to justice, the purity of their family
devotion were making a deep impression upon the bar-
baric gentile world.

The earliest church regulations, therefore, were intended to put an end to conversion to Judaism, and to
forbid Christians from engaging in any kind of social or
business relationship with the Jews. At the very first ecumenical council Emperor Constantine called upon Christians: "Henceforth let us have nothing in common with
this odious people. . . . Our Savior has shown us another
path."

Later church regulations and teachings of church fathers
were intended to place Jews in a position of contempt.
Basic Christian concepts were distorted as a conscious
effort was made to inflame Christians and gentiles with an
attitude of abhorrence toward the Jews. They were considered a people rejected by God because, according to the
Gospels, they had called for the crucifying of Christ. By
this act of deicide they had become accursed, and were to
wander the face of the earth, homeless and friendless, a
pariah people. Judaism was caricatured as a religion of
legalism and hypocrisy.

Church-wide sanction was given to several degrading
measures against the Jews at the Fourth Lateran Council
of the Church in 1215. These included an annual tax Jews
were to pay the Church and a requirement that Jews from
twelve years of age wear a badge distinguishing them
from Christians. In Germany Jews had to wear a pointed
hat, in Hungary a red cloth in the shape of a wheel, in
England fringes of two colors, in Italy a yellow hat, in

Spain Jewish males were prohibited from shaving their beards or cutting their hair.

In most Christian lands Jews were forced to live in ghettos or restricted quarters, were denied permission to build new synagogues, made to attend sermons on Christianity, and were refused the opportunity to enroll at a university, or own land, or obtain membership in a guild, which was required for work at a skilled craft in those days.

The animosity toward Jews and Judaism, planted so earnestly over the years, reaped ugly harvests during the Crusades when about 10,000 Jews were killed as enemies of the Church. And in many countries Jews were banished and forced to leave, often with little more than they could carry. Fortunately, not all rulers or bishops were harsh and violent toward the Jews under their jurisdiction. In fact several popes issued decrees intended to give the Jews protection, especially from enforced conversion. But it is only too true that for 1,500 years the Jewish lot was a most unhappy one in Christian Europe.

"If I had been a Jew and seen such blockheads and locusts ruling and teaching Christianity, I would have become a swine rather than a Christian, because they have treated Jews like dogs and not like human beings." This is how Martin Luther wrote when he hoped that the Jews would convert to the new form of Christianity that he had helped to develop. When they did not, however, he was as vociferous in his denunciation of the Jews "and their lies" as he was earlier in defending them. "I say to you lastly as countrymen, if the Jews refuse to be converted, we ought not suffer them or bear with them any longer." Thereafter, animosity and discrimination against the Jews continued, with but few exceptions, as the general policy in Protestant as well as Catholic Europe.

THE EMERGENCE OF LIBERALISM

With the arrival of the 18th century there emerged liberal voices who suggested that differences in religion

ought not to be the basis for civil disabilities. They urged
that all Jews be given freedom in economic and professional life, and unrestricted educational opportunities, for
then all society would benefit. But, unfortunately, most
Christian leaders continued to fear that political reform
would weaken the "Christian" character of the state.

Only revolution of enormous proportion could over-
throw this alliance of the clergy, the economically powerful, the politically conservative and the prejudiced faithful who intended to keep the Jews "in their place." The
French Revolution loosened this alliance and laid the
groundwork for Jewish emancipation. In 1790 and 1791
the Jews of France were granted the right to citizenship;
and in Italy, Germany, Holland, Spain, wherever the
French revolutionary forces carried their flag, Jews were
emancipated from the ghetto and given legal equality.

The powerful and the entrenched of medieval days
did not give up so easily. After the defeat of France in
1815, the reactionaries came back to power and the Jews
found themselves again the objects of persecution and discrimination. In Italy, Pope Pius VII restricted Jews to the
ghetto; and he permitted coercive missionary enterprises.
In Spain, the Inquisition was renewed; Germany reim-
posed medieval disabilities upon the Jews, and they were
expelled from Lubeck and Bremen, and from the faculty
of the newly established University of Berlin.

The situation in Eastern Europe continued to be bad
for Jews, since the liberating ideas of the French Revolution did not make much of a dent in that part of Europe.
Attacks, ghetto restrictions and pogroms remained the
order of the day for a longer period than in Western
Europe.

Not only the Jews, but the common folk of Europe
suffered from the stern rule of reactionaries and soon the
"liberals" made themselves felt and heard again. Revolutions and new political parties emphasized civil rights
and liberal democracy as the aim of the people of Europe.
The Jews were generally found in those parties and
movements that backed freedom of religion and equality

of rights and opportunities, and they shared in the victories that were won by the liberal forces.

THE SITUATION OF THE JEWS IN AMERICA

The largest migration of Jews to the United States came in times of great Jewish oppression in Europe. The first Jewish settlers of 1654 were refugees from the Inquisition in Brazil, the second wave came from Germany between 1815 and 1850, during the emergence of Jew-hatred as a reaction to the liberal reforms introduced in the country as a result of the French Revolution. The largest immigration came from Eastern Europe in the period from 1870-1910, when persecution of Jews was practically government policy there.

From the very beginning Jews found in this new land a greater measure of economic and social opportunity than they had ever experienced before. The frontiers were wide open and man was free to carve out his own destiny; nevertheless, the securing of complete religious and political freedom in the United States had to be fought for. The earliest settlers of colonial times brought with them European patterns of church-state establishment. The favorite church or churches were supported by public funds, church morality and practice was enforced by the civil magistrate, and the members of minority religious groups were restricted in their freedom.

Thus, in North Carolina, as late as 1808, an attempt was made to unseat a Jew who had been elected to the General Assembly. In Maryland it was not until 1828 that the State Constitution was changed to permit non-Christians to hold public office. And in 1860 there was an outcry in the Christian press when a rabbi was permitted for the first time to offer an invocation at the beginning of a session of Congress.

Antisemitism still exists in this country. It is an important part of the hate literature distributed wherever Negroes have engaged in any effort to achieve human dignity. As in Europe of old, any liberal effort to achieve

freedom is branded a "Jewish conspiracy," and Jew
hatred is evoked by those who would maintain status
quo patterns of discrimination.

A NEW TREND IN JEWISH-CHRISTIAN RELATIONS

Since World War II, especially in this country and in
Europe, a completely new revolutionary trend in Jewish-
Christian relations has become evident. Just as the French
Revolution brought with it political freedom for the
Jew, so the tragedy of the Hitler period and the later
development of the State of Israel, have overturned
all traditional Christian teachings concerning the Jews.

Meeting shortly after World War II in Amsterdam,
Protestant leaders confessed through their World Council
of Churches, "We must acknowledge in all humility that
too often we have failed to manifest Christian love toward
our Jewish neighbors or even a resolute will for common
social justice. We have failed to fight with all our
strength the age-old disorder of man which antisemitism
represents. The churches in the past have helped to foster
an image of the Jews as the sole enemy of Christ which
has contributed to antisemitism in the secular world. In
many lands virulent antisemitism still threatens and in
other lands the Jews are subjected to many indignities.
We call upon all churches we represent to denounce
antisemitism, no matter what its origin, as absolutely irre-
concilable with the profession and practice of the Christian faith. Antisemitism is a sin against God and man."

At its third assembly in New Delhi in 1961 the World
Council of Churches added to this statement this specific
recommendation: "The assembly urges its member
churches to do all in their power to resist every form of
antisemitism. In Christian teaching the historic events
which led to the crucifixion should not be so presented as
to fasten upon the Jewish people of today responsibilities
which belonged to 'corpus humanity' and not to one race
or community."

Recently, a world-wide Lutheran meeting called to

consider the relation of the church to the Jews, asserted: "Christian antisemitism is spiritual suicide. The phenomenon represents a unique question to the Christian church, especially in light of the long and terrible history of Christian culpability for antisemitism. No Christian can exempt himself from involvement in this guilt. As Lutherans we confess our own peculiar guilt and will amend with shame the responsibility which our church and her people bear for this sin. We can only ask God's pardon and that of the Jewish people." Then the church called upon its constituency "to examine their publications for possible antisemitic references and to remove and oppose false generalizations about Jews."

Similarly, Catholic scholars have begun to document how German bishops by their silence contributed to the Nazi murder of Jews. Now the Church, through an historic worldwide ecumenical council, has officially reconsidered its teaching on the Jews, its attitude toward antisemitism and the role of Church and State in a puralistic society.

The late Pope John XXIII, besides convening Vatican Council II, also ordered the revision of Catholic liturgy that contained words and expressions offensive to the Jews.

Here in America both Catholic and Protestant educators have reviewed their religious school texts and are now rewriting them so as to assure a greater measure of understanding of Jews and Judaism. Any reference to Jews having to suffer as a consequence of the crucifixion of Jesus is to be excised; for Church teaching is that Christ was killed by the sinfulness in the hearts of *all* men, and he is continually crucified when men harbor hatred against their brothers. Antisemitism is a sin against God and man, therefore, and cannot be countenanced by the Church.

The churches have come to recognize that they can no longer employ coercive measures to achieve the conversion of men. This violates the teaching of Christianity that God desires only that obedience which is freely given from the heart. Thus church officials in recent years have issued decrees acknowledging the importance of religious freedom for all men, and the right of man in good conscience to choose his own way in service of God.

Finally, church leaders have come to realize that if they are to overcome the scandal of Christian disunity, they must stop quarreling with each other and begin listening to each other. The ecumenical movement which has emerged in recent years acknowledges that some measure of God's truth is nurtured and maintained within other churches, and that Christians are called upon to engage in dialogue with each other in order to appreciate that which God may be saying to all men through differing religious groups.

This constructive attitude in the relations between Protestants, Eastern Orthodox and Catholics, is to be seen as operative also in the new relations between Jews and Christians. Christians are appreciating now, as they once did of old, that God had revealed Himself first to Abraham and through His people elect, the Children of Israel. Although the Jews suffered much in history, this was occasioned by their faithfulness to God, a suffering brought upon them cruelly by Christians and Gentiles. Church leaders have therefore issued calls for study and conversation with the Jews for the purpose of achieving mutual understanding and esteem. They wish to understand better that truth which is of the Jews.

This is not to assert that there are no problems or difficulties in the relation between Jews and Christians. There is still antisemitism to be found among some church leaders. There are many in the Church, in one country or another, who have not yet recognized the significance of the separation of church and state, nor the importance of religious freedom for all men, nor the vital contribution that Jews in their Judaism have to make to the religious vitality of our civilization.

Yet, so radical has been the change in attitude within world Christendom that many Jews, on their part, have now become willing for the first time in history to engage in religious conversation with Christians without fear or anxiety. And as a result one can expect that Jews will attain to a deeper understanding of the meaning of the Christian faith for the Christian, and a truer awareness of how much it is that Jews and Christians share together.

Despite this new rapprochement, Jews and Christians will continue to remain in disagreement over the basic Christian claim that Jesus is the Christ. As part of the Hebraic Biblical tradition, Jews and Christians nevertheless share certain values and ideals together. These ought to influence our social outlook and our political judgments and lead us to work together in order to achieve human freedom for all men, economic security for the needy, and the guaranty of peace. In working for such purposes, Jews and Christians will not only fulfill God's will upon earth, but rediscover each other as brothers.

SUGGESTED READINGS

THE ANGUISH OF THE JEWS, *Edward H. Flannery,* The Macmillan Company.

THE TEACHING OF CONTEMPT: Christian Roots of Anti-Semitism, *Jules Isaac,* Holt, Rinehart and Winston.

WE JEWS AND JESUS, *Samuel Sandmel,* Oxford University Press.

THE HISTORY OF THE JEWS, *Solomon Grayzel,* Jewish Publication Society.

ANTISEMITISM IN PERSPECTIVE

by Oscar Cohen

OSCAR COHEN: National program director of the Anti-Defamation League of B'nai B'rith; graduate of the University of Toronto; editor of the **FREEDOM PAMPHLET SERIES** and the **ONE NATION LIBRARY;** has lectured widely and has written for many publications, including chapters for **SOCIAL PROBLEMS IN AMERICA** by Alfred M. Lee, and **THE NEGRO CHALLENGE TO THE BUSINESS COMMUNITY** by Eli Ginzberg.

WEBSTER'S International Unabridged Dictionary defines antisemitism as "opposition to, hatred of, or agitation against Jews." But it is hard to say when antisemitism as an historical act or movement began, for not every action against Jews can be referred to as antisemitic. When the patriarch Abraham, for instance, as the head of a fairly large tribe of Hebrews, fought against neighboring nomadic sheiks, the feelings that were aroused then about the Jews stemmed naturally from the conflict. We would not label those enemies of Abraham "antisemitic."

While students in the field disagree as to when antisemitism actually began, there is little difference of opinion as to the incidence of antisemitic outbursts in ancient times. In pre-Christian days the Jews served as an outlet for all kinds of pent-up angers and frustrations because they were different by virtue of their ethical monotheism from their pagan contemporaries. In the time of Christian ascendancy in western civilization, the Jews were once again in the minority, and were attacked for religious or economic and political purposes.

THE RISE OF CHRISTIAN ANTISEMITISM

The antisemitism that arose in Christian times was the most lasting and pervasive in the long history of the Jews. Early Christian antisemitism developed as Christianity changed from a sect within Judaism to a separate and competing religion outside it. The writings of the early Church fathers contain many instances of antisemitic sentiments. The charge of deicide was born then and became a primary source of antisemitism. The Jews suffered increasing re-

strictions on their opportunities to make a living, and faced
personal abuse, attacks and on occasion forced baptism.

The year 1096, the beginning of the First Crusade, was
the start of a series of massacres perpetrated by the Cru-
saders upon the Jews while on their way to capture Jerusalem from the pagans. "We desire to combat the enemies
of God in the East," they are quoted as saying, "but we
have under our eyes the Jews, a race more inimical to God
than all the others. We are doing this whole thing back-
wards." And on this premise they killed those Jews who
would not accept baptism, they burned synagogues and
destroyed *Torah* scrolls.

As "enemies of God" the Jews were accused of many
"crimes"—they were ritual murderers who used the blood
of Christians for the baking of *matzot,* they were poisoners
of the wells in the time of the Black Plague, they were
defilers of the holy wafers—a host of preposterous accusations that were nevertheless believed by the masses. And
how were they to know, when respectable people, even
men of the cloth, made these accusations? The result of
teaching that the Jews were deicides and enemies of Christianity, and of incessant agitation against them, was that
entire communities were burned, a great deal of Jewish
property was confiscated or destroyed, many Jews were
banished, some were massacred, and some were offered
their lives if they accepted baptism.

By the beginning of the 18th century a degree of enlightenment began to permeate the European communities.
With it came a loosening of restrictions against the Jewish
population. And although "incidents" and pogroms continued to take place, there was the other side of the coin—
greater mobility and choice of occupation, fewer wholesale
expulsions. But violent antisemitic acts still occurred.

The history of Europe is a record filled with antisemitic
restrictions, oppressions and attacks. Immigrants from that
continent to the United States brought with them the seeds
of anti-Jewish prejudice. In the United States, however,
different conditions altered and reshaped European customs and beliefs, including antisemitic attitudes.

THE COURSE OF ANTISEMITISM IN AMERICA

Most Americans fail to understand the nature, extent and inherent danger of anti-Jewish prejudice and discrimination in America. Research indicates that a significant proportion of the American population harbors unfriendly attitudes toward the Jew. Most of these people are shocked when violent anti-Jewish acts occur and they do not relate their own prejudices to these outrageous actions. Desecrations and violent acts are only symptomatic of less obvious widespread prejudices which provide a favorable climate for extremists. The crackpots, professional antisemites, and vandals in revolt against authority do not represent the greatest danger for Jews and for democracy in America. Property damage, violence and bodily harm are, of course, a grave menace and should be regarded with utmost gravity—but these are not the most damaging acts. Violent acts arouse one's anger, and synagogue desecrations bring expressions of outrage. However, it is the polite variety of antisemitism which is not only far more prevalent, but far more dangerous.

While antisemitic acts of discrimination have been part of the American scene for many years, this fact does not necessarily indicate that anti-Jewish feelings are more intense in this country than in others. Attitudes are difficult to measure, but overt acts and discriminatory practices are more readily evident. The noted Harvard psychologist, Dr. Gordon Allport, points out most cogently that "Prejudice, if not *acted out,* if kept to oneself, does no great social harm." But, as Dr. Allport indicates, prejudice can lead to action and always presents a potential menace.

It should be pointed out, too, and this may seem paradoxical, that in no other country have Jews been able to make greater economic and cultural contributions to society. The rewards which our country offers for enterprise and education, the mobility and opportunities America provides, make it possible for Jews in this country to rise to great heights in many avenues of endeavor. Yet, despite these great advances in the United States, restrictions against Jews are still comparable to, and in many cases higher than is the case in other democratic nations. Whatever the reasons for the phenomenon of anti-Jewish discrimination in America, the fact remains that in this country discriminatory practices against Jews exist on a large scale.

Up to the time of the Civil War, extensive antisemitism was not experienced by Jews in this country. A number of individual instances of prejudice and discrimination stand out in the pre-Civil War period, but there was little of the systematic restrictive practices which came into being as the century drew to a close. Jews, in this early period, did have to struggle to achieve the right to hold public office, for the argument was made that no one who was not a Christian could take a Christian oath of office. In 1850 the *New York Herald* featured a front-page story of alleged ritual murders by Jews in the Near East. Such a story by a reputable newspaper, unthinkable as it is today, is perhaps indicative of the nature of antisemitism prior to the Civil War, when it was chiefly religious in character rather than economic and social.

Antisemitism in its present form began to take shape in the 1870's. At that time Jews, numbering a quarter of a million, had already begun to achieve economic success. In addition, they were thrusting their way upward socially at a time when social status was of significant concern. In commenting on this phenomenon in our history, John Higham states that "If American society had kept its old openness, group discrimination might not have accompanied the new stereotype, at least as quickly as it did. But during the Gilded Age a general struggle for place and privilege upset the pattern of urban life. . . . At every level so many successful people clamored for admission to more prestigious circles that social climbing ceased to be a simple and modest expectation; it became a genuine social problem." Dr. Higham goes on to point out that "Practically, antisemitic discriminations offered another means of stabilizing the social ladder, while, psychologically, a society vexed by its own assertiveness gave a general problem an ethnic focus. . . . The evidence suggests that insecure social climbers rather than relatively more secure patricians first resorted to this means of reducing competition."

It is generally assumed that antisemitic social discrimination began with the well-known incident in which Joseph Seligman, a distinguished leader of commerce, was excluded from the Grand Union Hotel in Saratoga in 1877. Actually, resort hotel discrimination had been well under way before this time. As an indication of the manner in which exclusionary practices were developing, several years before the Seligman incident a New York National Guard Regiment decided to exclude Jews from membership. The restrictive movement spread to resorts, clubs, private schools, residential areas, colleges, and fraternities and sororities. Again to quote Dr. Higham: "The social life of many eastern private colleges fell in line, as the sons and daughters of East European Jews enrolled in large numbers and quickly demonstrated their intellectual prowess. They arrived at a bad time. An all-absorbing, extra-curricular life of sport and snobbery was overrunning the campuses at the turn of the century, making hard study and good grades unfashionable and creating an intricate status system dominated by the Ivy League. After 1900, extremely few Jews were elected to the Princeton clubs or to fraternities at Yale or elsewhere. The literary and gymnastic societies at Columbia kept Jews entirely out, and at Harvard one of the best college dormitories suffered a serious decline in reputation because a good number of Jews lived there."

Also of significance is the antisemitic tinge to some aspects of the Populist movement. This movement was basically anti-urban and Jews were identified with urban life. Today there are few evidences of political antisemitism. When candidates have run for office in recent times on an antisemitic platform, they have been overwhelmingly defeated at the polls. This is not to say that antisemitism has not existed in political movements, particularly right-wing extremism. Rather, public expressions of antisemitism have become largely unacceptable and politically unprofitable since the Nazi extermination of millions of Jews.

It is evident that immigration "waves" have had a great deal to do with the development of prejudice against Jews. Other groups, Irish, Italian, German, Scandinavian, also experienced opposition when they came to this country. Although employment discrimination made its appearance at a later date than social barriers, by World War I patterns of anti-Jewish discrimination in America had already been molded. Thus, antisemitism in America was nurtured because of conditions peculiar to this country. While much of the basic spirit of antisemitism was inherited from Europe, its characteristics were substantially different in this country. In Europe, it traditionally had a religious basis, and was often politically organized. In the United States, antisemitism has resulted from religious influences, or from social and economic causes. Political antisemitism has never been an enduring factor in American life. Perhaps the closest we have ever come to national political antisemitism was our experience with the anti-immigration movements in the 1920's, out of which grew the quota laws specifically discriminating, at least in part, against Jews.

CONTEMPORARY PATTERNS OF ANTISEMITISM

Antisemitism was absorbed into our culture many years ago. Antisemitism became institutionalized at a time when public opinion was less enlightened about, less sensitive to, the nature of anti-democratic practices than is the case today. Such institutions, once accepted by society, tend to linger on long after public support for them has diminished or disappeared.

Here are some examples of contemporary antisemitism which grew out of early patterns of anti-Jewish discrimination:

• John Dean, in a study made over a decade ago, recorded

discrimination against Jews in 248 cities of from 10,000 to 500,000 population. Dr. Dean proposed three tests for acceptance of Jews: Junior League membership; country and city club membership; availability of homes in exclusive residential areas. In one-third of the cities, all three were denied to Jews; 20 cities accepted Jews in all three (mainly smaller cities) and more than one-half of the largest cities denied all three. Only in one larger city were Jews acceptable in the three areas.

- A survey by the Anti-Defamation League of B'nai B'rith in 1957 indicated that one out of every four resort hotels in this country discriminated against Jews. This situation has changed radically, largely because of antidiscrimination laws and educational efforts on the part of such agencies as the League. We cite this survey to indicate the serious restrictions which existed against Jews just a few years ago.

- In a number of industries there is widespread discrimination against employment of Jews. A recent study of employment practices of insurance companies by the ADL indicates a concentration of Jewish executives in sales departments rather than in home offices.

- A study of executive and white collar personnel of the major automobile corporations revealed that little more than one half of one per cent of these employees were Jewish. The *Harvard Business Review* of March-April, 1965, estimated that less than one per cent of executive personnel in heavy industry are Jews.

- In the area of housing, an ADL survey indicated that our nation is dotted by innumerable islands of anti-Jewish housing bias. Recent studies in the Chicago area indicated that in 12 suburbs the percentage of homes not available to Jews for sale or rent ranged from four per cent to sixty per cent. Frequently the real estate agent is a major force behind the establishment of a restrictive community. Repeatedly, agents, brokers and salesmen have told prospective Jewish purchasers that they are

ANTISEMITISM IN PERSPECTIVE

not opposed to selling to Jews, but that the people in the neighborhood would not stand for it.

• Some national fraternal and civic groups permit local units to make decisions about membership qualifications, and in many communities these organizations do not admit Jewish members. Similarly, purely local clubs discriminate against Jews, although this situation varies from place to place. There is no systematic pattern; practice apparently depends upon historic precedent in the community concerned.

• Despite the fact that discriminatory clauses have disappeared from constitutions the *practice* of exclusion in fraternities and sororities still remains widespread.

• Within the area of private and social clubs, discrimination is at its highest. It is safe to say that in most communities of America there is at least one club of some kind which does not, as a matter of policy, admit any Jews regardless of how distinguished they may be.

• Wherever antisemitism reveals itself, the "professional" bigot is always prepared to cater to its whims for, over the years, he has found the monetary rewards for promoting prejudicial stereotypes quite gratifying. Insofar as the public records reveal, the most successful operator of an antisemitic organization grosses in the vicinity of $200,000 a year. At the present time there are a few dozen professional antisemitic organizations, excluding the various Ku Klux Klan groups.

The fortunes of the Klan have fluctuated and they now seem to be enjoying an upswing. There are five or six major Klan organizations with a hard-core membership of 10,000. In addition, there are perhaps 25,000 to 35,000 sympathizers who are involved in Klan type groups. It should be borne in mind that the Klan, as distinguished from antisemitic organizations, directs a large portion of its venom at the Negro and the Catholic.

The list of overtly antisemitic organizations does not include such groups as the Organization of Arab Students and the Arab Office of Information. It would be misleading, however, to ignore these groups in surveying the picture of organized antisemitism, since by their activities they have unquestionably stimulated antisemitism in the United States.

Perhaps the nature of discrimination, and the lingering character of stereotyped conceptions, is best illustrated by the story told by a college professor who was giving a series of lectures at a university to executives employed by a large industrial concern, all of whom were in the $15,000 to $25,000 salary class. At one point he said to the group, "I don't know for sure of course, but I assume there are no Jews present in this class. I wonder why?"

There was a silence for a while and then one of the men in the class spoke up and stated, "Well, you wouldn't expect Jews in our occupation, there isn't enough money in it for them." The professor responded, "I assume, then, that that is why there is such a large proportion of Jewish professors on this campus."

It has not been the professional bigots or vandals who have established these stereotypes in our nation. The people who deliberately participate in or acquiesce to antisemitic practices, which are part of our culture, are the real culprits. They are the ones who help to create and maintain the climate of discrimination. They may not desecrate buildings, but they demean the opportunities and dignity of a group in our society.

THE SITUATION IN THE SOUTH

Antisemitism in the South, in light of the current upheaval there, deserves a special note. One sociologist has remarked that the Jew is resented for almost the same reasons as Yankees are resented by Southerners. In the eyes of many Southerners, Yankees are allegedly sharp and keen business people, they are all out for education of their children, they are clannish and so forth.

Nevertheless, the South has almost always been hospitable to the Jew, particularly so before the Civil War.

This war marked a turning point after which, for the first time, antisemitism became a significant factor in the life of Southern Jewry. Prior to it, the Jew was not only accepted in Southern society, but he was favored. True, there were instances of hostility, but these were exceptions rather than the rule. In 1733, for example, Governor Oglethorpe of Georgia opposed the settlement of Jews in that state. Georgians, however, welcomed the Jews, who stayed there and prospered.

Harvey Wish, in his study *Society and Thought in Early America* states that "the antebellum South displayed marked hospitality toward Jews." Indeed, it is remarkable that the relatively small number of Jews in the South held so many high offices—the Quartermaster General and the Surgeon General of the Confederate Army were Jews, as was the Secretary of State of the Confederacy.

Except for a few, Jews in the South were largely in favor of slavery or at least played no significant role in the Abolitionist movement. Despite this, historians indicate a significant rise of antisemitism during and after the Civil War, especially as the fortunes of the South deteriorated. There are historical parallels between the rise of antisemitism in the South and mounting hostility toward Jews in other times and places. It is evident from even a casual analysis of history that in times of great social crisis, antisemitism tends to increase.

It is not surprising, therefore, that we find increased expression of antisemitism in those areas of the South where deep crises are today being experienced. Research in such areas as Clinton, Tennessee; Beaumont, Texas; Tallahassee, Florida; and Charlottesville and Norfolk, Virginia, would appear to support the hypothesis that a rise in community tensions is accompanied by an increase in prejudice against the Jews. The tension situations in Alabama and Mississippi have been frequently accompanied by the distribution of anti-Jewish literature by extremist anti-Negro groups.

THE IMPACT OF CUSTOM AND RELIGION

Much could be written about the psychological causes of American antisemitism. However, we believe that much more important than theories of the totalitarian personality or of frustration-aggression, is the manner in which American society has accepted and retained antisemitism. Many Americans go along with anti-Jewish prejudices because it is part of their social environment. They may not agree with the mores of their community or reference groups, but they tend to conform. Comparatively few people are inclined to be pioneers.

The ADL surveyed one discriminatory housing development in the Detroit area and another in the Washington, D.C. area, and found almost identical results. The real estate agents stated that people in these areas would not tolerate Jewish neighbors. However, a survey showed that at least two-thirds of the people questioned had no objection to Jewish neighbors and a substantial number thought it would be desirable to have Jews living in the area. This is an example of the way in which positive attitudes are curbed by custom.

However, one must not overlook the fact that there has been a great reduction in discrimination in the last fifteen years. College entrance discrimination is largely nonexistent. Areas of employment once barred to Jews, such as the field of engineering, are wide open today. The problem today is not so much at the hiring gate as it is in advancement to executive positions.

There seems also to be reasonable evidence pointing to a betterment of attitudes toward Jews, as well as a lowering of barriers against them. While there is little scientific evidence available on which to base conclusions about attitude changes over the years, there is in progress at the University of California a five-year study of American antisemitism, from preliminary findings of which we can get some insights into the extent and nature of this problem.

One finding that emerges from these preliminary data indicates wide acceptance of unfriendly attitudes toward Jews. The study is uncovering a noteworthy lack of contact between Jews and Christians. Three-quarters of the Christians in America have not had a Jewish neighbor or contact with Jews in clubs and organizations. More than half have had no contact with Jews at work or in business. On the other hand, more than 80 per cent said it would make no difference to them if they had Jewish neighbors. And there are other encouraging indicators.

Another aspect of the study which demands attention is the role of religion in the development of anti-Jewish beliefs. The widespread belief that Jews are guilty in greater or lesser degree of the charge of deicide predisposes Christians to hold negative feelings about Jews. A significant number of Christians believe that "the reason the Jews have so much trouble is because God is punishing them for rejecting Jesus." In other words, these people believe that the persecutions of Jews have divine approval. Religiously based antisemitism will evidently require much more attention than has been given this problem in the past. The University of California study will perhaps focus attention on the unspectacular, non-violent kind of anti-Jewishness which always represents a danger, particularly in times of crisis.

In 1960 a wave of swastika smearings and other acts of vandalism of an anti-Jewish nature swept across the country. In an eight-week period over 700 incidents were reported. Public opinion was shocked at the time, and it seems that the desecrations were widely accepted as the most significant manifestation of antisemitism, rather than as the symptom of a more malignant disease. The problem we face is not the catching and punishing of the swastika painters and vandals, although this is also necessary. The problem is to root out, to expose and to educate the polite bigots. The enemy is complacency on the part of people, a lack of knowledge of the problem, and the hesitancy people have to stand up and oppose that which is indecent and immoral. These tendencies have to be combatted if we are to make greater progress in the struggle against antisemitism.

A number of years ago, H. A. Overstreet wrote in the *Saturday Review of Literature* that "it is the mild and gentle people of prejudice, with their compulsive effortlessness, who must bear the burden of the moral guilt. They have given the green light, and the legion of low hostilities has broken through on the run." The main problem stems not from those who carry out actions against the Jews, but from those who acquiesce to them. The bystanders are not innocent.

There could be no more appropriate way to conclude this brief account of American antisemitism than to quote these eloquent words of Dr. Overstreet:

"He who permits evil commits evil. This is what makes for the haunting sense of guilt in our culture. Many a member of the dominant group will earnestly aver that *he* never intended it that Negroes should be insulted and maltreated on buses, on railroad stations, and on public streets; that *he* never intended it that the Mexican-Americans should be brutally beaten up; that *his* heart is sore and ashamed when he reads of the defiling of Jewish synagogues by hoodlums. He did not intend these things. *But he created the social sanction for these things.* By adopting a twisted principle of human association he and the people like him opened the Pandora's box out of which have flown the intolerances and cruelties that have defiled our culture."

SUGGESTED READINGS

THE ANGUISH OF THE JEWS, *Edward H. Flannery,* The Macmillan Company.

ANTI-SEMITISM IN THE GILDED AGE: A Reinterpretation, *John Higham,* Anti-Defamation League.

AN ENEMY OF THE PEOPLE: Anti-Semitism, *James W. Parkes,* Penguin Books.

JEWS IN SUBURBIA: Tension and Unrest, *Albert I. Gordon,* Anti-Defamation League.

SOME OF MY BEST FRIENDS, *Benjamin R. Epstein* and *Arnold Forster,* Farrar, Strauss and Cudahy.

INTERMARRIAGE AND THE JEWISH FUTURE

by Marshall Sklare

MARSHALL SKLARE: Director, division of scientific research of the American Jewish Committee; lecturer, School of Social Work, Yeshiva University; he received his M.A. from the University of Chicago, and his Ph.D. from Columbia University; author of **CONSERVATIVE JUDAISM: AN AMERICAN RELIGIOUS MOVEMENT** and editor of **THE JEWS: SOCIAL PATTERNS OF AN AMERICAN GROUP.**

AMERICAN Jews have always had a reputation for resisting intermarriage, and they still serve as a model in this respect for other ethnic and religious groups who worry about their future in a pluralist society. Just as the Jewish alcoholic or juvenile delinquent is thought to be a rare exception, so the Jewish son who brings home a Gentile bride is generally considered a "sport." Within the Jewish community itself the danger of intermarriage is always felt to be there, of course, but the prevailing attitude—even among those who are knowledgeable about Jewish matters or professionally concerned with Jewish welfare—is that the threat of the problem has been surprisingly well contained in America.

The earliest study of intermarriage was Julius Drachsler's *Democracy and Assimiliation,* which received a good deal of attention at the time of its publication in 1920. On the basis of an examination of about 100,000 marriage licenses issued in New York City between 1908 and 1912, Drachsler found that of all white groups in the city, the Jews were least prone to marry outsiders. The Jewish intermarriage rate of 1.17 per cent was scarcely higher than that of interracial marriages among Negroes, and Drachsler bracketed the two together as a "low-ratio group," as opposed to the "middle-ratio" groups (Italians and Irish) and the "high-ratio" groups (English, Germans, Swedes, and others).

A second investigation that was influential in confirming the Jewish reputation for endogamy was conducted in New Haven by Ruby Jo Reeves Kennedy. Published in the *American Journal of Sociology* in 1944 (a follow-up article appeared in 1952), the Kennedy study was to reach a wide audience through Will Herberg's extensive use of it in *Protestant-Catholic-Jew*. Kennedy's conclusions were in close keeping with those of Drachsler. She found that for all the years investigated—1870, 1900, 1930, and 1940 —Jews had the lowest intermarriage rate in the city. The Italians were the only ethnic group which approached them in endogamy, and even their rate of intermarriage was several times higher.

All this must have seemed impressive evidence to the leaders of the Jewish community, just as it did—and does —to the scholars themselves. For example, the most recent sociological investigation of American-Jewish life, C. B. Sherman's *The Jew within American Society,* continues to take a highly optimistic view of the intermarriage problem. Comparing newer statistics with those collected by Drachsler, Sherman remarks that "considering the degree of acculturation to which the Jewish community has attained during the period, the surprise is not that the increase has been so big, but that it has been so small." Much the same point is made by Nathan Glazer and Daniel P. Moynihan in *Beyond the Melting Pot.* Commenting on the Kennedy study, the authors note that the persisting pattern of endogamy "sharply distinguishes the Jews of the United States from those of other countries in which Jews have achieved wealth and social position, such as Holland, Germany, Austria, and Hungary in the twenties. There the intermarriage rates were phenomenally high." (According to the statistics of Arthur Ruppin, these rates were as high as 20 and 30 per cent).

EARLY STUDIES LEAD TO COMPLACENCY

But even more influential, perhaps, than the Drachsler and Kennedy studies in establishing the Jewish reputation for continued endogamy was a report by the Bureau of the Census based on its Current Population Survey of March 1957 that only 7.2 per cent of the husbands or wives of Jews were of a different faith. The comparable figure for Protestants was 8.6 per cent, and for Catholics it was 21.6 per cent.

These statistics gave many people within the Jewish community reason to believe that the Jews were still doing quite well: after all, the Catholics, who had made a much more conscious effort than Jews to foster separatism, were faced with an intermarriage rate that was almost three times as high. Moreover, the Jewish rate was all the more heartening in view of the absolute size of the group and the insignificant percentage it comprised of the population as a whole. In his annual review of demographic data in the 1959 *American Jewish Year Book,* Alvin Chenkin, statistician for the Council of Jewish Federations and Welfare Funds, described 7.2 as a "nominal" percentage; if marital selection had taken place entirely at random, Chenkin pointed out, the Jewish intermarriage rate would have approached 98 per cent.

However, almost everyone who had cited the figure has failed to heed the Bureau's *caveat* that its statistics on intermarriage were probably subject to a larger margin of error than would result from normal sampling variation. (In an unusual aside, the Bureau noted that while it had told its personnel not to assume the same religion for all members of a given family and directed them to ask about each adult member of a household separately, some interviewers might have overlooked this instruction).

Other implications of the 7.2 per cent figure have also been ignored. No one has bothered to relate it, for instance, to the well-known fact that considerably more Jewish men intermarry than do Jewish women (at least seven out of every ten Jews who intermarry are men), so that as a consequence some Jewish women must either marry Gentiles or remain single. Spinsterhood does not, to be sure, affect the intermarriage rate, but it does influence another crucial demographic factor: the birth-rate.

However, the most crucial point which has been generally overlooked in evaluating the 7.2 figure is that it represented the *ratio* of intermarried to inmarried couples and not the *current* rate of intermarriage among Jews. The statistic, in other words, was cumulative—included were people who had taken their vows in Czarist Russia where intermarriage was forbidden, as well as people who had married in the United States; people belonging to the virtually closed community of the immigrant generation, as well as people living in the wide world of the fourth generation. The *current* rate, then, may well be at least double that of the Bureau's cumulative ratio. And even the cumulative ratio is bound to soar in the decades ahead with the thinning-out of the ranks of those who are presently keeping it down—first-and second-generation Jews.

In short, the grounds for the American Jewish community's optimism are by no means as firm as they have been assumed to be by laymen and sociologists alike. Interestingly enough, the present state of Jewish endoagmy seems to have been grasped more firmly by the novelists than by the sociologists. Even a hasty run-down of the work of such writers as Bernard Malamud, Saul Bellow, Philip Roth, Leslie Fiedler, Bruce Jay Friedman, Herbert Gold, Jack Ludwig, Myron Kaufmann, Neal Oxenhandler, etc., reveals how much recent American fiction has dealt with marriage or the strong possibility of it between a Jew and a Gentile.

CURRENT STATISTICS CAUSE CONCERN

Within the organized Jewish community itself, the publication in the 1963 edition of the *American Jewish Year Book* of Erich Rosenthal's article "Studies of Jewish Intermarriage in the United States," is one of the first signs that this community may at last be preparing to recognize that a problem does exist. Another work published at the same time—*Intermarriage and Jewish Life* edited by Werner J. Cahnman—consists of papers read at a conference organized by the Herzl Institute and is the first book on the subject sponsored by any American Jewish organization.

In his pioneering study, Rosenthal provides a sophisticated analysis of statistical data concerning intermarriage in the state of Iowa and in the city of Washington, D.C. According to Rosenthal's findings, during the years 1953-59, only 57.8 per cent of the marriage licenses applied for by Jews in Iowa *listed both applicants* as Jewish. Religion, then, still plays a role in the marital choices of Iowa Jews —42.2 per cent, after all, represents a far smaller inter-marriage rate than would be produced by randomization. Nevertheless, as Rosenthal suggests, unless the figure drops sharply in the future, the final chapter in the history of Iowa's Jewish community will have been reached by the end of this century.

Of course, the current situation in Des Moines, Daven-port, and other Iowa communities is not an accurate re-flection of what is happening in the major cities and their suburbs, where the great majority of American Jews still live. But at the very least this section of Rosenthal's study does point up the fact that the problem is most critical where the Jewish population is small both in absolute and relative terms. Moreover, in the other section of his study, Rosenthal reminds us that even in a middle-sized Jewish community like that of Washington, D.C. (with 81,000 members it ranks as the seventh largest Jewish community in the nation), the cumulative ratio is now almost twice the Census Bureau's figure. It was found that in 13.1 per cent of the households including a married Jew, either the husband or wife was Gentile. This per-centage is probably somewhat higher than the average for middle-sized Jewish communities—Washington's Jews not being known for the intensity of their Jewish com-mitment. But that does not really modify the import of the figure, particularly since there is reason to believe that the current rate of intermarriage in Washington substan-tially exceeds 13.1 per cent. Rosenthal himself does not offer a current rate, but he does provide tabulations on the rate for successive generations: 1.4 per cent for the first generation; 10.2 per cent for the second; and 17.9 per cent for the third. Since it can be assumed that the great majority of Washington's Jews who are now marrying belong to the third generation, the 17.9 figure is probably very close to the current rate.

SOME CAUSES OF INTERMARRIAGE

Besides offering a sharp corrective to Jewish complacency about the rate of intermarriage today, these statistics provide an occasion for calling into question a good many dated notions about the psychological and social conditions under which intermarriage now takes place. One traditional view, for example, holds that the Jew who marries a Gentile often does so to escape the social disabilities of being Jewish (the prototype here is someone like August Belmont). Though this motive was no doubt decisive in the marital choices of a fair number of mobile, *nouveaux riches,* or socially ambitious Jews of an earlier period, it seems to have much less force in the present age when many traditional status distinctions are being swept away and the old-time social arbiters are becoming increasingly ineffective. And as the hospital boards, country clubs, suburbs, and corporations that were once the exclusive preserve of the Protestant upper class become more democratic in their admission policies, we can expect that this reason for intermarriage will become even less significant.

Along with the habit of interpreting intermarriage as a form of status-seeking, there is still a tendency to view it as a form of escape from the burdens of Jewishness and the harassments of antisemitism—as, in short, the most effective method of assimilation. This explanation, too, undoubtedly had some relevance at an earlier period in American Jewish history (though never nearly as much as it did among European Jewry), but it is increasingly beside the point at a time when the penalties and risks of being Jewish are obviously on the wane. Indeed, if intermarriage were a response to the threat of antisemitism, particularly in a state as remote from the scenes and memories of Jewish persecution as Iowa is, there should currently be less, rather than more, of it.

Other standard explanations of intermarriage take psychological rather than social factors as the governing ones, finding the source of the impulse to intermarriage not in the confrontation of the Jew with the Gentile society, but in the early relationship between parent and child. Serious conflicts at this stage—so the notion goes—will be expressed later on in the attempt by the child to avoid a marital pattern similar to that of his parents. In its more simplistic form, this theory holds that marriage to an outsider is a gesture of hostility toward the parents, the point being to rob them of the pleasure they would obtain from a "suitable" match, shame them before relatives and friends, and deprive them finally of the consolation of Jewish grandchildren. The more complex form of the same theory regards intermarriage as part of a syndrome of general revolt from the mores and aspirations of the parents, often manifesting itself in bohemianism, political radicalism, or other types of identification with socially alienated and/or dissident groups.

But were this theory particularly pertinent, one would expect Jewish-Gentile marriages to be most prevalent in the second generation, where the trauma of acculturation was most decisively experienced and the generational conflict was at its most intense. However, intermarriage rates, as we have already noted, are clearly higher in the third generation; and in addition, as we shall soon see, Jewish-Gentile marriages are particularly prevalent among certain Jewish groups who are very much at home in the culture.

At best, the existence of a correlation between childhood conflicts and marital choices is easier to assume than it is to demonstrate. In analyzing the data on intermarriage contained in the recent "Midtown Manhattan Study" the sociologist Jerold Heiss began with the standard idea that those whose early family life showed marked signs of disruption or had otherwise been unsatisfactory would be more likely to intermarry than those with relatively stable childhoods. But he discovered that this idea could not be sustained. The family backgrounds of the exogamous Jews in the study were not exceptional in terms of conflict, and actually showed fewer cases of parental divorce, separation, and desertion than did the backgrounds of the endogamous Jews surveyed.

The few studies and essays allowing one to draw certain limited inferences about the personal motives and social context that foster exogamy happen to involve professional groups—mainly in the academy—which are marginal to the community life of American Jewry. Therefore, one cannot regard these findings as telling us anything definitive about the "typical" behavior of American Jews who choose to marry outside the faith. On the other hand, there is good reason not to discount them altogether, since most of the people concerned are Jews who grew up in metropolitan Jewish communities, who lead fairly conventional lives, and who practice highly respected professions.

According to a recent study conducted by Rabbi Henry Cohen, approximately 20 per cent of the Jewish faculty members at the University of Illinois—well over twice the national average—are married to Gentile women. This is a significant figure because Illinois has a reputation for academic and social conservatism, being neither particularly adventurous in its curriculum nor particularly "highbrow" in its faculty. We can therefore assume that the pattern here is more typical than it would be at experimental colleges like Antioch or Reed, or fashionable universities like Yale or Chicago. There is also a comparatively large Jewish student body on the Illinois campus; in contrast to a college such as Swarthmore, for example—which has been described as an "intermarriage mill"—the University of Illinois is a favorite choice of Midwestern parents eager to avoid this peril. (In fact, it was on the Illinois campus that America's first Hillel Foundation was established some forty years ago).

The Jewish population of Champaign-Urbana numbers about 250 families, which are almost equally divided be-

tween town and gown. One of Rabbi Cohen's most suggestive findings on intermarriage was the unexpected disparity between the 20 per cent ratio for the faculty members and a 6.5 per cent ratio for the Jewish townspeople.
The contrast between town and gown is even more striking in view of the respective family backgrounds of both
groups, which, if anything, would have led one to expect
their respective intermarriage rates to be reversed. Most
of the Jewish faculty members (chiefly mathematicians,
physicists, psychologists, and sociologists) arrived in
Champaign-Urbana during the last few years; they are
mainly sons of East European immigrants and grew up in
predominantly Jewish neighborhoods; almost all described
their parents as affiliated with either Orthodox or Conservative synagogues. The townspeople, on the other hand
—chiefly manufacturers, wholesalers, retailers, and professionals—include a group descended from "old" German-Jewish families who are firmly rooted in the community and whose predominant background is Reform.

What lies behind the disparity in the intermarriage rates
of these two groups? Rabbi Cohen points out that many of
the Jewish teachers and researchers at the University of
Illinois (and presumably the overwhelmingly majority
of the intermarried couples) hold to a point of view—
"Academic Commitment" he calls it—which fulfills a
function analogous to that of religious faith:

> How many more aspects of religious faith and fel-
> lowship we find in the Academic Commitment! There
> is the dominant philosophy of naturalism. Its method
> is scientific; its faith, that all being can be explained in
> terms of a single order of efficient causation in which
> a supernatural Deity has no place; its **morality**, the
> ideals of humanism rooted in infinite human experi-
> ence; its messianic hope, that man—through under-
> standing the consequences of his actions—can build
> a better world.

As against the case of the Gentile society of Champaign-
Urbana, there are a number of Gentile academicians on the

Illinois campus who do not consider affiliation with a religious institution to be a necessary sign of respectability. Furthermore, Jewish life in Champaign-Urbana—ethnic, religious, or cultural—depends largely on the town community, most of whose members are attached in one way or another to Jewish organizations. The academicians, on the other hand, range, according to Rabbi Cohen, from "the strongly identified who are trying to preserve Jewish culture in a Midwestern cornfield (to) the cosmopolite who feels that there are enough barriers between people . . . without the clannishness of the Jews." Once the memories of Jewish culture become vague, he writes, the town Jew can still find reasons to remain within the fold: he retains a latent supernatural faith, and the larger community expects him to be Jewish. By contrast, once the faculty Jew ceases to find meaning in the ethnic fellowship or the folkways, he has neither traditional belief nor strong social pressure to help him maintain his commitment.

If intermarriage among academicians on a campus as conservative as the University of Illinois is so high, it should not surprise us that there are cities with larger and more active Jewish communities where intermarriage rates among special segments of the Jewish population are even higher. New Haven is a good example. Champaign-Urbana has many Jewish physicians, but New Haven also has a fairly substantial group of psychoanalysts. In a study which appeared several years ago under the title *Social Class and Mental Illness: A Community Study,* A. B. Hollingshead and Frederic C. Redlich studied the therapists as well as the patients. They found that 83 per cent of New Haven analysts "came from Jewish homes," and of these some 64 per cent were intermarried. This startling figure exceeds even the current level of the geographically isolated Jewish community of Iowa, and is, of course, many times higher than the general rate in New Haven itself.

In our context, perhaps the most interesting fact to emerge from the New Haven study is that apart from marital choice and the lack of religious affiliation, the analysts do not appear to be alienated in any profound sense from the culture in which they live. Far from exhibiting any left-wing political beliefs and sympathies, they tend toward the attitudes of the old-fashioned American who started from humble beginnings and achieved success as a result of hard work. Living in the best residential areas of New Haven, enjoying high incomes which they have earned (unlike many Protestants in the same area) "largely through their own efforts and abilities," their individual social mobility has been such that 73 per cent of them have won a higher station in life than their fathers, 79 per cent have surpassed their brothers-in-law, and 83 per cent have outdistanced their brothers.

Their essential conformity to middle-class ideals is nowhere better shown than in their attitude to their children's education. While denying any desire to impose their own values upon their offspring, their typical response to the question "How much education do you want for your children?" was: "As much as they want; college is the minimum." On the whole, they have no contact with Jewish life, yet as Hollingshead and Redlich put it: "Doubt and confusion is apparent in their response on how they would like to have their children trained religiously." Presumably the rate of intermarriage among the children of these analysts will be very high, although the children's motives will obviously be different from those which led their fathers to intermarry. But even where both parents are Jewish, there will no doubt be a high rate of intermarriage among the children in this group.

CHANGING ATTITUDES TOWARD INTERMARRIAGE

Thus far we have concentrated on the behavior of the Jew in relation to intermarriage, but perhaps the newest factor in the situation is the change in the position of the Gentile. It becomes evident that intermarriage is increasing not only because the Jew is moving out into the general society, but also because the tastes, ideas, cultural preferences, and life-styles preferred by many Jews are more and more coming to be shared by non-Jews. In the Herzl Institute volume referred to above, this process is commented upon by Richard Rubenstein, a well-known Hillel rabbi currently at the University of Pittsburgh. As Rubenstein sees it, in the course of "emancipating" themselves, many of the bright middle-class Gentile girls who attend the better colleges are attracted by the political liberalism characteristic of Jewish students or by their equally characteristic avant-gardism in intellectual and aesthetic matters. To the allure of the "Jewish" cultural style is added the fact that Jews are in, but still not completely of, the society. In other words, where Jewish alienation used to inhibit contact with Gentiles (several decades ago, the heavily Jewish radical movements on the college campuses experienced considerable difficulty in appealing to the rest of the student body), it now operates in a subtle way to foster them. For, as Rabbi Rubenstein says, it is precisely this delicate balance between acceptance and marginality which is sought after by girls who do not want Bohemian husbands but rather respectable ones who are somewhat "different." In addition, the marked rise in egalitarianism on the college campuses following World War II has done much to promote a climate in which dating, and in some cases marrying, outside one's social group is no longer regarded as deviant behavior, and on the more "advanced" campuses even confers some degree of status. And finally, these changes in the social atmosphere of the college community run parallel to developments in the occupational world, for to a greater extent than ever before, Jews are now working with Gentiles as colleagues instead of serving them as merchants or free professionals.

What all this suggests is that the old notions about the causes of intermarriage are beginning to look as outmoded as the causes themselves. Both on the folk level and in more sophisticated terms, these notions invariably involved the imputation of some defect in the contracting parties. If a Gentile girl agreed to marry a Jew, it must be because no Christian would have her, or because she had made herself sexually available as no Jewish girl would deign to do. Similarly, if a Jewish man married a Gentile girl, it must be because no Jewish girl would have him, or because he was a self-hater or a social climber. Whatever their applicability to individual cases, it takes no great insight to realize that approaches like these—which stress the deviancy and inferiority of the person who intermarries—serve the dual function of reinforcing the practice of endogamy and allaying fears about the threat of intermarriage. By impugning the motives of exogamous Jews, or by attributing them to dark forces outside the Jewish community, the challenge that intermarriage poses to the prevailing values of the group is vanquished—at least for the moment. The difficulty, however, is that these assumptions of pathology—social or personal—no longer explain either the rate or the reasons for exogamy among Jews. This is not to say that intermarriage can already be considered a routine phenomenon and that the motives which impel Jews to choose Gentile mates are basically no different from those which lead them to marry Jews. Nevertheless, from the evidence that has begun to accumulate, it is becoming impossible to view intermarriage as an indication either of personal aberration or of social persecution. In a recent study of middle-class intermarried couples residing in the Boston area, Maria and Daniel Levinson conclude that:

> *intermarriage is not . . . a unitary phenomenon. It occurs under a variety of psychological and social conditions and has varying consequences. Psychologically it is not purely a neurotic manifestation, although neurotic motives may enter to varying degrees. Nor is it to be seen solely as an "escape" from the Jewish group or as a means of securing social or financial gain, although motives of this kind play a part in some cases.*

Heiss's analysis of the Midtown Study supports this conclusion. Surveying the mental-health rating assigned each

respondent by a board of psychiatrists, he found that there
was no significant difference between the mean rating
achieved by those who had intermarried and those who
had not.

THE DILEMMA OF JEWISH PARENTS

It is precisely the "healthy" modern intermarriages
which raise the most troubling questions of all to the
Jewish community in general, and Jewish parents in particular. When his child intermarries, the Jewish parent
guiltily feels that in some way he must be responsible. Yet
how is he to oppose the match? Chances are that he believes that love is the basis of marriage, that marriage is
the uniting of two individuals rather than two families,
and that the final determinaiton of a mate is his child's
prerogative. This complex of ideas (which constitutes a
radical departure from the norm, if not always the practice, of traditional Jewish society) came to be embraced
by some of the more advanced members of the first generation in America, by a majority of the second generation,
and by an overwhelming proportion of the third. How
then can the parent ask his child to renounce what he himself believes in? Moreover, the liberalism of the Jewish
parent—his commitment to the idea of equality and his
belief in the transitory character of the differences which
distinguish people from one another—serves to subvert
his sense of moral rectitude in opposing intermarriage.
For if he is at all in the habit of personal candor, he must
ask himself if the Gentile is any less worthy of the Jew
than the Jew is of the Gentile.

The second-generation parent or adviser usually man-
ages to escape this dilemma by falling back on the argument of happiness. Experience, he will say, is the best
teacher, and what it teaches is that intermarriage seldom
works out well. And he will cite figures to show that exogamous couples have higher divorce rates than those who
marry within the fold. Thus the need to confront the pain-

ful contradictions in his own position is evaded, and he can oppose his child's intermarriage with a good conscience.

In the writings of such founding fathers of the contemporary American Jewish community as Isaac Mayer Wise or Solomon Schechter, the asumption is that Jewish survival is entirely possible in a free society. But having finally established themselves in such a society, Jews are now coming to realize that their survival is still threatened— not by Gentile hostility but by Jewish indifference. This is what finally makes intermarriage so bitter a dilemma to confront. On the one hand, it signifies the fulfillment of the Jews' demand for acceptance as an individual—a demand he has been making since the Emancipation; on the other hand, it signifies a weakening of Jewish commitment. In short, it casts into doubt American Jewry's dual ideal of full participation in the society and the preservation of Jewish identity. And once the rate of intermarriage is seen to be growing, the contradiction in the basic strategy of American-Jewish adjustment is nakedly exposed.

A more realistic confrontation is necessary, and that requires a much larger body of research than we now possess on the current rate of intermarriage in the country as a whole. It also requires much more information about the Jews who intermarry and about the causes and consequences of their doing so. So, too, there is a need for studies to evaluate the various methods in use to combat intermarriage, particularly those involving Jewish education. And demographic research will have to be done at regular intervals so that a reliable trend line can be established.

A candid and pertinent discussion of intermarriage will also require a more critical examination of Jewish attitudes than we have had in the past. One immediately thinks of the issue of conversion, which many Jews seem to regard as a token, last-gap measure in a developing process of assimilation; but is it? There is also the obvious, but usually ignored, problem of birth-rate. One reason why a rising rate of intermarriage is of such pressing significance is that the birth-rate of native-born Jews has been so low. If a greater proportion of second-generation Jewish parents had permitted themselves to have even three children rather than one or two, the present situation would be far more hopeful so far as Jewish survival is concerned. But the fact is that the fertility rate of the second generation dropped catastrophically, and with hardly a word of discussion about it among Jewish leaders. Reform and Conservative rabbis decided, for all practical purposes, to exempt the question of contraception from the area of the sacred, implying that a decision about family size was of strictly private concern. Orthodox spokesmen were not prepared to go this far in the direction of secularization, but they preferred to concentrate on other issues such as maintaining the practice of *kashrut*.

The threat posed by intermarriage may change all this, and there is a possibility that it will also change the way most Jews think about their Jewish responsibilities. Typically, the American-Jewish notion has been that to be a good Jew means doing something for some other Jew; it means, in short, philanthropy. As the problem of intermarriage grows in urgency, however, the Jewish community in America will for the first time have to face an issue which is highly personal—almost anti-philanthropic—in character. And if the emphasis on philanthropic activism has allowed American Jews to avoid confronting the stark question: "What do you stand for when you wish to remain separate?"—the defense against intermarriage will necessarily involve a coming to terms, sooner or later, with what one is defending.

As the evidence accumulates that Jewish survival in America literally depends upon each individual Jew—and in an entirely different way than it did in the past—the answer to the question, "What do you stand for when you remain separate?" may well demand the development of a new consciousness in the community. This will not be the first time in history that social conditions have impelled a people to philosophical discussion and involvement. If the problem of intermarriage should engender such a consciousness—the kind which has been foreign to the activism of American Jewry—it will have had a positive effect on the quality of Jewish life. If it does not, the negative consequences are indeed ominous to contemplate.

SUGGESTED READINGS

INTERMARRIAGE AND JEWISH LIFE, edited by *Werner J. Cahnman*, Herzl Press.

INTERMARRIAGE: INTERFAITH, INTERRACIAL, INTER-ETHNIC, *Albert I. Gordon*, Beacon Press.

INTERMARRIAGE AND THE FUTURE OF THE AMERICAN JEW, proceedings of a conference sponsored by the Commission of Synagogue Relations, The Federation of Jewish Philanthropies of New York.

JEWISH-GENTILE COURTSHIPS, *John E. Mayer*, Free Press.

BEING A JEW IN AMERICA

by Leon A. Jick

LEON A. JICK: Rabbi, Free Synagogue of Westchester, Mount Vernon, N. Y.; is a graduate of Washington University, with an M.H.L. from the H.U.C. in Cincinnati; his collection of sermons **A PAST FOR THE PRESENT—A PRESENT FOR THE FUTURE** was distributed by National Jewish Welfare Board to all Jewish Chaplains in the Armed Forces; has lectured at M.I.T., Bates University and other universities.

"AMERICA is different!" This has been the conviction of American immigrants from the Pilgrim fathers to the present day.

The experience of each successive wave of new arrivals has provided confirmation. Immigrants may have experienced discrimination and hardships in the new land, but they also found an open society and ample opportunity for advancement. In America there was no rigid "class system" and no "established church." Indeed, there was not even a clearly dominant majority group.

Religious worship was free and the nation as a whole was made up of a host of religious, ethnic and racial minorities. And as America continued to grow and develop, more and more groups were accepted into the "mix" that made up the emerging American nation.

Small wonder that Jewish immigrants plunged so eagerly into the life of America, and made such a phenomenally rapid adjustment. Unlike many other immigrant groups, Jews had come to America to stay. They had little nostalgia for the lands they had left, and the promise of American life gave even the most impoverished a vision of a more secure and prosperous future.

In addition, Jews possessed a tradition which stressed education and family solidarity. They began at once to avail themselves of the educational opportunities offered by the public schools and by city and state universities. Jewish parents labored diligently to give their children opportunities they themselves lacked. Helpful in the process of adjustment, also, were Jewish religious traditions which stressed discipline and individuality, and the Jewish historic experience which developed self reliance and business skills. These enabled Jews to make the most of the economic opportunities around them. In a relatively

short time, Jews had risen in economic, education and social position far more rapidly than was the norm, even in
America. Poverty, foreignness, exclusion, vanished like
the morning mist. American Jews belonged.

AFFLUENCE AND SURVIVAL

By the beginning of the 1960's the American Jewish
community had become the largest, most affluent, most
influential, Jewry in all history. Yet at the very height of
its strength and achievement, alarms have been raised
concerning its future. A popular magazine speaks of "The
Vanishing American Jew," and Jewish publications echo
the concern.

Thoughtful men and women wonder to what extent this
concern is justified. Is there reason to fear for the future
of Jewish life in America? If there is, it is not the result
of antisemitism or hostility. In free and prosperous America, the danger is not external pressure.

American Jews, like other minority groups, have learned
that America makes room for the survival of many diverse
groups. In fact this very diversity is a part of the greatness
of America. More than 40 years ago Louis Brandeis, who
later became the first Jewish Supreme Court Justice, explained that multiple loyalties are desirable as long as they
do not conflict with each other. A man who is a good citizen of his city and state and is loyal to his family and
school, is a better citizen of his country. In the same way
he added, a Jew who participates in Jewish causes becomes
a better American.

This view was widely accepted by almost all groups in
America. Social scientists called it "cultural pluralism."
The growing strength and creativity of America made it
clear that this nation could achieve unity without exacting
the price of uniformity.

The cultural heritage which diverse immigrant groups
brought to these shores contributed to the richness of
America. Thus far at least, America has not become a
"melting pot" into which all groups disappear and lose

their identity. It is better compared to an "orchestra" in which distinctive religious and ethnic groups make their own unique and recognizable contribution to the total harmony.

This does not mean that the expressions of Judaism have not changed in the American setting. American Jewish life reflects the American environment just as the Jewries of Eastern Europe, Spain, Babylonia and every other Jewish center were influenced by their surroundings. Many of the "folk" aspects of Jewish life which arose when Jews lived in autonomous, self-contained communities have disappeared; the Yiddish language and Yiddish culture have, be it said sadly, declined in importance. At the same time, new forms have appeared: the Jewish religious heritage has revitalized itself through Reform, Conservative and modern Orthodox Judaism. Clearly the Jewish group has established its place in the American setting. Judaism and America are not only compatible, they are congenial.

IS THERE A WILL TO PRESERVE JUDAISM?

The question which faces the new generation of American Jews is not: Is it possible for Judaism to survive in America? Of course it can.

The question is: Will young Jews want to preserve it? Will they have the commitment to Judaism and the determination to preserve Jewish values and assure creative survival in a free society? This is the issue which is in doubt. There is a growing conviction that only if young American Jews possess Jewish knowledge, only if they know what the Jewish tradition is and what the Jewish world view offers to enrich human life, only then will they have the necessary commitment and determination.

We need not look to the long and rich past for evidence of the strength which Judaism gives to those who hold fast to it. The achievements of the American Jewish Community itself provide the most obvious evidence of the power of the Jewish tradition.

In America, the percentage of Jews attending college is

three times as great as that in the general population. Jews
who constitute 3 per cent of the population, buy one third
of the books. Large numbers of Jews are distinguished
authors, dramatists, musicians, scientists, researchers, ar-
tists. In every phase of academic and educational work
Jews are active in great disproportion to their numbers.
This does not mean that Jews are superior in ability or
are "better" than other groups; it simply points up the
fact that Jews have a tradition of learning which still influences their behavior.

The Jewish tradition stresses the importance of education for every individual. Jewish religious practice em-
bodies this emphasis. In Judaism, every religious service
includes some learning and every man is expected to be
informed. "An ignorant man cannot be truly pious," said
Hillel. As a result of this pattern, Jews were literate in all
ages, even when those among whom they lived were illiterate. In America today, Jews still demonstrate the continuing effect of this part of the Jewish tradition.

Our tradition also stresses deeds and actions. From the
time of Sinai, Judaism has taught that man links himself
to God through his moral actions. The pattern of mutual
aid and concern for the unfortunate embodied itself in the
practices of the Jewish community throughout the ages.
It is still evident in the amazingly energetic program of
Jewish philanthropy and in the vigorous activity of large
numbers of Jews in the causes of social justice whether
the issues directly involve the Jews as a group or not.
While no group can claim a monopoly of devotion to
justice and every group has its share of the unscrupulous
and immoral, the participation of American Jews in movements for human betterment, from the Peace Corps to the
Anti-Poverty Program, continues to be far in excess of the
norm. The only explanation for this pattern of behavior
can be found in the special emphasis in Jewish tradition
on the pursuit of justice, and the unique experience of the
Jewish group.

Jewish teaching, and the customs that derived from it,
has always placed great stress on the family and on the

place of the home in developing values and attitudes. In
Judaism every home was to be a sanctuary, as important
as the synagogue or temple. Jewish family unity provided
the strength which enabled men and women in trying
times to face a hostile world with dignity and self respect.
The Jewish home became a means of bringing beauty,
reverence and even holiness into troubled lives. In Eastern
Europe, as Mendele Mocher Seforim wrote, even the poor
and harried peddler, who lived like a dog on the outside,
was a king at the Sabbath table in his own home. According to many social scientists it is this home and family
atmosphere which explains the low rates of alcoholism
and delinquency among Jews.

THE WEAKENING JEWISH COMMITMENT

If statistics provided evidence of the strength of Jewish
life in the past, recent studies dramatically illustrate the
consequences of weakening Jewish commitment. Sociologists have found that the rates of alcoholism and delinquency among Jews are rising rapidly. It may be that as
Jews become "acculturated" they tend to become conform-
ists who adopt whatever practices are common around
them. It may be that when Jewish content disappears, there
is less resistance to this type of "conformity."

It seems that American Jews, who have so many achievements to their credit, have thus far failed in one important
respect. They have not yet learned how to transmit to those
who will follow the Judaism which made their own
achievements possible. They are enjoying the powers with
which their tradition has endowed them, but they are not
renewing these powers. American Jewry is "spending its
capital," using up its resources without replacing them.

There are many indications that as Jews abandon the
ideals, practices and standards of their Jewish tradition
they risk betraying not only themselves, but also the essential spirit of America. They are denying that in the future
as in the past America can be enriched by variety. They
thus repudiate the fact that America found its greatness in

diversity, and requires that each group contribute its own and its best qualities to society. Jews without Judaism are intellectually poorer, morally weaker, culturally less interesting. A homogenized, "pudding" America, without Jews and other diverse groups, is an intellectually poorer, morally weaker, culturally less interesting America.

Only if they communicate to their children the ideals, values and living patterns of Judaism will this generation of prosperous, American born and educated Jews transmit the same qualities which they received from their immigrant parents and grandparents.

Many sensitive and thoughtful young American Jews are aware of the power and life-giving worth of the tradition they have inherited. They are conscious of the growing spiritual problems which the complex modern world presents. And they do seek ways of reclaiming Jewish values for themselves, the better to transfer them to those who will follow. The Jews of America need the strength and guidance of Judaism; America needs the moral power and the variety that such committed Jews give to the country.

WHAT IS JEWISH COMMITMENT?

Jewish commitment does not require isolation or self segregation. It does not require that Jews separate themselves from the mainstream of American life. It does mean the reassertion of the importance of diversity and the right of groups and individuals to pursue their own destiny within the framework of freedom. Only in a totalitarian society, or in prison, does equality mean sameness. Under freedom, equality means the right to be distinctive without discrimination. Throughout our history, including centuries of tyranny, Jews maintained their own ideals and way of life, and by so doing upheld the right of all human beings to differ. In the time to come, Jews can again demonstrate that true universal brotherhood means the acceptance of diversity.

Jewish commitment in America today means recovery

of the Jewish world view. It is the very essence of Judaism that religion must be a way of life. In the Jewish faith man links himself to God through deeds *(mitzvot)*; what is "good" and what God requires of man is "to do justly and to love mercy and to walk humbly with God." Society, too, has a goal: the messianic age of peace between nations and security for individuals; a time when "nation shall not lift up sword against nation, neither shall they learn war anymore; but every man shall dwell under his vine and under his fig tree and none shall make them afraid."

In this age of speed without goals and plenty without purpose, we need the guidance of our tradition more than ever. Judaism cannot solve every problem, nor resolve every dilemma which we face in our complex times, but it can provide us with direction and standards to help us find our way.

Judaism demands of us commitment to life and to justice for all men. It moves us to involvement in tasks and movements which implement our ideals. Judaism affirms that this could be a better world, and reminds us that when we help make it so, we are doing God's work. In the words of our sages: "Man's job is to be God's partner in continuing the work of creation."

As Jews in America we are not only involved in religious ideals and actions, we are linked to a history, a people and a culture. Our history, with all its trials and triumphs, is a demonstration of man's ability to overcome adversity. Jewish history is evidence of the power of the human spirit to overcome force and repression. Our history gives us a special sensitivity to discrimination and persecution; it fills us with concern for freedom of expression and for the separation of the state from religion. This history needs to be understood and lived and continued.

As Jews, we are linked to a people which in our own times has suffered and achieved. We can grow in strength and in worth as we share the experiences of our fellow Jews in Europe, in Israel and around the world.

These special ties of kinship and destiny need not diminish our involvement with the larger family of mankind.

On the contrary, our concern for the welfare of our fellow Jews everywhere in the world must widen our horizons, sharpen our sensitivity and intensify our concern for our fellowman. In the words of Hillel: "If I am not for myself, who will be for me? But if I am for myself alone what good am I? And if not now, when?"

Jewish culture, too, adds a dimension to our understanding. There is a vast treasure house of Jewish learning, from the prophets and Psalms to Sholom Aleichem and Saul Bellow. When Jews in America share in these riches, their vision is enlarged, their power to understand and to contribute is increased.

In addition Jewish life offers the discipline and the poetry of Jewish observances and the enlightenment of Jewish institutions. Sabbaths and festivals not only represent our ethical ideals and our historic expriences, they bind families together in shared experiences. They provide us with symbolic actions which bring beauty and holiness into our lives. They serve as reminders and tokens of our link to God and to our tradition.

Synagogues and schools serve not only as the setting for religious services and classes. They are the instruments through which our ideals, values, history and culture are preserved, communicated and transmitted. Even if it were true that individual "spiritual geniuses" could fulfill their own spiritual and prayer needs without synagogues and schools, and this is doubtful—it nevertheless is true that a religious heritage cannot be sustained without religious institutions. Those who believe they are so learned, so ethical, so perfect that they do not "need" synagogues, are needed in synagogues to inspire and enlighten ordinary mortals. Men have the responsibility to participate for what they can give as well as for what they can receive. Clearly the support of Jewish institutions of worship and learning is an obligation for everyone who is concerned about the survival of Judaism and the Jewish people.

Ideals, history, people, culture, observances — all of these and much more constitute the Jewish heritage. They are a part of what Judaism brings to the lives of Jews in America.

American Jews must learn that, unlike an inheritance, a heritage cannot be given. It can only be made available. In order for a heritage to continue, it must be accepted and renewed. Jews who wish to claim their heritage must deepen their knowledge. Many areas of belief need clarafication; many Jewish institutions need reconstruction; many causes require action.

Being a Jew in America offers a great challenge and a great opportunity. The challenge is to fulfill the promise of both our Jewish and our American heritage. The opportunity is to raise ourselves and our world closer to the goals of freedom and justice and holines which both our American and Jewish traditions share.

As Rabbi Tarphon once said: "The day is short, the work is much, the laborers are slothful, and the Master is urgent. It is not incumbent upon you to complete the task, but neither are you free to abstain from it."

SUGGESTED READINGS

AGENDA FOR AMERICANS, *Eli Ginzberg,* Columbia Univ. Press.

THE AMERICAN JEW: A Reappraisal, Edited by *Oscar Janowsky,* Jewish Publication Society.

AMERICA IS DIFFERENT, *Stuart E. Rosenberg,* Thomas Nelson and Sons.

THE JEWS WITHIN AMERICAN SOCIETY, *Bezalel Sherman,* Wayne State University Press.

AMERICAN JUDAISM, *Nathan Glazer,* University of Chicago Press.

INDEX

301

303

309

X-Y-Z